Effective Instruction for Middle School Students with Reading Difficulties

Effective Instruction for Middle School Students with Reading Difficulties

The Reading Teacher's Sourcebook

by

Carolyn A. Denton, Ph.D.
Children's Learning Institute
University of Texas Health Science Center at Houston

Sharon Vaughn, Ph.D.
Meadows Center for Preventing Educational Risk
University of Texas at Austin

Jade Wexler, Ph.D.
University of Maryland, College Park

Deanna Bryan

and

Deborah Reed, Ph.D.
University of Texas at El Paso

·P·A·U·L·H·
BROOKES
PUBLISHING CO.®

Baltimore • London • Sydney

KH

Paul H. Brookes Publishing Co.
Post Office Box 10624
Baltimore, Maryland 21285-0624
USA

www.brookespublishing.com

Typeset by Auburn Associates, Inc., Baltimore, Maryland.
Manufactured in the United States of America by
Versa Press, Inc., East Peoria, Illinois.

The individuals described in this book are composites or real people whose situations are masked and are based on the authors' experiences. In all instances, names and identifying details have been changed to protect confidentiality.

Cover photo © iStockphoto.com/asiseeit.

Library of Congress Cataloging-in-Publication Data

Effective instruction for middle school students with reading difficulties : the reading teacher's sourcebook / by Carolyn A. Denton … [et al.].
    p.   cm.
    Includes bibliographical references and index.
    ISBN-13: 978-1-59857-243-8 (pbk.)
    ISBN-10: 1-59857-243-1 (pbk., layflat)
    1. Reading (Middle school)—United States. 2. Reading—Remedial teaching—United States 3. Middle schools—United States. I. Denton, Carolyn A.
    LB1632.E33 2012
    428.4071′2—dc23
                                             2012020406

British Library Cataloguing in Publication data are available from the British Library.

2016   2015   2014   2013   2012
10   9   8   7   6   5   4   3   2   1

11/12/13

Contents

About the Authors

Carolyn A. Denton, Ph.D., is Associate Professor in the Children's Learning Institute, part of the Department of Pediatrics at the University of Texas Health Science Center in Houston. A former teacher, she conducts research in schools focused on reading intervention, response to intervention models, coaching as a form of professional development, and reading comprehension. Her current projects include a study of reading comprehension in middle and high school students, a study of interventions for elementary-age children who have both attention-deficit/hyperactivity disorder and severe reading difficulties, and a project developing a Tier 2 first-grade intervention that targets both decoding and comprehension. She has served as the head of the Texas Adolescent Literacy Project, an initiative of the Texas Education Agency focused on the development of intervention approaches for struggling middle school readers. Dr. Denton is the coauthor of three other books, including a reading intervention program for the early grades and two books on the role of the reading coach, as well as numerous articles and book chapters. She has made presentations and provided training to teachers, administrators, coaches, researchers, and university faculties throughout the United States and in Europe and Hong Kong.

Sharon Vaughn, Ph.D., holds the H.E. Hartfelder/Southland Corp. Regents Chair in Human Development and is Executive Director of the Meadows Center for Preventing Educational Risk, an organized research unit at the University of Texas at Austin. She was Editor in Chief of the *Journal of Learning Disabilities* and Co-editor of *Learning Disabilities Research and Practice*. She is the recipient of the Council for Exceptional Children Special Education Research Award, the American Educational Research Association Special Interest Group Distinguished Researcher Award, the International Reading Association Albert J. Harris Award, and the University of Texas Distinguished Faculty Award. Dr. Vaughn is the author of numerous books and research articles that address the reading and social outcomes of students with learning difficulties. She is currently the principal investigator or co-principal investigator on several Institute of Education Sciences, U.S. Department of Education, and *Eunice Kennedy Shriver* National Institute of Child Health and Human Development research grants investigating effective interventions for students with reading difficulties and students who are English language learners. She is the author of more than 10 books, 150 peer-reviewed research articles, and 50 chapters.

Jade Wexler, Ph.D., is Assistant Professor in the Department of Counseling, Higher Education, and Special Education at the University of Maryland, College Park. Dr. Wexler has almost 15 years of experience as a teacher and researcher in the field of special education. She earned her Ph.D. in Special Education (Learning Disabilities and Behavior Disorders) in 2007 from the University of Texas at Austin, where she remains a fellow in the Meadows Center for Preventing Educational Risk Dropout Prevention Institute. She has extensive experience directing large-scale studies (funded by the National Institutes of Health, the Institute of Education Sciences, the Meadows Foundation, and the Greater Texas Foundation) investigating high-quality interventions for students with significant reading difficulties and students at risk for dropping out of school. Her current research focuses on investigating effective practices for adolescents with reading difficulties, including those in the juvenile justice system. She also investigates methods to decrease dropout rates and increase school engagement for students at risk for dropping out of school.

Deanna Bryan began her teaching career working with children with severe disabilities. While teaching in a life skills classroom, she met a student that she believed could learn to read. She began tutoring this student one on one and this is where her passion for teaching reading began. Ms. Bryan spent most of her teaching career working with middle school students. She was a public school special education reading teacher for 9½ years before going to work for the Vaughn Gross Center for Reading and Language Arts at the University of Texas at Austin. At the Vaughn Gross Center, she worked as a research assistant and then as an instructional coach. She was also a member of the development team for the Texas Adolescent Literacy Academies. Ms. Bryan believes middle school teachers are special and feel they are called to work with this unique age group. She hopes that this book will serve these teachers well. Ms. Bryan currently resides in Austin, Texas, with her husband and two children.

Deborah Reed, Ph.D., is Assistant Professor in the Department of Teacher Education at the University of Texas at El Paso. She has spent 19 years working with adolescents as a middle and high school teacher, technical assistance provider, and researcher. While at the Meadows Center for Preventing Educational Risk, Dr. Reed served as Principal Investigator of the Texas Adolescent Literacy Academies, which resulted in the training of more than 21,000 content area and intervention teachers. She has also assisted the Florida Center for Reading Research and the IRIS Center at Vanderbilt in developing teacher-friendly resources for addressing adolescent literacy issues in both general and special education settings. Her publications have appeared in *Scientific Studies of Reading, Reading Psychology, Preventing School Failure, Research in Middle Level Education, Learning Disabilities Research and Practice, Journal of Adolescent and Adult Literacy, Learning Disability Quarterly,* and *Educational Assessment.*

Acknowledgments

We would like to thank Dr. Susan Ebbers for her generous contributions to the vocabulary chapter and Wendy Hickman for her assistance in preparing the manuscript for publication. We would also like to thank all the many students, teachers, and researchers with whom we have worked over the course of many years for all they have taught us about providing effective instruction for students who struggle with reading.

To the Meadows Foundation,
aiming to improve the quality and circumstances of lives

Introduction

We hope that this guide provides middle school reading teachers some much-needed and welcome insight into improving reading outcomes for middle school students with reading problems. As middle school teachers know, reading problems are not eliminated when students move from elementary to secondary settings. In 2011, the National Assessment of Educational Progress (NAEP) was administered to eighth-grade students across the nation. Although some gains were made in eighth-grade NAEP reading scores from 2009 to 2011, the NAEP data showed that 24% of eighth-graders overall (about 40% of African American and Hispanic students and students eligible for free or reduced lunch) are not able to read at a basic level (National Center for Education Statistics, 2011). Clearly, many students in middle school still require reading remediation. Ultimately, reading becomes an unpleasant obligation for these students as they struggle to keep up in school and society in general.

Middle school students have become responsible for learning increasingly more complex content at a rapid pace to meet state benchmarks. Despite any reading difficulties a secondary student might have, the U.S. educational system expects students to be able to decode fluently and comprehend material with challenging content. For this reason, it is essential that teachers and school administrators are knowledgeable about reading instruction and ways to help older struggling readers. This requires high-quality and ongoing professional development to improve the knowledge and practice of teachers. To ensure success for students, teachers need guidance about best practices.

Teachers should be well informed about how to interpret assessment data and design instruction according to student needs. Having a system in place to assess students in order to identify struggling readers and guide decision making regarding instructional needs, grouping, and scheduling can help older struggling readers achieve success. This guide will focus on the assessment of struggling middle school readers, determining instructional needs and setting short- and long-term goals based on assessment results, and designing instruction to address student needs. We include many sample lesson plans for research-supported instructional activities that have a track record of success with struggling readers.

The assessments and lessons in this guide reflect what we know about the critical elements of reading for students with reading difficulties. Knowing best practices for teaching and integrating critical reading elements allows teachers to design appropriate instruction.

As a reminder, no one program will be an easy fit for all, and providing the appropriate instruction for struggling adolescent readers is no small task. It is our hope that this guide will serve as just that—a *guide* to inform educators about best practices for adolescents with reading difficulties so that educators can better serve this special group of students.

Section I ||| Assessing Struggling Readers at the Secondary Level

Section I provides an overview of the process of assessment for secondary struggling readers. We introduce a fictitious teacher, Ms. Lopez, to illustrate the process.

Ms. Lopez is a reading teacher in a middle school. Last year, she had a challenging class in which all 20 students were reading below grade level and seemed to have different needs. Because she did not have a specific reading curriculum, she was expected to develop her own lessons or modify whatever materials she could find. As a result, she did not feel that she was able to adequately meet the needs of her students.

In addition to the self-imposed pressure she felt to help her students, Ms. Lopez was faced with the increasing demands of the state assessments. She wants to avoid this situation this year by learning how she can provide more effective instruction, but she is still unsure about how to get started.

TERMS TO KNOW

alphabetic principle	Understanding that the sequence of letters in a written word represents phonemes, or sounds, in a spoken word and can be recombined to form other words
anecdotal records	Quick notes taken by teachers during or immediately after instructional time to record students' responses to instruction, particularly evidence of students' strengths and needs to guide future instructional planning
cloze test	An assessment of reading comprehension in which students read a passage with words systematically deleted; students must supply the deleted words
comprehension	The ability to understand what is read—the ultimate goal of reading
curriculum-based assessment	A type of assessment developed to measure progress in mastering the objectives of a curriculum; closely reflects instructed skills and content and is typically used to inform instruction; may be timed or untimed
diagnostic assessments	Assessments designed to refine a teacher's understanding of student strengths and weaknesses to inform instructional decisions

fluency	The ability to read with speed, accuracy, appropriate phrasing, and expression
frustration reading level	Text that is too difficult for students; when students repeatedly read text at this level, they typically develop counterproductive habits
independent reading level	Text that the student can read on his or her own, without support (also called the "homework level")
informal reading inventory	An assessment consisting of text passages at increasing levels of difficulty used to determine students' independent, instructional, and frustration reading levels and to measure comprehension (and sometimes fluency) in increasingly difficult text; students read passages at different reading levels and answer questions while teachers take notes regarding the students' reading behaviors
instructional reading level	Text that students can read with assistance or instruction; best for teaching students how to become better readers
intervention	Intensive instruction designed to help remediate a student's difficulties; usually provided in addition to the student's regular instruction
letter–sound correspondence	The relationships between letters or letter combinations and the sounds they represent
maze test	An assessment of reading comprehension, often timed, in which students read a passage with words systematically deleted; for each deleted word, students select the appropriate word from three possible words so that the passage makes sense; a multiple-choice cloze test
phoneme	The smallest unit of sound in a language; English has about 40 phonemes, which are represented by about 250 letters or letter combinations (e.g., the long *a* sound [one phoneme] can be represented by the letter *a* with a silent *e* [lake], *ai* [rain], *ay* [day], *a* [paper], *eigh* [eight], *ey* [they], *ea* [steak], *ei* [vein], and *aigh* [straight]).
phonemic awareness	One kind of phonological awareness; the ability to hear and manipulate sounds within words, usually demonstrated by segmenting words into their individual sounds and blending sounds to form words; an auditory skill, but should be linked with instruction in letters or letter sounds (phonics)
phonological awareness	Awareness of components of spoken language, including the ability to identify words in spoken sentences, to segment words into onset–rime units and syllables, and to manipulate discrete sounds in words; an auditory skill
progress-monitoring measures	Brief assessments of growth toward a particular academic goal, given frequently and used to guide instructional decision making
screening measures	Brief assessments that focus on the critical skills of reading for the purpose of identifying students who may need additional support
sight word	A word that is recognized immediately as a whole, without applying word analysis or decoding strategies
vocabulary	The words a student is able to recognize and use orally or in writing
word recognition	The accurate reading of words

Chapter 1

A Schoolwide Approach to Reading Intervention

Educators who work with middle school students are all too aware that not all children learn to read by the time they leave elementary school. Many students in Grades 6, 7, and 8 have reading difficulties. The purpose of *Effective Instruction for Middle School Students with Reading Disabilities: The Reading Teacher's Sourcebook* is to provide middle school reading teachers with an overview of research-based instructional approaches for teaching struggling readers. We recognize that writing is an essential component of literacy instruction; however, in this sourcebook, we focus primarily on reading.

Our goal for this sourcebook is to provide reading teachers with the strategies necessary to integrate reading instruction into a coordinated, comprehensive, schoolwide approach. The goal of this schoolwide effort is to ensure that all students are able to read and learn from academic text—including content-area textbooks and literature—and are motivated to engage in reading for many different purposes. To address this goal, the schoolwide approach is designed to meet the needs of all students by providing them with instruction designed to help them read and comprehend the complex vocabulary and content of academic text and to increase their motivation to read. These elements are essential if students are to be successful at learning from text. The components of the schoolwide approach include the following:

- Common instructional routines and strategies implemented across content areas (i.e., math, social studies, science, English language arts) to promote students' learning of content-area vocabulary and comprehension of academic text; provided in a school context of strong leadership, and a commitment to high standards, instructional excellence, and maintaining a safe and positive school environment
- Strategic instruction provided in reading classes or intervention settings
- Intensive intervention for students with more serious reading difficulties

These components are described in detail in the following sections. Figure 1.1 presents an overview of essential elements of each component. Table 1.1 outlines a schoolwide reading intervention approach for middle schools.

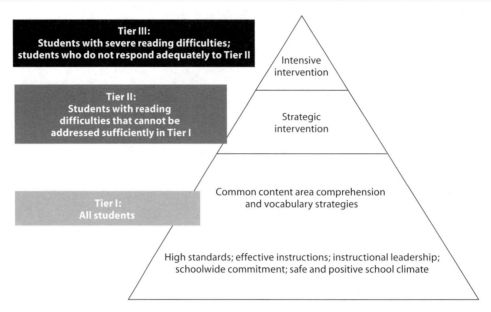

Figure 1.1   3-Tier diagram. (Adapted with permission from the Vaughn Gross Center for Reading and Language Arts at the University of Texas at Austin. [2005]. *Introduction to the 3-Tier reading model: Reducing reading difficulties for kindergarten through third grade students* [4th ed.]. Austin, TX: Author.)

TIER I: SCHOOLWIDE STRATEGIES AND ROUTINES

Tier I, *schoolwide strategies and routines*, affects all students in the school. It consists of the following:

- Assurance of a safe and positive schoolwide environment in which all students receive quality instruction based on high academic standards; this often includes a schoolwide approach to behavior management

- A schoolwide commitment to support the reading development of all students, supported by strong instructional leadership

- A limited set of research-validated reading comprehension and vocabulary instructional routines and activities implemented consistently across all content-area classes

- Benchmark testing of all students two to three times per year to identify students who need supplemental reading instruction

- Quality, sustained professional development related to evidence-based vocabulary and comprehension strategy instruction in middle school content areas, with time and opportunities for teachers to collaborate within and across subject areas

Most schools in which students are successful in spite of serious challenges such as poverty and language differences share some common characteristics. Educators in these schools have high standards—based on grade-level expectations—for all of their students and are committed to providing effective instruction in all classes; when necessary, educators work together to develop solutions to problems and overcome obstacles. Educators in effective schools have a sense of urgency in their approach to reading intervention for students who are still behind when they reach middle school. Successful schools also have strong instructional leadership, either from the principal or other individuals such as team leaders or professional development coordinators. These leaders understand the components of effective instruction for students who perform above average levels, those who perform according to grade-level expectations, and those who struggle. In effective

Table 1.1. A schoolwide reading intervention approach for middle school

	Tier I	Tier II	Tier III
	Strong schoolwide foundation and consistent reading strategies and routines	Strategic intervention	Intensive intervention
Definition	A limited, powerful, and consistent set of instructional routines used to teach content-area vocabulary and comprehend content-area text, implemented by all content-area teachers; implemented within a safe and positive school environment in which there is a schoolwide commitment to excellence	Reading classes or small-group instruction specifically designed to accelerate the reading growth of students with moderate reading difficulties	Specifically designed and customized reading instruction delivered in small groups or individually to students with serious and persistent reading difficulties
Students	All students in content-area classes	Students with moderate reading difficulties; usually students performing 1–2 years below grade level; most will have needs primarily in comprehension, vocabulary, and, sometimes, fluency; some will need short-term, focused instruction in multisyllable word reading*	Students with severe and persistent reading difficulties; usually students performing more than 2 years below grade level; students with seriously impaired decoding ability, very low fluency, and poor text comprehension*
Focus	Academic vocabulary and comprehension of academic text	Reading comprehension, vocabulary, fluency (as needed), multisyllable word reading (as needed)	Explicit and systematic instruction in word reading and decoding, fluency, vocabulary, and comprehension; individualized to address students' specific needs
Program	None	Research-based reading program(s) emphasizing comprehension and vocabulary, fluency, and word recognition	Specialized, research-based reading program(s) emphasizing word recognition, fluency, vocabulary, and comprehension that can be used to provide individualized instruction
Instruction	Implementation of a consistent set of evidence-based instructional routines and activities	Carefully designed and implemented explicit, systematic instruction	Carefully designed and implemented explicit, systematic instruction, individualized to address student needs
Teachers	Science, social studies, math, reading, and English language arts teachers	Intervention provided by personnel determined by the school; usually a reading teacher or other interventionist	Intensive intervention provided by a reading teacher, special educator, or other intervention teacher
Setting	Science, social studies, math, reading, and English language arts classrooms	Appropriate setting designated by the school; usually a reading class or supplemental tutoring	Appropriate setting designated by the school; usually a reading class or supplemental tutoring
Grouping	Regular content-area class groupings; collaborative activities in small groups and peer pairs to support active involvement	Homogeneous small groups and peer pairs; instruction provided within class sizes of 12–18 students	Homogeneous small-group instruction (no more than 1:5), peer pairs, individual instruction
Time	In all content-area classes throughout the school day	30–50 minutes per day for one or two semesters	50–60 minutes (or more) every day for 1 or more school years
Assessment	Schoolwide benchmark assessments at the beginning, middle, and end of the school year	Progress monitoring one or two times per month on target skills to ensure adequate progress and learning, with instructional changes made when students do not demonstrate adequate growth; diagnostic assessment to determine the focus and pacing of instruction	Progress monitoring between two and four times each month on target skills to ensure adequate progress and learning, with instructional changes made when students do not demonstrate adequate growth; diagnostic assessment to determine the focus and pacing of instruction

Adapted with permission from the Vaughn Gross Center for Reading and Language Arts at the University of Texas at Austin. (2005). *Introduction to the 3-Tier reading model: Reducing reading difficulties for kindergarten through third grade students* (4th ed.). Austin, TX: Author.

*For information on using assessments to identify students who need instruction in fluency and word identification, see Chapters 2–4.

schools, administrators prioritize academic achievement in budgeting and scheduling and support teachers who work with challenging students. Finally, effective schools support a safe and positive environment that is conducive to learning; if students, teachers, and/or others in the school do not feel that this is the case, the first step in the schoolwide intervention process is to implement comprehensive positive behavioral supports or other consistent and effective strategies to address student behavior problems and ensure a comfortable atmosphere for all.

The second part of Tier I is the implementation of a limited set of effective instructional routines and practices within content-area classes to teach students strategies for reading, understanding, and learning from content-area text. Implementing these routines should both increase active student involvement and support the learning of all students in the class. Several of the vocabulary and comprehension strategies in this sourcebook are appropriate for content-area instruction. What matters is that students are asked to use the same strategies throughout the school day so that they may internalize these strategies and use them independently whenever they are reading.

Tier I is not designed to turn content-area teachers into reading teachers but rather to teach students how to read and comprehend content-area text. For example, consider that math text, which is dense with sample problems and concepts, is different from the more narrative format often found in social studies text. Social studies and science texts often include diagrams and other graphic sources of information that are essential to understanding the content. Finally, literature texts used in English classes include both complex expository pieces and narratives that often are characterized by literary forms of language usage that are unfamiliar to students. In addition, each content area has its own specialized vocabulary. Teachers who are knowledgeable in a particular subject area *are best able to teach students how to learn from content-area text*. The Tier I instructional routines are designed specifically to give content-area teachers the tools for this instruction.

Tier I of the schoolwide model has three basic goals. The first goal, essentially, is to support the development of vocabulary and reading comprehension in all students. Many middle school students, even those achieving at average levels, are unable to understand and use the specialized vocabulary and comprehend the complex text structures found in academic texts in the various content areas. Williamson (2006) found that texts students typically are asked to read in postsecondary settings, including community colleges, universities, the workplace, and the military, are significantly more demanding than high school textbooks. High school textbooks are, in turn, more complex than those used in middle school classes.

The second goal is to encourage students with reading difficulties to apply the vocabulary and comprehension strategies emphasized in supplemental intervention lessons throughout the school day and in different kinds of text. Typically, struggling adolescent readers develop habits in the ways they approach reading and writing tasks. These habits often are counterproductive and have been practiced over a period of years. For example, these students may skip difficult words or even entire sections of challenging text. Some students may attempt to complete assignments such as answering questions about text by searching the text for specific words they find in the questions and then copying from the text in the hope that this will result in acceptable answers. Other students are disruptive or disrespectful to escape reading or writing tasks that are too difficult for them. Even though these students may learn key reading skills and productive reading strategies in a reading intervention class, they do not tend to apply these new strategies automatically whenever they read and write in other classes. It is far easier to fall into old habits. Incorporating a small but consistent set of the same reading routines and practices into content-area teachers' instruction encourages struggling readers to apply important reading skills and strategies each time they encounter text in school. Students then have multiple opportunities to practice and apply skills and strategies in different kinds of text and are more likely to replace old, inefficient habits with newer, more productive habits.

The third and final goal is to provide content-area and reading teachers with the tools and support they need to teach students who may be difficult to teach. The schoolwide approach is based on a commitment to improving literacy for all students. Collaboration among teachers is a key element of the approach and has a large impact on the success of schoolwide intervention in any school.

The section of this sourcebook titled "Assessing Struggling Readers at the Secondary Level" describes benchmark testing. In addition, several of the vocabulary and comprehension activities described in this sourcebook are appropriate for content-area instruction and may be adopted by a school or grade-level team. It is important that content-area teachers receive appropriate professional development and ongoing support (e.g., coaching, peer coaching, regular study groups) so that they are able to implement the instructional routines correctly and feel comfortable and confident with this approach.

TIER II: STRATEGIC INTERVENTION

Tier II, *strategic intervention,* is designed specifically to provide supplemental reading classes or tutoring to students who need focused instruction in reading. Typically, these students are reading 1–2 years below grade level and need short-term (usually lasting for one or two semesters), targeted instruction in comprehension and vocabulary. Some students also need instruction in reading fluency and in identifying multisyllable words; many benefit from instruction in recognizing common prefixes and suffixes and using knowledge of these word parts to read unfamiliar words. The goal of strategic intervention is to provide explicit instruction and practice in a set of strategies that will enable striving readers to be successful in their content-area classes and increase their motivation to read. This sourcebook provides information about assessing and instructing striving readers along with sample lesson plans to guide teachers who provide strategic intervention.

Elements of Strategic Intervention

To implement strategic intervention, educators need to do the following:

- Use the results of benchmark assessments to identify students who need supplemental intervention.
- Administer diagnostic assessments to learn about the instructional needs of individual students.
- Provide regular explicit, systematic instruction to homogeneous groups of students within reading classes or supplemental tutoring sessions.
- Use materials and instructional approaches validated by scientific reading research.
- Focus on teaching vocabulary, reading comprehension, reading fluency, and multisyllable word identification, depending on student needs.
- Monitor student progress one to two times per month and use the results to make instructional decisions.

- Receive quality, sustained professional development related to scientific research-supported instruction for struggling readers, with time and opportunities for reading teachers to collaborate to support the progress of all students.

TIER III: INTENSIVE INTERVENTION

The purpose of Tier III, *intensive intervention,* is to provide intensive, targeted intervention to students with more severe reading difficulties, usually those who are performing more than 2 years below grade level.

Research indicates that secondary-level students who are performing substantially below grade level will not meet grade-level standards without highly intensive intervention. Contrary to common practice in elementary schools, we suggest that students who perform more than 2 years below grade level be placed directly into Tier III intensive intervention without first receiving less intensive strategic intervention. These students have an urgent need for instruction that will accelerate their progress to enable them to close the gap between them and their typically developing peers. Teachers who provide intensive intervention should keep in mind that students requiring intensive support must learn *faster* than typical students if they are going to be prepared to succeed in high school and beyond.

Elements of Intensive Intervention

Intensity of an intervention is increased when educators do the following:

- Decrease group size. It is recommended that intensive intervention be provided to homogeneous groups of five or fewer students. This enables the teacher to monitor each student closely and provide him or her with immediate feedback, and it increases each student's opportunities to respond and interact with the teacher.

- Increase instructional time. Instructional time may be increased in three ways: 1) by extending length of intervention sessions, 2) by providing intervention every day of the week, and 3) by extending the duration of the intervention to an entire school year or longer.

- Increase student time on task with active student involvement in relevant activities and many interactions with the teacher.

- Make instruction more explicit and systematic. Implement a research-based reading program designed to provide direct and carefully sequenced instruction but that can be individualized to meet student needs.

- Use the results of frequently administered diagnostic assessments to individualize instruction.

- Monitor student progress every 1–2 weeks and use the results to revise instruction to meet student needs.

IMPLEMENTING A SCHOOLWIDE READING INTERVENTION APPROACH

Schools must address key questions as they begin to implement a schoolwide reading intervention approach. Figure 1.2 includes some of these questions. Figure 1.2 is a checklist that can be used to guide school personnel as they plan to implement a three-tiered

Planning Checklist for Implementing Schoolwide Reading Intervention

STEP 1. SELF-EVALUATION: REVIEW CURRENT READING PRACTICES WITHIN THE SCHOOL TO DETERMINE NEEDS AND PRIORITIES

☐ Does the school have a unified vision and plan for ensuring that all students are able to read and learn from academic text and are motivated to read? Are administrators and teachers committed to implementing the plan?

☐ Is there a safe and positive school environment that is conducive to learning?

☐ Do teachers and administrators have high academic standards for their students based on grade-level expectations?

☐ Do teachers provide effective instruction supported by strong instructional leadership from the principal or another person or persons in the school?

☐ Is academic achievement given priority in scheduling, budgeting, and allocation of personnel?

☐ Do content-area teachers consistently teach and encourage students to implement evidence-based vocabulary and comprehension strategies? Is the same limited set of strategies used across all classes?

☐ Are benchmark reading assessments administered three times per year to identify students who need supplemental reading classes or intervention?

☐ Do reading teachers or tutors implement research-supported programs and teaching approaches to provide strategic intervention to students who perform somewhat below grade level and have problems comprehending academic text?

☐ Do reading teachers or other teachers implement research-supported, explicit, systematic reading programs to provide intensive intervention to students with more severe reading difficulties?

☐ Is the progress of students in strategic and intensive intervention monitored regularly to determine whether they are responding adequately to intervention?

STEP 2. DEVELOP A PLAN FOR COLLECTING, MANAGING, AND USING BENCHMARK AND PROGRESS-MONITORING DATA

☐ Who will administer benchmark assessments?

☐ Who will organize the results and analyze them to determine which students need strategic or intensive intervention?

☐ Reading teachers or interventionists should administer progress-monitoring assessments but may need some assistance. If so, who will assist them?

☐ Who will compile progress-monitoring data and display them as easily interpreted graphs or in other accessible formats?

☐ It is recommended that groups of reading teachers, other teachers, and, ideally, administrators meet regularly to examine the progress-monitoring data so that they can identify students who are not making adequate progress and collaborate to make plans for accelerating the progress of these students. Who will organize these meetings?

(continued)

Figure 1.2.   Planning Checklist for Implementing Schoolwide Reading Intervention. (Adapted with permission from the Vaughn Gross Center for Reading and Language Arts at the University of Texas at Austin. [2005]. *Introduction to the 3-Tier reading model: Reducing reading difficulties for kindergarten through third grade students* [4th ed.]. Austin, TX: Author.)

STEP 3. DEVELOP A SCHOOLWIDE PLAN FOR IMPLEMENTING CONTENT-AREA STRATEGIES AND ROUTINES

☐ If there is a need for professional development in a system of positive behavioral supports to ensure a safe and positive school environment, then who will provide this professional development and who will ensure that the system is implemented?

☐ Is there a plan for providing quality professional development to content-area teachers to prepare them to incorporate evidence-based vocabulary and comprehension strategies and to use collaborative grouping to increase active student involvement? Does this plan include ongoing support in the form of regular study group sessions and/or coaching?

☐ Are content-area teachers committed to implementing research-based strategies and routines across classes to ensure that students learn key vocabulary and are able to read and understand academic text in each discipline?

☐ Are content-area and reading teachers given adequate time to plan and collaborate to overcome obstacles to integrating these strategies and routines into their instruction?

☐ Is a system established for problem solving and decision making related to this component of school-wide intervention?

STEP 4. DEVELOP A PLAN FOR IMPLEMENTING STRATEGIC INTERVENTION

☐ Who will provide strategic intervention?

☐ Will strategic intervention take place in reading classes or in tutoring sessions?

☐ How will class sizes of 12–18 students be ensured?

☐ When will strategic intervention be provided?

☐ Where will strategic intervention be implemented?

☐ Is a system in place for monitoring the progress of strategic intervention students between one and two times per month and using the results to guide instructional decisions?

☐ Are criteria established for entry and exit from strategic intervention?

☐ How will assessment data be used to group and regroup students, to plan targeted instruction, and to make adaptations to ensure students meet grade-level benchmarks and/or objectives?

☐ Is a system established for problem solving and decision making related to strategic intervention?

☐ Is time provided for collaboration among reading intervention teachers?

☐ Who will ensure that reading interventionists receive quality professional development emphasizing scientific research-based programs and practices in teaching students with reading difficulties? Who will provide them with ongoing support?

Figure 1.2. *(continued)*

STEP 5. DEVELOP A PLAN FOR IMPLEMENTING INTENSIVE INTERVENTION

☐ Who will provide intensive intervention (e.g., reading teacher, special education teacher, other well-qualified teacher)?

☐ When and how often will intensive intervention be provided?

☐ Where will intensive intervention be implemented?

☐ What scientific research-based, explicit, systematic program(s) will be used to provide intensive intervention?

☐ Has the relationship of intensive intervention with Section 504 and special education services been clarified?

☐ Is a system in place for monitoring the progress of intensive intervention students between two and four times per month and using the results to guide instructional decisions?

☐ Are criteria established for entry and exit from intensive intervention?

☐ How will assessment data be used to plan targeted instruction and to make adaptations to ensure students meet grade-level benchmarks and/or objectives?

☐ Is a system established for problem solving and decision making related to intensive intervention?

☐ Is time provided for collaboration among intervention teachers?

☐ Who will ensure that intensive intervention teachers receive quality professional development emphasizing scientific research-based programs and practices in teaching students with reading difficulties? Who will provide them with ongoing support?

Figure 1.2. *(continued)*

schoolwide approach. We suggest that schools begin with a self-assessment to determine their current levels of implementation of the schoolwide approach. The first section of Figure 1.2 provides sample questions that can guide this self-assessment process. The remaining sections concern the implementation of the three tiers of intervention described in this chapter. (A photocopiable version is available in the Appendix.)

The next section in this sourcebook provides information about administering assessments to collect student data and how administrators and teachers can use the data to inform decisions about placing students in strategic and intensive interventions and to the instruction provided to those students.

Chapter 2

Overview of Assessment at the Secondary Level

Remember Ms. Lopez? She wants to provide more effective instruction to struggling readers in her middle school classes. The first priority to improve instruction for struggling readers is to conduct reading assessments. Conducting assessments allows teachers to do the following:

- Identify students who need additional support or intervention.
- Determine an instructional focus for each student.
- Determine how to group students appropriately for instruction.
- Plan instruction according to student strengths and needs on an ongoing basis.
- Monitor student progress toward goals.
- Evaluate the outcomes of instruction.

Teachers can use the diagram in Figure 2.1 to guide the assessment process for secondary students. The elements of this diagram are explained in the following paragraphs.

In the early elementary grades, **screening measures**, brief assessments that focus on the critical skills of reading, usually are administered at the beginning of the school year to all students to determine which students may require **interventions**. Often, screening assessments provide the first opportunity for teachers in the primary grades to identify potential struggling readers. When teachers determine through screening measures that a student needs intervention, they may decide to conduct more in-depth assessments so that they can analyze a student's strengths and needs to guide instructional decisions. These more detailed assessments are called **diagnostic assessments**.

Students in middle school may begin the school year already identified by the school district as struggling readers. Many reading teachers in the upper grades already know that their students have reading difficulties when the students are assigned to their classes. Typically, middle school struggling readers are identified when they fail to demonstrate adequate reading comprehension proficiency on high-stakes tests or standardized achievement tests. When struggling readers are identified at the end of the school year, schools can make decisions about scheduling accordingly. Schools also may screen any new students who come into the school district once school has started.

Although secondary teachers may not need to administer screening measures to decide who needs reading support, it is still important for them to conduct diagnostic assessments to determine what types of support students need. Diagnostic assessments

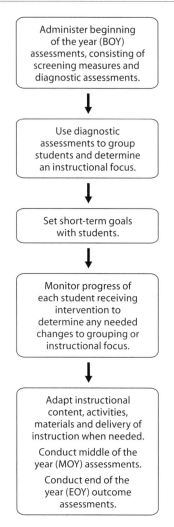

Figure 2.1. Guide to reading assessment for secondary students.

can provide teachers with valuable information about how to group students and plan instruction designed to accelerate student progress.

Progress-monitoring measures may be given a minimum of three times a year or as often as once a week using multiple test forms. Use a progress-monitoring tracking form and have students chart their own progress toward their goals (see Chapter 3). Seeing the information will help to determine which goals have been met and to set new goals, if appropriate. Teachers can use the progress-monitoring data to determine whether students are making adequate growth and whether instruction needs to be changed.

Between semesters and at the end of the year, give an outcome assessment—such as year-end standardized tests—to determine whether students will need to continue with intervention or change their instructional focus. Outcome assessments provide information about whether students met annual benchmarks and mastered objectives at their grade levels. The outcome assessments should reflect the instruction given during the semester and/or year; often, these assessments are accountability assessments required by states.

THE SEQUENCE OF ASSESSMENT

In the primary grades, teachers typically use assessments that will measure a student's knowledge and skills in **phonological awareness**, the **alphabetic principle**, **letter–sound correspondence**, and word reading. Educators tend to assess young students in a sequence that starts with beginning skills such as letter recognition, sound recognition, and word reading and then progresses along a continuum to more complex skills such as fluency and comprehension (see Figure 2.2). For example, in kindergarten and first grade, teachers may assess letter-naming ability and phonemic awareness. Being able to rapidly name letters is highly correlated with future reading success (Wagner et al., 1997). **Phonemic awareness**, including the ability to orally segment a word into individual **phonemes** (i.e., saying the sounds in the word *cat* one at a time: /c/ /a/ /t/), is an important predictor of reading progress (National Institute of Child Health and Human Development [NICHD], 2000). As students begin to read connected text, primary-grade teachers begin to assess oral reading fluency, vocabulary, and comprehension. It is important to realize, however, that even though more complex reading behaviors such as comprehension come later in the reading continuum, instruction in these areas is not delayed until students are proficient readers. For example, listening comprehension strategies can be taught very early as precursors to later reading comprehension strategies.

In the upper grades, students are expected to read fluently and accurately so that they can comprehend text. Despite any reading difficulties a secondary student might have, the educational system in the United States has expectations that these students will be able to decode fluently and comprehend material with challenging content (McCray et al., 2001). Older students who struggle with reading tend to dislike reading and to read infrequently (Moats, 2001). As a result of reading less, they tend to experience further regression in reading and to have poorly developed vocabulary and background knowledge (Stanovich, 1986). Often, difficulties for readers who fall behind their peers start as early as the first or second grade. By middle school this gap often widens, and students who should be reading at least 10,000,000 words during the school year may be reading as few as 100,000 words (Lyon & Moats, 1997).

Many middle school students with comprehension problems also demonstrate very poor word reading. Some students may disguise word-reading difficulties through well-developed sight-word knowledge; however, without adequate decoding skills, students are likely to read many words inaccurately, particularly in content-area text that includes unfamiliar words and concepts.

With secondary students, instead of assessing their skills "from the bottom up," as is often done in the early grades, teachers assess them beginning with the most complex skills (see Figure 2.3). Secondary students' oral reading fluency and comprehension may be assessed to determine whether further assessments are necessary in the area of **word recognition**. As stated in the beginning of this chapter, students in need of reading inter-

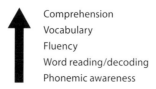

Comprehension

Vocabulary

Fluency

Word reading/decoding

Phonemic awareness

Figure 2.2. Elementary sequence of assessment. (From Wexler, J., Wanzek, J. & Vaughn, S. [2009]. Preventing and remediating reading difficulties for elementary and secondary students. In G.D. Sideridis and T.A. Citro [Eds.], *Strategies in reading for struggling learners*. Lanham, MD: Rowman & Littlefield; reprinted by permission.)

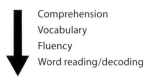

Comprehension
Vocabulary
Fluency
Word reading/decoding

Figure 2.3.   Secondary sequence of assessment. (From Wexler, J., Wanzek, J. & Vaughn, S. [2009]. Preventing and remediating reading difficulties for elementary and secondary students. In G.D. Sideridis and T.A. Citro [Eds.], *Strategies in reading for struggling learners.* Lanham, MD: Rowman & Littlefield; reprinted by permission.)

vention may first be identified because of their failure to demonstrate competence on state accountability tests or other assessments of reading comprehension.

Intervention teachers may assume that most secondary struggling readers have needs in the area of reading comprehension. The question, however, is *why* are students struggling with comprehension? They may lack one or more of the following:

- Effective strategies to help them understand, organize, and remember information
- The ability to make inferences to integrate ideas across a text
- The ability to monitor their own understanding and repair errors when they occur
- Adequate knowledge of word meanings
- The ability to read fluently enough to understand what they are reading
- The ability to accurately identify words
- Interest in or motivation for reading

Each of the above can affect comprehension. For example, students who read very slowly often have difficulty remembering and integrating information from text, and they usually read less than more skilled readers, resulting in limited vocabulary and background knowledge. Therefore, if a student has limited comprehension, it is important to assess reading fluency.

If a student has low fluency, teachers may probe further to understand issues that may influence the student's fluency development. Is the student in the habit of reading slowly or inaccurately and not monitoring whether what he or she is reading makes sense, or does the student lack fluency because he or she has problems identifying, or decoding, the words in the text? Some students have problems directly related to slow processing of language in general. These students not only read slowly but also may have problems retrieving words that they want to say. To help answer questions about why a student may read slowly or inaccurately, it may be helpful to give the student an assessment of word identification. This may be an assessment of quick recognition of **sight words**, words that are recognized automatically on sight, or it may be an assessment of the student's ability to use phonics and recognize common sound–spelling patterns to decode unknown words of differing complexity. Both of these domains should be assessed if there is an indication that a student has significant problems with decoding.

Chapter 3

Selecting and Administering Assessments

Perhaps one of the biggest challenges teachers of secondary students encounter is to accurately and quickly assess the reading **comprehension** and **vocabulary** knowledge of their students. Because teachers have relatively little time to determine what students know about word meanings and how well they understand text, they require measures that are relatively brief to administer and score. Researchers are still working to determine effective and efficient practices for assessing vocabulary and comprehension that are useful for teachers to diagnose specific student difficulties and monitor students' progress. Below-average scores on high-stakes criterion-referenced tests and standardized achievement tests as well as general teacher observations and low grades in reading and language arts classes provide indications that certain students struggle to comprehend text. Some schools administer alternate forms of the year-end high-stakes test at regular intervals throughout the year. Although these tests provide insight into students' levels of progress on the kinds of items included on the tests, they may not be sufficient to inform a teacher about specific aspects of vocabulary or comprehension on which students need instruction.

If a teacher is using a systematic reading program or a supplemental program for struggling readers that includes assessments linked directly to the objectives being taught, then the teacher may track outcomes of these assessments by using a form that indicates whether students have mastered each objective. For example, if the program includes instruction in and a related assessment of identifying cause-and-effect relationships in text, then a teacher may use the results of the assessment to determine whether students need further instruction and practice in that skill.

Another tool that may be used to monitor students' progress in comprehension is close, ongoing observation of the student's successful or unsuccessful responses to instruction in the reading and/or language arts classroom. For example, students may be taught to apply comprehension strategies such as inference making and summarization, and teachers may observe the ease or difficulty with which students apply these strategies successfully. (See Chapter 7: Comprehension for examples of instructional approaches that can be used to teach these strategies.) Students who struggle to master comprehension objectives probably need more or different kinds of instruction in those aspects of comprehension.

Similarly, students who use a limited vocabulary in writing and speaking and who have difficulty understanding or remembering words in reading and listening probably require instruction designed to help them learn and remember words. (See Chapter 8: Vocabulary for examples of vocabulary instructional activities.) Whether students learn and master specific vocabulary words can be assessed with tests of those words' meanings, but it is important to ensure that these tests are cumulative, including words taught in the past along with those recently taught. It is not productive for students to memorize a list of words for a test and then promptly forget them. If quality vocabulary instruction is part of the reading curriculum, then students actively *use* the words they learn and remember them over time.

It may be useful for teachers to take notes about their observations of students' responses to vocabulary and comprehension instruction during regular reading classes using **anecdotal records**, because it can be difficult to remember details about student responses from day to day (or even from minute to minute) when teaching many sections of reading or language arts throughout the day.

ASSESSING READING FLUENCY

Fluency is the ability to read with speed, accuracy, appropriate phrasing, and expression. Reading fluency usually is measured as a combination of the rate and level of accuracy at which a student reads.

Silent Reading Fluency

Secondary-level students typically spend most of their engaged reading time reading silently, but silent reading fluency can be difficult to assess because a teacher cannot directly observe whether the student actually reads the text passage in its entirety or listen directly to the number of errors the student makes while reading.

Group-administered standardized tests of silent reading fluency that can be used for screening and monitoring students' progress over time include the Test of Silent Reading Efficiency and Comprehension (TOSREC; Wagner, Torgesen, Rashotte, & Pearson, 2010), the Test of Silent Word Reading Fluency (TOSWRF; Mather, Hammill, Allen, & Roberts, 2004), and the Test of Silent Contextual Reading Fluency (TOSCRF; Hammill, Wiederholt, & Allen, 2006). In the TOSREC, students are given a list of increasingly complex statements that can be identified as true or false using general world knowledge (e.g., *Houses can jump*). The score is the number of items the students get correct in 3 minutes. In one research study, Denton and colleagues (2011) found that the TOSREC was more predictive of reading comprehension standardized test scores than assessments of oral reading fluency (ORF) for middle school students. The TOSREC has four equivalent forms at each grade level; therefore, it can be given repeatedly throughout the year to track student progress. In the TOSWRF and TOSCRF, students are given printed words with no spaces between them and asked to put slashes between the words to separate them; their score is then the number of words correctly identified in 3 minutes. The TOSWRF, which consists of isolated words of increasing difficulty with no spaces between them (e.g., *weweaway-seesher*), has two equivalent test forms so that it can be given at the beginning and end of a period of time to measure student growth. The TOSCRF has four equivalent forms so that it can be given at intervals over a school year, and it consists of actual text presented with no punctuation or spaces between words (e.g., *thesesmallgreymiceranaway*).

Another kind of assessment sometimes used to measure silent reading fluency with comprehension is a **maze test** or **maze assessment**. In a maze assessment, students read text in which words have been removed at regular intervals (e.g., every seventh word) and replaced with blanks. For each blank, the student is given a choice of three words and must select the correct one (i.e., a multiple-choice format). Maze assessments can be administered timed or untimed. Preliminary evidence validates the maze test as a reliable way to monitor growth in some aspects of comprehension (Espin & Foegen, 1996). The timed administration of maze passages may be used to evaluate the rate at which a student reads silently along with the accuracy of selection of words that make sense; however, much of the research on the validity of this assessment has been done with students at the elementary rather than secondary level (Shin, Deno, & Espin, 2000; Wiley & Deno, 2005). Computerized maze assessments have been developed and may be practical for use in middle schools to monitor student progress in fluency.

Oral Reading Fluency

Teachers assess students' ORF by listening to students read brief passages aloud for 1–2 minutes and recording the number of words read and errors made. By subtracting the number of error words from the total number of words read, the teacher can determine the number of words correct per minute (WCPM). This kind of brief assessment can be used for the following:

- Screening students to identify struggling readers
- Determining students' **instructional reading level** in order to match students with text of appropriate difficulty
- Monitoring student growth over time in fluency and word recognition

How can using a 1- or 2-minute measure of ORF be so beneficial? It has been found that scores on brief measures of ORF are highly predictive of scores on standardized tests of reading comprehension such as the Stanford Achievement Test, particularly in the elementary grades (see Fuchs, Fuchs, Hosp, & Jenkins, 2001). This strong relationship between fluency and comprehension decreases as students are asked to read and comprehend increasingly complex text, but very low fluency at the middle school level can be a sign of serious reading problems.

On average, students in Grades 6–8 are able to read grade-level material at about 120–150 WCPM, but researchers have not yet determined fluency benchmarks for struggling middle school readers. We provide broad guidelines for evaluating fluency scores below. Figure 3.1 describes the procedures for administration of assessments of ORF using a digital kitchen timer. Note that these directions include locating passages for students to read. Alternatively, published sets of ORF passages are commercially available.

When giving an ORF assessment, it can be useful to administer more than one passage and take the average score to get a more accurate score for each student. For example, using multiple forms, a teacher may have students read three eighth-grade ORF passages and take the average score from all three. Because students' background knowledge about certain passages will vary, their scores may vary; taking an average will provide more accurate results.

Teachers may use the same ORF assessment to determine a student's reading accuracy level. This information can help a teacher decide what level of text a student can read independently and on what text a student may need more support in order to be

1. **Find passages** of approximately 250 words, written on grade level. If you are assessing a student in seventh grade, the passage should be written on the seventh-grade level. (Note: Published passages for this purpose are commercially available for Grades 6–8.)

2. **Prepare the passage** so that it is easily readable. Make a master copy on cardstock. The students will read from this copy, and it will not be marked. Make several copies on regular paper. You will use these regular copies to mark student errors.

3. **Sit next to or across from the student.** Give the student the master copy of the passage, and hold your copy on a clipboard. Struggling readers can be anxious about making mistakes, so it is important that you mark errors discreetly so as not to distract the student.

4. **Ask the student to read the passage until you say "stop."** Remind the student to read quickly and accurately and to pay attention to what he or she is reading.

5. **Say "begin," and start the timer** for 1 minute as soon as the student begins reading the first word.

6. **Mark errors by slashing through incorrect words,** including mispronunciations, substitutions, reversals, or omissions (skipped words). If a student does not say a word in 3–5 seconds, say the word, and mark that word as an error. If the student skips one or more lines, point back to the line that was skipped and count this as one error. DO NOT count self-corrections or insertions (extra words) as errors.

7. **Mark where the student stopped reading after 1 minute.** If the student is in the middle of a sentence when the timer goes off, allow the student to finish reading the sentence; however, do not count any words read after 1 minute.

8. **Determine the student's oral reading fluency score** (words correct per minute, or WCPM) by subtracting the number of error words from the total number of words the student read in 1 minute.

   Example:
   Your seventh-grade student Alex read 65 total words in 1 minute and made six mistakes. Subtracting his six error words from the 65 total words results in a score of 59 WCPM (65 total words read in a minute − 6 error words = 59 WCPM).

9. **Determine the student's reading accuracy level** by dividing the WCPM by the total number of words the student read in 1 minute.

   Alex read 59 words correctly in 1 minute. Dividing that number by the total words possible (or the total words read in the minute) and moving the decimal point two places to the left produces his percent accuracy score. Of the 59 words that Alex read, 91% were read accurately.

   59 (correct words) / 65 (total words read in 1 minute) = .907, rounded to .91, or 91% accuracy.

10. **Compare student accuracy** to the benchmarks in Figure 3.2.

    By comparing Alex's accuracy to the benchmarks in Figure 3.2, you can see that grade-level material is at an instructional level for Alex. This material is actually nearly at frustration level for Alex. Thus, Alex probably will need support when reading grade-level material. A logical goal would be for Alex to read grade-level material at 95% accuracy or higher by the end of the school year.

11. **Examine the student's fluency score.**

    Alex's reading rate is 59 WCPM with 91% accuracy. This suggests that Alex can accurately decode most of the words in grade-level text but that he read the selection very slowly. The answers to the following questions would help guide the instructional plan for Alex:
    - Does Alex's rate of reading vary depending upon his interest in the text? When Alex selects the text he would like to read, does he read at a faster rate?
    - Does Alex's rate of reading improve when you ask him to read more quickly?
    - Does Alex understand what he reads?

    Assuming that the rate of reading for Alex is low under most conditions, then establishing goals of improved rate of reading is appropriate. If Alex's rate of reading is dependent on his interests, then targeting motivation to learn a wider range of content may be an appropriate goal.

    If Alex has a generally low reading rate, he may need opportunities to practice reading to build fluency. Instructional activities for this purpose are provided in Chapter 9: Fluency.

Figure 3.1. Procedures for the administration of an oral reading fluency assessment. (From Rasinski, T.V. [2004]. *Assessing reading fluency.* Honolulu, HI: Pacific Resources for Education and Learning; adapted by permission.)

successful. See Figure 3.2 for accuracy levels commonly associated with the independent, instructional, and frustration reading levels (photocopiable version in the Appendix). (Note that these levels are determined differently in various published **informal reading inventories** but that the ones we have included are in common use. These are meant to be guidelines—not "hard and fast" rules.) The **independent reading level** (also called the "homework level") is usually described as the level of difficulty of text that the student can read on his or her own, without support. Text at the **instructional reading level** is best for teaching students to be better readers. This level includes text that students can

Accuracy Guidelines

INDEPENDENT LEVEL

No more than 1 in 20 words is difficult.   95%–100% accuracy

INSTRUCTIONAL LEVEL

No more than 1 in 10 words is difficult.   90%–94% accuracy

FRUSTRATION LEVEL

Difficulty with more than 1 in 10 words.   ≤ 90% accuracy

Figure 3.2. Accuracy Guidelines. (*Source:* Betts, 1946.)

read with assistance, or instruction. Text at the **frustration reading level** is probably too difficult for the student. When students are repeatedly asked to read frustration-level text, they typically develop counterproductive habits. Most individuals can read more difficult text if the topic is one in which he or she is highly interested and/or has good background knowledge. For this reason, there is likely not just one reading level that is appropriate for a student. The student's reading level will vary somewhat depending upon the text.

For example, Ms. Lopez gives an eighth-grade ORF measure to Jeremy, an eighth-grade boy, and he reads it with 96% accuracy. Jeremy is able to read eighth-grade text at an independent level, and this level of text is appropriate for assignments that will be done with little or no teacher or parent support. Ms. Lopez gives the same eighth-grade passage to Alicia, another eighth-grade student. Alicia reads the passage with only 92% accuracy. The eighth-grade text is on Alicia's instructional reading level, so Ms. Lopez can assign eighth-grade text to Alicia if Alicia will receive support or instruction as she reads it. Ms. Lopez also asks Alicia to read a seventh-grade passage. Alicia can read this passage with 97% accuracy, so her independent reading level is seventh-grade text. Ms. Lopez also gives the eighth-grade passage to Michael, who can read it with only 82% accuracy. The eighth-grade text is at Michael's frustration level, and unless Michael is highly interested in the text and is willing to struggle through it with guidance, he should not be asked to read this text. If Michael is regularly required to read eighth-grade text, he may display low motivation to read or even behavior problems. Ms. Lopez gives Michael the seventh-grade text and finds that it is at his instructional reading level, because he can read it at 90% accuracy. Michael reads a sixth-grade text with 97% accuracy, indicating that this is his independent reading level.

An easy way to apply this process to any text a student reads is to use the "One-to-Ten Rule": If a student misses more than one word for every ten words read, the text is probably too difficult. So if a student reads 50 words and misses 5, he or she read the text with 90% accuracy, indicating the instructional reading level. But, if the student misses seven words in the same text, the text is at the frustration level for that student. A student can read 10 words and miss 1, read 20 words and miss 2, and so forth, and still be at the instructional level. Keep in mind, though, that these are rough guidelines. It is important to use good "teacher judgment" when placing students in text but to be sure to listen to them read orally from time to time to verify that they are able to read most of the words accurately.

As with assessing ORF, it is helpful to have students read more than one passage to assess their oral reading accuracy levels. The accuracy levels on different passages are then averaged. Sometimes, students will struggle on a particular passage because of a name or concept with which they are not familiar but are able to read other text at the same level with better accuracy. If oral reading accuracy is determined at the same time as ORF, giving two to three brief 1-minute passages is sufficient to find both students' accuracy and fluency on grade-level text.

Using the Results of Oral Reading Fluency Assessment

Researchers have not determined whether having somewhat low ORF is reason for concern at the secondary level. Our best advice is to pay attention to students who score below 100–125 WCPM, as students who score below these levels may need fluency instruction.

Ms. Lopez will need to conduct more assessments to find out about her students' reading difficulties and to plan appropriate instruction. After assessing each reader's fluency ability, Ms. Lopez examines the results and determines which students have difficulties. She then conducts further assessments of these students to devise an instructional plan for each student. Further assessments usually include measures of word recognition. Besides indicating whether a student needs word-recognition instruction, word-reading assessments also can tell a teacher about a student's *specific* areas of need; for example, whether the student lacks a strategy for reading multisyllable words or has problems reading words that contain specific sound–spelling patterns (e.g., vowel combinations such as *ai* or *oa*, *r*-controlled vowels such as *ar* or *ur*).

Remember, if a middle school student's fluency is a little below average, this may not be reason for concern unless it seems to keep the student from understanding or remembering what he or she reads or from completing reading assignments. As a general rule, we recommend that students with ORF rates below 90–100 WCPM be given additional assessments of word recognition.

ASSESSING WORD RECOGNITION

Some systematic decoding programs designed for secondary students include assessments that can be used to evaluate student mastery of the different phonic elements or skills that are being taught in these programs (e.g., the sound of the letter combination *ai*, reading vowel team syllables such as *tain* in the word *maintain*, reading words with certain prefixes and suffixes). If such assessments are available with an instructional program, then they can be used to determine what students know and do not know to guide instruction (diagnostic assessment) and to monitor student progress over time. If no such assessments of word reading are available, the teacher may use a published assessment of **word-recognition** or phonics knowledge to determine student needs and track progress in mastering the elements being taught.

Note that not all difficulties with pronunciation are a result of poor word-recognition skills. Students with limited vocabularies, especially English language learners (ELLs), may recognize a word but not know how to pronounce it. Sometimes, ELLs may have trouble pronouncing a word because they have never heard it in English—not necessarily because they do not know what the word means. They also may mispronounce English words that bear a close resemblance to words they know in their native languages (e.g., the English word *literature* and the Spanish word *literatura*). Take care interpreting assessments with these students; similarly, interpret with care the oral reading assessments of students with speech-production difficulties and those who speak nonstandard English dialects.

MONITORING STUDENT PROGRESS OVER TIME

Throughout the year, Ms. Lopez may continue to use ORF measures to monitor improvement for students with low ORF scores. This can be done by administering passages at the same level of difficulty at regular intervals during the school year. Typically, it is helpful to monitor the progress of students with reading difficulties every 2–4 weeks. The scores on these assessments can be plotted as a line graph, resulting in a visual representation of a student's rate of progress over time. This can be done only if the assessments conducted throughout the year are all at the same level of difficulty. If students are given more difficult passages to read over the course of the school year, their fluency rates will drop when moved to a higher level, making it impossible to compare their rate of growth during one part of the year to that during another part of the year.

Typically, it is helpful to monitor students' progress all year long at the **goal level**, or the level of text that they should be able to read at the end of the school year. Then, teachers can examine their progress toward that goal. For example, let's say that Ms. Lopez has a student named Teresa in the seventh grade who begins the school year able to read sixth-grade–level text at 70 WCPM. Ms. Lopez may set a goal that, by the end of the school year, Teresa will be able to read seventh-grade–level text at 100 WCPM. Thus, Ms. Lopez would administer seventh-grade passages to Teresa every 2–4 weeks throughout the school year to see how Teresa is progressing toward this goal. These are not the same passages but rather different passages of approximately equal difficulty. To establish the approximate levels of difficulty of ORF passages, the developers of published assessments do extensive field testing with many students. Nevertheless, the difficulty of a particular passage will vary from student to student based on the student's knowledge of relevant vocabulary and background knowledge.

Besides monitoring ORF, Ms. Lopez also may want to monitor progress in the other specific reading domains that her instruction is targeting. For example, if a student's instructional focus is at the word-recognition level, it will be important for Ms. Lopez to monitor progress in this area. Ms. Lopez may administer an assessment of word recognition or decoding at regular intervals to evaluate student progress in mastering phonics elements or rapidly identifying words. Teachers also can create their own curriculum-based assessments by listing examples of all the different types of words (or all the sight words, letter–sound correspondences, or words with various syllable types) that will be taught throughout the year and administering this list at different points during the year (or semester) to see which elements students have learned and which students do not know or have forgotten.

Monitoring progress is essential so that Ms. Lopez knows how to adjust instruction and grouping. Typically, if a teacher is monitoring ORF every 2 weeks and three data points indicate that a student is not making progress, the teacher needs to adjust instruction in some way.

Having students chart their own progress in fluency can increase motivation and participation (Vaughn & Bos, 2012). A simple format for charting progress is a progress-monitoring tracking form (see Figure 3.3). After generating multiple scores, teachers may also have students plot their fluency scores on a line graph. Figure 3.4 shows an example of a progress-monitoring graph.

Student:				
	9/1	9/2	9/3	9/4
Text level	Fifth-grade text	Fifth-grade text		
Score	80	83		
Errors	7	3		
Accuracy	91% accuracy	97% accuracy		
Reading level	Instructional level	Independent level		

Figure 3.3.   Progress-monitoring tracking form.

CAVEATS ABOUT ORAL READING FLUENCY IN MIDDLE SCHOOL STUDENTS

Many of the guidelines about monitoring students' progress and establishing benchmarks in ORF for older students with reading difficulties are based on research with younger children in Grades 1–4. Considerably less is known about fluency practices for older students. Consider the following when interpreting fluency rates with older students:

• The most important outcome for students is that they can understand and learn from the text they read. If students have below-average fluency but demonstrate average or above-average comprehension, it may not be appropriate to spend considerable time on improving their rate of reading; however, students who read very slowly may have problems completing assignments and staying focused when asked to read long texts.

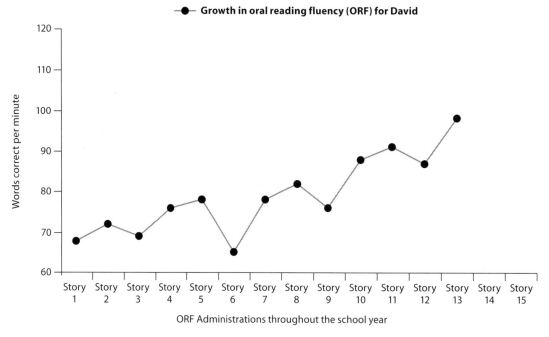

Figure 3.4.   Progress-monitoring graph.

- Students who read above 100 WCPM with 90% accuracy in grade-level text may benefit from time spent on enhancing their background knowledge, vocabulary, and/or comprehension rather than on fluency instruction.

- Consider the individual needs of adolescent learners, their interest in reading, and their motivation to learn as you interpret ORF scores and develop interventions.

OUTCOME ASSESSMENTS

After a semester or year is completed, it is helpful to administer outcome assessments to determine whether students have attained instructional goals. Some students may be making so much progress that they will not require additional reading instruction. For students who continue in the reading class, administer diagnostic assessments. These assessments may show that, for some students, word reading or fluency skills that were previously identified as "still developing" may now be classified as meeting grade-level benchmarks (see Chapter 4: Using Assessment Results to Plan Instruction). Based on these assessments, students would be regrouped and the focus of instruction adjusted.

Chapter 4

Using Assessment Results to Plan Instruction

As we described in Chapter 1, students with severely impaired decoding ability and very low fluency are best served in very small classes within the intensive intervention tier. However, we know that many middle school reading teachers, such as Ms. Lopez, will have these students assigned to the same class sections as students who do not need extended instruction in decoding and word recognition. In the following sections, we describe how Ms. Lopez can use the results of assessments to divide a class into small groups with similar instructional needs and determine the instructional focus for each group. In the last section of this chapter, we describe a potential instructional approach for a class that includes only students in the strategic intervention tier.

GROUPING STUDENTS FOR INSTRUCTION

Once Ms. Lopez determines the specific areas of instruction each student needs, she groups students accordingly and focuses instruction according to the needs of each group. Students benefit when teachers use a variety of grouping formats such as working with students individually, even for 1–2 minutes; small-group and whole-group instruction; and pairs (Elbaum, Vaughn, Hughes, & Moody, 1999, 2000). Pairing peers to work together can be beneficial to students while freeing up the teacher to work with small groups. Smaller groups and paired peers make it possible for a student to receive more immediate feedback from a teacher or a peer and increase active student engagement; both feedback and active engagement have been related to improved student outcomes.

It is challenging to adequately instruct students with a variety of needs in a whole-group setting. Often, this is not as productive as using smaller, homogeneous groups with instructional goals based on the needs of students in the group, as reflected in diagnostic and progress-monitoring assessments. Although it is not possible to form perfectly homogeneous groups, the more similar the needs of the students in each group, the more efficiently Ms. Lopez will be able to instruct her students. Ms. Lopez also remembers that group assignments are based on a dynamic process in which changes are made according to student progress (Mastropieri & Scruggs, 2002). Students do not remain in the same group for every activity or for months across the school year. Typically, secondary struggling readers can be grouped into four categories, as illustrated in Table 4.1.

Table 4.1. Categories of secondary struggling readers

Student profile	Focus
Adequate word-reading skills and reading fluency, average or limited vocabulary knowledge, poor text comprehension	Comprehension strategies + vocabulary
Low fluency level and poor text comprehension but adequate word recognition	Comprehension strategies + vocabulary + fluency practice with connected text
Weak decoding ability; slow, dysfluent reading; poor text comprehension	Comprehension strategies + vocabulary + multisyllable word recognition instruction and practice and fluency practice with connected text
Seriously impaired decoding ability, very low fluency, poor text comprehension	Explicit, systematic instruction in decoding and word recognition + fluency + vocabulary + comprehension (at this level, each daily lesson includes instruction in word reading as well as opportunities to apply decoding and comprehension strategies reading instructional-level text)

DETERMINING THE INSTRUCTIONAL FOCUS

Next, Ms. Lopez determines her instructional focus based on the results of her assessments. One way to approach this task is to organize all of a class's assessment data in a table to identify students with similar needs. Figure 4.1 shows sample eighth-grade data. Ms. Lopez gave an ORF measure to her students and then determined who was reading below 100 WCPM. For those students, she gave additional measures to determine why they were not reading fluently. In the figure, the letters *MB* stand for *meets benchmark* and the letters *SD* stand for *still developing*, indicating dimensions of reading for which students have attained grade-level competence or have not yet developed to that level, respectively.

The following are the steps Ms. Lopez followed to form groups in her class:

1. After determining from previous assessments and grades that all students in her class had comprehension needs, Ms. Lopez administered a measure of ORF to each student.

Student name	ORF	Plan of action	Test of Word Reading Efficiency	Plan of action	San Diego Quick Assessment of Reading Ability
Elizabeth S.	77	Continue testing	SD	Continue testing	SD
Ryan W.	62	Continue testing	SD	Continue testing	SD
Aaron S.	162				
Jose D.	103				
Bernardo K.	179				
Juan G.	85	Continue testing	SD	Continue testing	SD
Maria P.	52	Continue testing	SD	Continue testing	SD
Rueben S.	154				
Ghani R.	155				
Antonio Z.	89	Continue testing	MB		
Isabella B.	170				
Andre S.	95	Continue testing	MB		
Alexandra D.	87	Continue testing	MB		
Justin B.	98	Continue testing	MB		
Jacob B.	99	Continue testing	MB		

Figure 4.1. Results of Ms. Lopez's assessments. (Adapted with permission from the Vaughn Gross Center for Reading and Language Arts at The University of Texas at Austin. [2005]. *Introduction to the 3-Tier reading model: Reducing reading difficulties for kindergarten through third-grade students* [4th ed.]. Austin, TX: Author.) (*Key:* ORF, oral reading fluency; SD, still developing; MB, meets benchmark.)

2. Ms. Lopez identified that six of her students (Aaron, Jose, Bernardo, Rueben, Ghani, and Isabella) were reading above 100 WCPM. Ms. Lopez determined that these students' needs were primarily in the areas of comprehension and vocabulary. She will continue to monitor Jose's reading fluency and accuracy because his score is close to the 100 WCPM benchmark.

3. For the remaining nine students whose ORF scores fell below 100 WCPM, Ms. Lopez administered more specific measures to assess the sources of the students' comprehension and fluency needs. She gave these nine students the Test of Word Reading Efficiency (TOWRE; Torgesen, Wagner, & Rashotte, 1999) to test individual word-reading fluency and the San Diego Quick Assessment of Reading Ability (LaPray & Ross, 1969) to test knowledge of phonics and syllabication.

4. Then, Ms. Lopez recorded all the scores in a table so that she could appropriately group her students. Teachers use the guidelines for interpreting scores on individual assessments along with individual judgment to determine whether students' skills are still developing (SD) or whether students have met benchmarks (MB). Generally, if a student scores below the 25th or 30th percentile on a standardized test like the TOWRE, the student will be considered "still developing."

5. Based on the scores recorded in the table, Ms. Lopez was able to group her students into three groups and determine the instructional focus for each group, as shown in Figure 4.2.

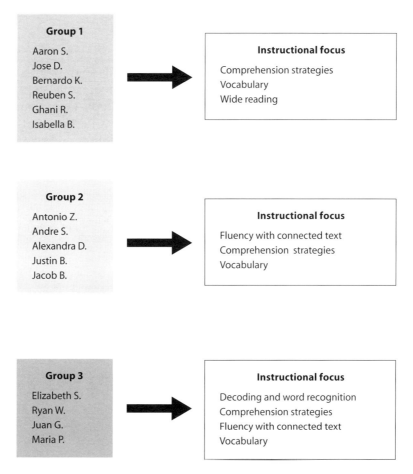

Figure 4.2. Ms. Lopez's groupings.

Ms. Lopez will meet with each of these small groups for a portion of the class at least two or three times per week so that she can provide instruction to target their particular needs. She will meet with the group with greatest needs every day for a few minutes of systematic instruction in phonics and word reading. Because all of her students need work on comprehension and vocabulary strategies, Ms. Lopez will provide instruction in these areas to the whole class. Although she will focus primarily on the same strategies (i.e., summarizing, making inferences, questioning) for all students, students will practice applying the strategies in instructional-level text. Thus, different students will be applying the same strategies using different text.

If a student is working independently, it can be helpful to have the student apply a comprehension strategy in independent-level text until he or she becomes proficient at that strategy. However, if the student is learning through guided practice, instructional-level text is appropriate. With a great deal of support (e.g., having students engage in partner reading in which a higher-performing student reads a section of text aloud followed by the lower-skilled reader reading the same section of text aloud), students may apply comprehension strategies in frustration-level text. Exposing students to more challenging text is important so that students come in contact with more advanced vocabulary and sentence structures (Stahl, 2003). However, it is important to keep in mind that reading frustration-level text with no support can promote use of ineffective strategies and decrease motivation to read. Constantly reading frustration-level text is—well—frustrating! Table 4.2 provides a list of factors to be considered when selecting text for students.

SETTING SHORT-TERM GOALS WITH STUDENTS

Work with students to set short-term intermediate goals so that both you and the students can monitor progress toward larger goals through manageable steps. Using a task analysis procedure, large goals can be refined into smaller steps. For example, a goal of reading multisyllabic words made up of closed, open, and vowel-consonant-*e* syllable types (e.g., *amputate, monopolize*) might be broken down into the following manageable steps:

Table 4.2. Factors to consider when selecting text for students

Student-related factors	Text-related factors
Word-recognition ability How accurately does the student read the words in the text?	**Text format** How much print is on the page? How complex are the sentences?
Fluency Can the student read the text fluently enough to understand and remember what is being read and to enjoy reading?	**Vocabulary** Are there challenging vocabulary words that will make comprehension difficult? Is it necessary to understand the challenging words in order to comprehend the text? If so, can difficult words be pretaught?
Comprehension strategies Is the student a strategic reader? Does the student monitor and self-correct errors? Does he or she connect ideas within the text and interpret the text using background knowledge?	**Genre** What type of material is it? Is it narrative or expository? If it is expository, is it well organized with clearly presented ideas in coherent paragraphs?
Interest and motivation What is the student interested in? What topics will keep his or her attention? Can you give the student a choice of reading material?	**Content and concepts** What is the topic of the text? Is the subject matter accessible to the students? If the students do not have sufficient background knowledge to relate to the text, can ideas be pretaught to make it easier for students to access the text?
Background and vocabulary knowledge What background knowledge does the student bring to the text? How familiar is the student likely to be with the vocabulary that is essential to understanding the text?	**Illustrations and/or graphics** Do the graphics support the text? What is the quality of the graphics?

- Recognize and read closed syllables (e.g., *am*).
- Apply these skills to read multisyllable words.

It is possible for these steps to be broken down even further. Students benefit when they are aware of their goals and track their progress. See Chapter 10: Word Recognition for a description of instruction in multisyllable word reading.

SCHEDULING SMALL-GROUP INSTRUCTION

After dividing her class into appropriate groups and determining each group's instructional focus, Ms. Lopez can design a weekly schedule. A sample schedule based on a 50-minute period is shown in Figure 4.3. Detailed suggestions about the content of instruction, along with instructional activities that can be used to teach the content, are included in Sections II and III of this sourcebook.

	10-minute blocks	Monday	Tuesday	Wednesday	Thursday	Friday
1st 10 minutes	Grouping and focus: teacher led	Whole-group instruction: comprehension strategy	Whole-group instruction: review comprehension strategy	Whole-group instruction: vocabulary strategy	Whole-group instruction: review vocabulary strategy	Whole-group instruction: review comprehension or vocabulary
	Grouping and focus: student led	n/a	n/a	n/a	n/a	n/a
2nd 10 minutes	Grouping and focus: teacher led	Whole-group instruction and guided practice: comprehension	Group 2 with teacher: multisyllable word reading	Whole-group instruction and guided practice: vocabulary	Group 3 with teacher: decoding and word recognition	Group 1 with teacher: vocabulary and comprehension
	Grouping and focus: student led	n/a	Groups 1 and 3 independent practice (pairs): comprehension	n/a	Groups 1 and 2 independent practice (pairs): vocabulary	Groups 2 and 3 partner reading: fluency
3rd 10 minutes	Grouping and focus: teacher led	Whole-group instruction and guided practice: comprehension	Group 2 with teacher: multisyllable word reading	Group 3 with teacher: Guided practice: vocabulary	Group 3 with teacher: decoding and word recognition	Group 1 with teacher: vocabulary and comprehension
	Grouping and focus: student led	n/a	Groups 1 and 3 independent practice (pairs): comprehension	Groups 1 and 2 independent practice (pairs): vocabulary	Groups 1 and 2 independent practice (pairs): vocabulary	Groups 2 and 3 partner reading: fluency
4th 10 minutes	Grouping and focus: teacher led	Group 3 with teacher: decoding and word recognition	Group 3 with teacher: decoding and word recognition	Group 2 with teacher: multisyllable word reading	Group 1 with teacher: vocabulary and comprehension	Group 3 with teacher: decoding and word recognition
	Grouping and focus: student led	Groups 1 and 2 independent practice (pairs): comprehension	Groups 1 and 2 partner reading (pairs): fluency	Groups 1 and 3 independent practice (pairs): vocabulary	Groups 2 and 3 independent practice: comprehension	Groups 1 and 2 independent practice (pairs): comprehension
5th 10 minutes	Grouping and focus: teacher led	Group 3 with teacher: review comprehension; guided practice	Group 3 with teacher: decoding and word recognition	Group 2 with teacher: fluency	Group 1 with teacher: vocabulary and comprehension	Group 3 with teacher: decoding and word recognition
	Grouping and focus: student led	Groups 1 and 2 independent practice (pairs): comprehension	Groups 1 and 2 partner reading (pairs): fluency	Groups 1 and 3 independent practice (pairs): vocabulary	Groups 2 and 3 independent practice: comprehension	Groups 1 and 2 independent practice (pairs): comprehension

Figure 4.3.   Ms. Lopez's class schedule.

This schedule is just one example. There are many other ways to design a weekly schedule for effective instruction. Teachers must consider the needs of each student, each small group, and the class as a whole. The needs of the students will dictate the balance between small-group and whole-class instruction as well as the instructional focus of each lesson.

AN ALTERNATIVE SCHEDULE FOR READING INTERVENTION CLASSES

For classes that include only students who are receiving strategic intervention or when- ever students in a reading class have very similar needs, a schedule such as the one in Figure 4.4 may be appropriate (photocopiable version in the Appendix). The number of minutes dedicated to each activity may be adjusted (or whole activities eliminated) ac- cording to the needs reflected on student assessments. At the same time, if many students in the group have severe word-reading difficulties, more time should be devoted to sys- tematic instruction in word recognition (see Chapter 10: Word Recognition).

MANAGING SMALL-GROUP INSTRUCTION

Teachers who have not previously implemented small-group instruction may feel over- whelmed by such a schedule. It can be helpful to begin by incorporating small-group in- struction a little at a time, working with small groups 1 or 2 days a week at first and then gradually adding small-group lessons as the teacher and students become comfortable with this instructional arrangement.

As you plan lessons, keep in mind that even though students need direct instruc- tion in reading skills and strategies, they also need daily practice reading interesting text at their independent or instructional reading levels. This reading may be done indepen- dently or in pairs and may provide opportunities to apply comprehension strategies, vo- cabulary strategies, or word-reading skills or to build fluency. When students engage in guided and independent practice of strategies and skills, most of this practice occurs in the context of reading text. Practicing *does not* mean completing worksheets. This manual contains many examples of lesson plans with guided and independent practice activities designed to support student learning.

Classroom management is very important in small-group instructional formats. While the teacher works with a small group, other students must be able to work without direct teacher supervision. Implementing this model successfully requires that students learn and practice regular routines. Directly teaching these routines is the key to sanity for the teacher and successful progress for the students. In other words, teachers directly teach students what they want the students to do as they work in pairs, when they have completed an assignment, or in other situations in which students will be expected to work independently of the teacher.

By middle school, some students who struggle with reading are several years be- hind their typically developing peers. To catch up, struggling readers must learn at a faster rate than higher-performing students. This means that there is absolutely no time to waste. Every minute of class time is precious. While the teacher is working with a small group, the other students must be actively engaged in practicing strategies and skills they are learning. Students are not given "seatwork" to keep them occupied. Every activity is

Sample Instructional Sequence for Reading Instruction (Based on a 45-minute class)

EVERY DAY FOR THE FIRST 4–6 WEEKS OF INTERVENTION

COMPONENTS	TIME RANGE (IN MINS.)
Fluency (partner reading)	7–10
Vocabulary instruction (prefixes, suffixes, base words, and roots)	8–10
Multisyllable word reading instruction and practice	18–24
Spelling dictation	4–6

SAMPLE WEEKLY SCHEDULE FOR REMAINDER OF INTERVENTION

COMPONENTS	TIME RANGE (IN MINS.)
MONDAY	
Fluency (if needed) or other text reading (partner reading)	7–10
Multisyllable word reading practice or vocabulary word part review	6–8
Vocabulary instruction	15–25
Spelling dictation	6–8
TUESDAY	
Fluency (if needed) or other text reading (partner reading)	7–10
Vocabulary review and practice	5–7
Comprehension strategy instruction (modeling and guided practice)	10–15
Passage reading, applying comprehension strategy	15–20
WEDNESDAY	
Fluency (if needed) or other text reading (partner reading)	7–10
Vocabulary review and practice	5–7
Comprehension strategy instruction, continued	8–10
Passage reading, applying comprehension strategy	20–25
THURSDAY	
Fluency (if needed) or other text reading (partner reading)	7–10
Multisyllable word reading practice or vocabulary word part review	6–8
Vocabulary review and practice	8–10
Comprehension strategy instruction, continued; passage reading, applying comprehension strategy	25–35
FRIDAY	
Fluency (if needed) or other text reading (partner reading)	7–10
Comprehension review	6–8
Expository writing (Write a summary of the passage or write an essay using the same text structure as the passage, guided by a graphic organizer.)	25–35

Figure 4.4. Sample Instructional Sequence for Reading Instruction (based on a 45-minute class).

purposeful and directed at the critical skills students need to be competent, successful readers.

Note that students may change groups as often as appropriate, depending on their rates of progress in comprehension, vocabulary, fluency, and word recognition. It is important to monitor progress carefully so students are not held back, receiving instruction that no longer meets their needs.

Section II

Effective Instruction for Struggling Readers

Chapter 5

Components of Effective Instruction

After conducting assessments, Ms. Lopez should be aware of her students' needs in the following areas:

- Comprehension
- Vocabulary
- Fluency
- Word recognition

By this point, Ms. Lopez has designed a flexible grouping system that will allow her to work with homogenous, small groups when necessary. She feels that she has a grasp on what her students need to learn but is overwhelmed by the challenge of giving them the help they need. She is not sure how to structure her lessons to meet her students' needs. This chapter discusses how to organize and plan effective instruction.

Researchers have identified key lesson components that make instruction more effective for struggling readers (Mastropieri & Scruggs, 2002; Swanson & Deshler, 2003). The components, explained in more detail later in this chapter, are as follows:

- Statement of objective or purpose
- Daily review
- Explicit modeling and teaching
- Guided practice
- Independent practice
- Teaching for generalization
- Monitoring student learning
- Periodic review (multiple opportunities for practice)

TERMS TO KNOW

automaticity   Automatic processing; implementing a skill, strategy, or process with little or no conscious attention to it

corrective feedback   Specific clarification provided by the teacher to give students information about their errors

distributed practice   Providing many opportunities to practice a skill or apply a strategy distributed across time; distributed practice sessions are typically shorter than massed practice sessions, in which students practice a skill in a single extended lesson

generalization   The application of a rule or behavior to a new context or setting (e.g., applying a comprehension strategy learned in reading class to a social studies assignment)

objective   The aim or goal of the lesson; what the teacher wants the students to learn

overlearning   Learning to the point of mastery, or automaticity

positive feedback   Specific praise provided by the teacher to reinforce students' correct responses and encourage student effort

prior knowledge   Background knowledge or knowledge that students already have from previous experience

scaffolding   Adjusting or extending instruction so that students are able to be successful with challenging tasks; this support is temporary and removed when no longer needed

think-aloud modeling   A type of modeling in which the teacher verbalizes what he or she is thinking in order to make the thought process apparent to students

STATEMENT OF OBJECTIVE OR PURPOSE

The **objective** of the lesson must be clear to the teacher before it can be clear to the students. Be aware of what you want your students to learn and teach with that goal in mind. Provide students with a step-by-step presentation of information. Present only a few ideas at once, and connect new material to **prior knowledge**. During this stage of the lesson, an effective teacher will provide a supportive framework illustrating how the new information being presented is related to information that students already know. Using this framework, students are able to gain access to prior knowledge and then connect it to the new subject matter being introduced (Swanson & Deshler, 2003).

DAILY REVIEW

A daily review is more than just checking to see whether homework assignments are complete. A review of material covered the day before gives the teacher the opportunity to see whether her students have mastered the material and provides students with an opportunity to **overlearn**—to learn to the point of mastery, or automaticity. When students overlearn a skill or strategy they are able to apply it with little or no conscious attention. For example, fluent readers develop automaticity in word recognition; they can recognize words without conscious attention to the task, freeing up their mental resources to focus on the meaning of the text. Overlearning leads to long-term retention and provides connections for future learning (Mastropieri & Scruggs, 2002). During the daily review, do the following:

1. Review quickly the material taught in the previous lesson.

2. Review previous learning with specific consideration for whether students have retained key concepts.

3. Present information visually and explicitly. In other words, present information clearly enough that your students have no doubt about what it is you want them to recall. One method of presenting information in this way is to post information such as definitions of key concepts or essential steps of previously taught strategies around the classroom. If students do not display adequate knowledge of the material already covered, adjust instruction or reteach material as needed.

EXPLICIT MODELING AND TEACHING

Model the strategy or demonstrate the skill clearly. Show students what you want them to do. Strategies can be modeled through a **think-aloud** process. During think-aloud modeling, the teacher actually carries out each step of the strategy while talking about his or her own thought processes. This type of modeling allows the thinking process to become observable and gives students a clear picture of what the strategy being taught looks like. The sample lesson plans in this book provide many examples of think-aloud modeling. It is important that teachers not simply assume that students understand the execution of a skill or the thinking process involved in applying a strategy. Therefore, careful modeling is essential. In addition to this modeling, repeated questioning throughout the presentation of new information gives the teacher an opportunity to assess the students' levels of understanding and correct any misconceptions before moving on (Swanson & Deshler, 2003).

Finally, after teaching a skill or strategy, carefully monitor student understanding and adjust instruction accordingly. If students are not fully grasping a concept, it is important to adjust instruction to meet their needs. This usually involves modeling the process again and providing explicit feedback as students practice it.

In summary, when presenting new information, be sure to do the following:

- Be mindful of what you want your students to learn.
- Connect new material to students' prior knowledge.
- Model and/or demonstrate the new strategy or skill.
- Question the students' understanding of the new material.
- Monitor the students' understanding and adapt instruction as needed.

During the modeling phase of instruction, try to ensure that ELLs and others with limited oral vocabularies are directly observing the teacher—not trying to listen, write, copy, and watch at the same time. Because of their limited English skills, they benefit from having their full attention on the teacher.

GUIDED PRACTICE

Guided practice gives students the opportunity to demonstrate what they have learned with guidance from the teacher. It is important that the teacher provides guidance while students work on their assignments—not wait until they are finished to check for accuracy. This is the time to give students helpful hints and clarify any misconceptions they might have. Providing this type of guidance while students are working ensures that students are practicing a skill or learning a concept correctly. Without guidance, some students will practice a skill incorrectly and, consequently, become confused. When students practice their mistakes, those mistakes become bad habits.

An effective teacher provides **scaffolding**, or support, to students in the initial stages of learning a new strategy or skill. Scaffolding allows students to apply a new strategy or skill in a safe environment by providing specific support directly where assistance is needed. For example, if a student is having difficulty with the concept of asking themselves questions during reading to monitor his or her own comprehension, a teacher may scaffold by starting a question for the student (or students) and then having the student finish the question. For example, while reading text about the Civil War, the teacher may start a question as follows:

Teacher: Where did Abraham Lincoln…?

Student: …give his speech?

Through supported application of skills and strategies, a student will be able to reach the goal of mastery. Scaffolding will be discussed further in Chapter 6.

Guided practice should directly reflect the objective of instruction. During this time, the teacher's job is to ensure that students have a clear understanding of the strategy or skill that has just been presented. Students who have problems remembering new material often benefit from practicing in a variety of formats and contexts. Teachers should ensure that students are given ample time to understand new concepts before moving on to independent practice. Overall, students may need multiple opportunities to practice with guidance from the teacher.

This phase in the lesson is an excellent time to involve students in actively responding to questions. Student responses should guide the teacher in making decisions about how best to scaffold or support student learning. In addition to providing extra practice opportunities, questioning can help teachers assess student progress and knowledge of concepts.

Teachers can have students respond in several different formats:

- **Choral response:** All of the students answer together.

- **Partner response:** Each student responds to a partner. Assign each student in a pair a number. Then say, for example, "Ones tell twos why the character…."

- **Silent response:** Students point thumbs up or down to indicate agreement or disagreement or engage in some other type of silent response.

- **Individual selection:** Pose a question to the whole class and then strategically select an individual student to answer the question. Remember to say the student's name *after* asking the question so that all students think they might be called on and rehearse an answer in anticipation of being selected.

It is critical for students to practice correct responses. When a student gives a correct response, restate the correct response and have the class repeat the correct response as well. This will give the students an opportunity to practice correct reading and responding. Consider the following examples:

Point to a word on the board.

Teacher: What is this word… (short pause) Justin? (This is an example of individual
               selection.)

Student: *Island.*

Teacher: That's right—*island.* Everyone, what is this word?

Class: *Island.* (This is an example of choral response and practicing correct responses.)

Or:

Teacher: What does it mean that he was *elated*... (short pause) Sara?

Student: It means he was very happy and excited.

Teacher: That's right. *Elated* means very happy and excited. Everyone, what does *elated* mean?

Class: Very happy and excited.

During guided practice, it is essential to offer **positive** and **corrective feedback**, as appropriate. When students read a word incorrectly or give an incorrect response, they are essentially practicing and reinforcing that incorrect response. Positive and corrective feedback will be discussed further in the next chapter. One example of providing corrective feedback is provided below

Student (reading orally): She longed to see the is-land....

Teacher: That word is *island.* Say the word.

Student: *Island.*

Teacher: Good. Please reread the sentence.

Student: She longed to see the island her grandmother told stories about....

INDEPENDENT PRACTICE

Once students are consistently responding to questions and applying a skill or strategy correctly during guided practice, then they are ready to apply their new knowledge independently. Independent practice reinforces concepts taught and allows students to learn information on their own. Independent practice should parallel the goals of the lesson and be directly relevant to guided practice.

When planning for independent practice, a teacher may reflect, "Am I giving the students an opportunity to apply the strategy or skill that was taught without support?" If, through direct instruction and guided practice, students were taught how to categorize vocabulary words, they should have several opportunities to practice categorizing words independently. Sometimes, teachers make the mistake of asking students to practice a related skill during independent practice instead of the exact strategy or skill that was taught. For example, a multiple-choice worksheet asking students to choose the category to which a word belongs is related to categorization; however, this activity is not as effective as giving students a list of words and asking them to categorize them appropriately. Many students will not be able to accomplish a task such as categorization independently unless they have had sufficient explicit instruction, modeling, and guided practice.

The goal of independent practice is for students to develop automaticity, or mastery of a strategy or skill. Once the strategy or skill becomes a habit, it will be easier for students to generalize their new knowledge.

TEACHING FOR GENERALIZATION

Generalization occurs when students apply strategies and skills they have learned in the reading class whenever they read in other contexts or settings. Struggling readers usually do not generalize automatically.

To promote generalization, teachers can plan instruction so that students have ample practice applying their new skills and strategies with a variety of texts, including texts that are similar to those that students read in English language arts, math, social studies, and science classes. Teachers can also tell students explicitly that they should apply skills and strategies to a wide range of circumstances and can lead discussions in which students verbalize ways that they can generalize strategies they have learned. For example, a teacher may ask questions such as, "Can you think of a time you might use this strategy outside of this class?" Examples of teaching for generalization are provided in the lesson plans included in this sourcebook.

If content-area teachers are aware of the vocabulary and comprehension strategies students learn in the reading class, then they can show how these strategies apply in different disciplines and remind students to use the strategies throughout the school day. See Chapter 1 for a description of coordinated strategy instruction across content areas to support continuity and generalization.

MONITORING STUDENT LEARNING

Monitoring student learning refers to the process of gathering information regularly through student assessments. The information gathered should be directly connected to a student's instructional focus. For example, if diagnostic assessments establish that a student needs to work on fluency or word recognition, then a teacher may monitor student growth through repeated assessments of ORF or word list reading.

Once you establish a routine of regular progress monitoring, you can use the data collected as a guide to planning instruction. The data will help you know when you need to reteach concepts and when you need to adapt instruction. Four ways to adapt instruction are defined in Figure 5.1 (photocopiable version in the Appendix). For further discussion of progress monitoring and adapting instruction, please refer to Chapters 3 and 4.

PERIODIC REVIEW AND/OR MULTIPLE OPPORTUNITIES FOR PRACTICE

A teacher who wants students to have long-term retention of the material they have learned must plan and provide for daily, weekly, and monthly review of strategies and skills. Swanson and Deshler (2003) took a "big-picture" look at what research says about instructional practice. They found that students need to practice newly learned material thoroughly but that **distributed practice** is better for retention. Distributed practice means that concepts learned in one unit of study are carried over for review and connection to new information in another unit of study. Connections between related materials should be pointed out explicitly to students. In their book *Effective Teaching Strategies That Accommodate Diverse Learners*, Kame'enui and Carnine (1998) suggested that teachers keep a cumulative list of strategies and skills covered and then space the review of this material

Guide to Adapting Instruction

ADAPTATION CATEGORY	DEFINITION	EXAMPLES
Instructional Content	Skills and concepts that are the focus of teaching and learning	Determining main ideas Reading words with closed syllable patterns Summarization
Instructional Activity	The actual lessons used to teach and reinforce skills and concepts	Semantic mapping Main idea strategy lesson Teaching the multisyllable word reading strategy
Delivery of Instruction	The procedures and routines used to teach instructional activities	Grouping—whole class, small group, or partners Modeling and thinking aloud Connecting to background knowledge Multiple opportunities for practice
Instructional Materials	Supplemental aids that are used to teach and reinforce skills and concepts	Narrative or expository text Manipulatives Charts Flashcards Recorded text

Figure 5.1. Guide to Adapting Instruction. (Adapted with permission from The University of Texas Center for Reading and Language Arts. [2003b]. *Special education reading project [SERP] secondary institute—Effective instruction for secondary struggling readers: Research-based practices.* Austin, TX: Author.)

over time through a variety of activities. Effective teachers understand that it is their job to find out what their students know, to teach them what they do not know, to guide them and support them as they learn, and to provide several opportunities for students to apply their newly learned skills or strategies (see Figure 5.2).

Figure 5.2. Steps to long-term retention.

Chapter 6

Delivering Effective Instruction

Are there teacher behaviors that make a difference in student learning? Absolutely. Teachers who have a repertoire of certain teaching behaviors are more effective than teachers who are unaware of these practices. The teaching skills and strategies proven to improve student learning can be thought of as "features of effective instruction." Through learning and practicing these skills, teachers can have a positive impact on the progress of their students, especially those with learning difficulties, often resulting in a heightened sense of empowerment and confidence for the teachers.

Some important elements of effective instruction for students with reading difficulties (Mastropieri & Scruggs, 2002; Vaughn & Bos, 2012) include the following:

- Explicit instruction
- Targeted instruction
- Time on task
- Quick pacing of lessons
- Positive feedback
- Corrective feedback
- Student motivation

TERMS TO KNOW

autonomy	Personal independence
corrective feedback	Specific clarification provided by the teacher to give students information about their errors
explicit instruction	Instruction that is clear and obvious so that students do not have to guess what they are expected to learn
motivation	A feeling of interest or enthusiasm that makes a student want to complete a task or improve his or her skills
positive feedback	Specific praise provided by the teacher to reinforce students' correct responses and encourage student effort

quick pacing of lessons	Instruction that moves at a manageable pace for students while taking advantage of every minute; minimizes unnecessary teacher talk and transition time between activities
scaffolding	Adjusting and extending instruction so that students are able to be successful with challenging tasks; temporary and removed when no longer needed
scope and sequence	The content and objectives included in a curriculum and the order in which they are presented
self-regulation	A student's ability to monitor his or her own progress and make adjustments to complete a task as necessary
targeted instruction	Instruction that is based on assessments; targets student weaknesses, builds on strengths, and is designed to teach students exactly what they need to learn
time on task	Time when students are actively engaged in learning and applying what they have learned

EXPLICIT INSTRUCTION

When instruction is explicit, students know exactly what they are expected to learn. To provide a clear objective to the student, the objective must first be clear to the teacher. That is why the instructional planning discussed in the previous chapter is so important. **Explicit instruction** is provided through the following:

- A clear statement of the objective
- Modeling
- Demonstration
- Understandable explanation

The following is an example of explicitly teaching the sight word *through*: *Point to the word* through *on a flashcard or the board.*

> **Teacher:** This word is *through*. It is an irregular word because the "o-u" makes the sound /ew/ and the "g-h" is silent. Let's read a sentence with the word *through* in it.
>
> **Students:** When the Prince of Wales went through the door, he realized everyone was there to make him King.
>
> **Teacher:** Great reading. You remembered that "t-h-r-o-u-g-h" is *through*.
> In this sentence *through* means that he passed into the room.
> Now, each of you think of a sentence with the word *through* in it.

The teacher calls on 2–4 students (including nonvolunteers) and they use the word *through* in sentences.

Still pointing to the word.

> **Teacher:** What word?
>
> **Students:** *Through.*

The teacher may ask individual students to read the word and then ask the group to read a list of previously learned words including the new word. The teacher also may ask the students to read sentences or paragraphs containing the word *through*.

The previous scenario is a simple example of explicit instruction. The main idea is this: Teachers should not make students guess or infer what they are supposed to learn; therefore, it is important to know the objectives of lessons and to express these objectives simply and clearly to your students.

TARGETED INSTRUCTION

Targeted instruction is instruction based on the results of ongoing student assessments. Essentially, teachers use the information gathered from assessments to determine what students need to learn. Assessment should be the first order of business at the beginning of the year or when a student first begins the reading class. Refer to Section I: Assessing Struggling Readers at the Secondary Level for an in-depth discussion. Assessment is essential for identifying each student's strengths and needs. Following the initial assessment, it is important to collect relevant data regularly to define students' progress or lack of progress in areas such as fluency, comprehension, and word recognition. This regular observation of students' learning should guide the teacher's design of instructional objectives and adaptations and indicate when reteaching is needed.

One way to support students' specific learning needs is through **scaffolding**. An effective teacher scaffolds to help a student move from what he or she already knows to new learning. With appropriate scaffolding or support, a student will be able to accomplish tasks that would otherwise be impossible to accomplish independently. Teaching struggling readers requires that the teacher be constantly aware of where students are in their learning and where they need to be. Instructional support, or scaffolding, is temporary and should be taken away as soon as a student is able to perform a task without help. Just as a father hanging onto the seat of his daughter's bike while she is learning to ride will eventually let go and watch her glide down the street on her own, an effective teacher must know when to support a student and when to encourage independence. Subsequently, once a task has been mastered, an effective teacher will raise expectations and provide necessary support, thus repeating the cycle of scaffolding.

Examples of scaffolding include but are not limited to the following:

- Choosing text at the student's instructional level so that the text is challenging for the student but he or she is capable of reading it with support
- Providing a partial response to a question and asking the student or students to complete it
- Acknowledging a partially correct response and helping the student correct or refine it
- Organizing tasks into smaller steps
- Connecting the topic of instruction to students' prior knowledge and experience
- Providing hints rather than telling a student an answer or moving on to another student when the first student does not respond

TIME ON TASK

Time on task refers to the time students are actively engaged in learning and applying what they have learned (Carroll, 1963). On-task behavior is usually observable. Student behaviors that would indicate time on task include the following:

- Making direct eye contact with the teacher
- Giving answers to the teacher's questions that are directly relevant to instruction
- Asking the teacher to clarify instructional information
- Applying a strategy or skill appropriately
- Performing an instructionally relevant task appropriately

Effective teachers continually monitor their classrooms for active engagement in the lesson and know how to employ techniques designed to increase time on task. Some effective techniques include the following (Mastropieri & Scruggs, 2002):

- Plan activities that require students to be actively involved, with a minimum amount of time spent sitting and listening.
- Provide positive feedback to students who are on task.
- Question students frequently. To maximize student engagement, ask the question first, then pause briefly before selecting a student to answer. This will help ensure that all students think actively about the question because they do not know who will be called on to answer it.
- Set a timer to ring at random intervals, and award students who are on task when the timer rings.
- Provide ample visuals and materials to make learning concrete.
- Have classroom routines in place to minimize transition times and ensure that all students know and practice the routines.

If struggling readers are to close the gap with their peers, they must make progress at a faster rate than average readers, which requires increased instructional time (Vaughn & Bos, 2012). It is imperative, therefore, that instruction be designed deliberately to decrease downtime and increase students' time on task.

QUICK PACING OF LESSONS

Quick pacing of lessons increases time on task and instructional time (Vaughn & Bos, 2012). Effective teachers are constantly aware of their instructional pacing in relation to the responsiveness of their students. Planning is a prerequisite to quick pacing. To move at a pace that is manageable for students but that also keeps them actively engaged, an effective teacher must adequately plan the content to be covered and the instructional activities used to teach and practice the objectives.

It is important that teachers use data from assessments to help plan their lessons. Effective teachers know their students' strengths and needs and set objectives based on those needs. Next, they must consider the **scope and sequence** of the curriculum. This refers to the amount of material to be covered and the order in which it will be presented. It is difficult to modify the pacing, or speed of instruction, if the scope and sequence are not clear. Some school districts have curriculum guides with a suggested scope and sequence for each grade level. This may be an excellent resource. Remember, however, that struggling readers may need a modified curriculum that takes into account their areas of need. Teachers might want to think of themselves as emergency room doctors who treat their students' greatest needs first. For example, perhaps a teacher has a student who is unable to write a multiparagraph essay and also is unable to read more than 60 WCPM on grade level text. Which is more critical? Although there are important writing standards for middle school students, the greater need is fluent reading. Assessment and progress monitoring can lead a teacher to a "diagnosis," and strong instructional design can help the teacher provide the "treatment" effectively.

Besides quick pacing across lessons, pacing within lessons should be energetic with little downtime. Pacing is improved when teachers are well organized and when students know and use routines for transitions and activities. Furthermore, adequate planning for active student involvement reduces behavior difficulties. Behavior problems may increase if students are bored or lessons are too easy or too difficult.

POSITIVE FEEDBACK

Positive feedback is authentic and specific. For example, "Good job! Well done!" and "Way to go!" are less meaningful to students than, "I can see that you are previewing the chapter by looking at the charts and graphs; good strategy" or, "You recognized the open syllable in that word; nice work." If a teacher continually gives out praise with no observation to back it up, then older struggling readers will notice. They may assume that empty praise from a teacher is a sign that they are not doing anything worthy of sincere praise. It can be useful to praise an unsuccessful effort provided you specifically praise the *attempt* but also correct the mistake. For example, if a student misreads a word, you may say, "You read the first syllable of the word correctly. The word has three syllables; try reading the second and third and putting them together to read the word."

Appropriate statements for positive feedback include the following:

- "You recognized the parts of that word. Good work."
- "Very impressive that you remembered how to write that word."
- "You are following the steps of the strategy so carefully! That should help you understand what you are reading."
- "Nice job of making notes while you read. That should help you remember what you are reading."
- "You read that passage with so much expression. Nice work."

CORRECTIVE FEEDBACK

Corrective feedback provides students with information about their mistakes. If a student continually performs a task, applies a strategy, or reads a word incorrectly, then the student essentially is practicing the mistake and the mistake will become a bad habit.

When giving corrective feedback, there are a few things to remember. Corrective feedback is simply providing information and, therefore, should be given in a neutral tone. Your classroom needs to be a place where older struggling readers are not afraid to make mistakes—a place where students know that you understand their instructional needs and that you will support and challenge them appropriately. When giving corrective feedback, try not to provide the feedback too quickly. Give the student time to self-correct.

Appropriate statements for corrective feedback include the following:

- After pointing to the paragraph where important information about a comprehension question resides: "This paragraph will tell you why the octopus is often near larger fish. See if you can reread the paragraph and find the answer."

- "The word you wrote is *signal*. Can you write *single*?"
- "That's not quite right. Can you take another look?"
- "Yes, that is partially correct. Can you give me more information?"
- "Very close. This word is *special*."

To give corrective feedback, you may simply provide a correct model and have students repeat the correct response two or three times: "Watch me. I'll show you how to use the strategy." (Model the strategy again.)

ENGAGED READING PRACTICE

Even though it is very important to teach students strategies and skills to improve reading outcomes, it is absolutely essential that students are given ample time every day to actively engage in reading. To be engaged in reading, students need to have a purpose for reading, as well as interesting text that is at an appropriate level so that they can appreciate and understand what they are reading. Sustained silent reading (SSR) is popular but is not associated with improved reading outcomes, perhaps because many students are not engaged appropriately in reading. If a student chooses a book to read during SSR that is not at an appropriate level, the student will most likely be looking at pictures instead of reading. The student might be quiet but will probably not be reading.

Students may engage in reading in a variety of formats. Individual silent reading is appropriate if text is on the students' instructional or independent reading levels. With difficult text, it may be more appropriate to have students read orally with the support of a peer (as in partner reading), but "round robin" reading in which students take turns reading a paragraph or section while others follow along is not likely to actively engage students in reading. Other, more useful grouping formats for engaged oral reading practice include peer partners and small groups that meet with the teacher. Partner reading is described in detail in Chapter 9. When students read orally in a small group, the teacher is able to provide appropriate text, scaffold students when they struggle, and prompt students to apply the reading skills and strategies they are learning.

ADDRESS STUDENT MOTIVATION

When designing instruction for middle school readers, it is essential to think about **motivation**. One of the greatest challenges that teachers of older struggling readers face is motivating these students to persevere in their quest to improve their reading. Teachers can help increase student motivation by encouraging **autonomy**, or personal independence; making learning relevant; and teaching students how to self-regulate.

Generally speaking, adolescents are in search of control, autonomy, and independence. Adolescence is a time of exploring how to gain and handle this control. By creating a classroom environment that encourages autonomy, teachers can support the urge for independence in their students. First, teachers can be aware of this need and create opportunities for their students to make their own choices. For example, teachers may allow their students to choose their own reading material when appropriate (Biancarosa & Snow, 2004; Reed, Schallert, Beth, & Woodruff, 2004). Simply giving students a choice between two passages to read when practicing a new strategy or skill may encourage student engagement.

Another way to encourage student autonomy is to develop a classroom library. The presence of diverse and abundant reading material in the classroom is invaluable (Guthrie, Schafer, Von Secker, & Alban, 2000). As teachers get to know their students, they become aware of their students' interests and can keep these interests in mind while ordering books for the classroom or walking the aisles of a discount bookstore. Students are appreciative when they know teachers have added a book to the classroom library "for them." It may take some time to collect and/or purchase reading material that is of high interest to students. A classroom library is a work in progress, growing each year with the needs and interests of different students. This type of library may consist of books from several different genres such as fiction, nonfiction, action and adventure, mystery, poetry, joke books, classics, childhood favorites, autobiography and/or biography, short stories, sports, and historical fiction. A classroom library also may include baskets of comic books, magazines, newspapers, and books by popular authors. Teachers must focus on the high demands of the curriculum, and, as noted earlier, SSR programs cannot replace effective instruction. However, even 10–15 minutes of independent reading time each week gives students the opportunity to select their own reading material and to feel a sense of empowerment. It is not uncommon for students to get hooked quickly when reading books of their own choosing and then want to check out the books to finish reading at home. Middle school students often will check out books to read to a younger sibling at home.

Another aspect of motivation is relevance. If you can show students how the content of the lesson is truly relevant or important to them, then they will be more likely to tune in and engage in the lesson. To show students this relevance successfully, teachers must first determine students' needs and try to understand what is relevant to them. Swan (2004) gives several examples of how teachers can help their students make concrete connections to what they are learning. For example, as an introduction to the concept of *revolution,* a social studies teacher might show his class a 10-minute video clip from an episode of the cartoon *The Simpsons* in which the character Bart and his friends take over a summer camp run by abusive camp counselors. The more teachers listen to students and understand what is important to them, the easier it will be to adapt teaching to make classroom activities relevant to students (Biancarosa & Snow, 2004). Although motivation is important, teachers must take care not to shortchange instructional time. Motivation alone will probably not improve reading outcomes.

A primary goal of teachers' efforts to motivate students is to encourage them to develop **self-regulation**. Students with high self-regulation are able to monitor their own performance and redirect their approach to a task when they realize that their current approach is not productive (Reed et al., 2004). For example, imagine a group of students working together to complete an assignment. They are sitting by the window and are able to see several of their friends running around the track for gym class. The conversation drifts from the assignment to social conversation about their friends. A self-regulating student might suggest that the group find somewhere to sit away from the window so that they can concentrate and complete their task. It is important to instill in students this ability to self-regulate so that they will not only self-regulate in reading class but also in other classes, at home, and one day at college or work. One activity that may promote self-regulation is to have a class discussion to identify and list the smaller goals or substeps necessary to complete a particular assignment. Then, as students are working on the assignment, the teacher periodically may direct them to stop and ask themselves whether they are being productive. Is their current approach helping them to accomplish the substeps? Do they need to change how they are working in any way? By talking through this process with students, teachers give them guided practice in self-regulation (Reed et al., 2004).

Biancarosa and Snow (2004) noted that students must be competent to improve their reading performance but that competence alone is not enough. Competence must be accompanied by engagement to make reading performance gains, and neither is sufficient without the other. Fostering an environment that encourages both autonomy and self-regulation supports student engagement in learning, but this environment must be coupled with instructional support and guided practice designed to build reading competence (Biancarosa & Snow, 2004). It is not enough to provide instruction to struggling middle school readers, but neither is it enough to attend to student motivation without providing effective instruction. The next section includes a description of instructional principles that are particularly important in teaching struggling readers. The following sections describe reading strategies and instructional practices that are supported by research. We hope these tools will be part of the foundation of effective instruction in your classroom.

Section III Research-Supported Instructional Practices

As struggling readers get older, the performance gap between them and average students their age typically continues to widen (Stanovich, 1986). In addition to basic skills instruction, struggling middle school readers also may need explicit instruction in strategies that will help them think about and understand what they read (Bryant, 2003). Many struggling readers are inefficient processors of information and therefore need to be directly taught strategies to improve their reading skills (Swanson & Deshler, 2003). Swanson and Deshler, in their analysis of recent research on adolescents with learning disabilities, state that the overall goal of strategy instruction for older readers is to empower students to apply these strategies independently. Teachers of struggling readers must remember the goal of enabling students to be independent readers. When delivered as described in Section II, Effective Instruction for Struggling Readers, instruction in reading strategies in the areas of comprehension, vocabulary, fluency, and word recognition will allow students to move from relying heavily on teacher guidance to becoming independent learners.

It is clear that reading teachers need to know the major components of reading, but it is also helpful if struggling middle school readers understand these terms. At the start of the year, teachers can define **comprehension**, **vocabulary**, **fluency**, and **word recognition** simply and clearly for students. (See Terms to Know for student-friendly definitions.) This way, the teacher and students will have a common language to use when talking about reading strategies. Explain to the students that assessments you have given them helped to determine their strengths and needs in comprehension, vocabulary, fluency, and word recognition. This may be a good time to talk with students individually about their assessment scores and to develop short-term and annual goals. Perhaps students can work independently in small groups or with partners while you speak with other students one to one. It is important to be both honest and encouraging when talking with older struggling readers. Most of the time, these students know that they have trouble reading, but they may have never been told their specific strengths and needs. Be sure to emphasize both. Students often are reminded of their weaknesses; it is encouraging for them to also be aware of their strengths. In addition, it is possible that they have never had instruction in strategies designed to improve their reading. It is helpful for an older struggling reader to take ownership of his or her needs. For example, a student might be able to clearly recognize and state, "I read fluently but I need to work on understanding what I read, and there are strategies I can use to help me with this."

Once students understand the terms, post definitions for *comprehension*, *vocabulary*, *fluency*, and *word recognition* in your room. These are the components of reading in which your students should improve.

Before beginning to teach specific strategies or skills, do the following:

- Explain to students that throughout the school year, you will be teaching them several strategies in the areas of comprehension, vocabulary, fluency, and word recognition. The Appendix includes a handout called Characteristics of Effective Readers. You may want to distribute this to your students as part of your discussion of strategies.

- Tell students that you will give them a lot of practice and provide guidance when they first learn a strategy; however, as they begin to catch on, you will expect them to use these strategies independently.

- Emphasize that the strategies you teach are not just for your reading class—they are for all reading. Ask students to brainstorm places and settings in which they will need to be able to read. Encourage students to practice using the reading strategies they learn in your class in the following situations:
  - In another class
  - While they are working on homework
  - When they are reading a magazine, newspaper, or book

TERMS TO KNOW

comprehension	The ability to understand what is read—the ultimate goal of reading
fluency	The ability to read text quickly, accurately, and with expression
skill instruction	Teaching students to perform a specific activity (e.g., recognizing closed syllables in words)
strategy instruction	Teaching students to use a series of steps to work through solving a problem or completing a task (e.g., a multistep plan for reading multisyllable words)
think-aloud	A type of modeling in which the teacher verbalizes what he or she is thinking in order to make the thought process apparent to students
vocabulary	Words a person recognizes and uses orally or in reading and writing
word recognition	The accurate reading of words

SAMPLE LESSONS IN THIS BOOK

Sample lesson plans target comprehension, vocabulary, word recognition, and fluency. The lessons are complete and can be implemented as they are or adapted to meet the needs of a particular class.

Following is a list of *very important notes* about the sample lessons:

- Each plan is intended to be *an example of one lesson in a series* of **skill instruction** and **strategy instruction** lessons. For example, one of the lesson plans included in this section teaches students how to summarize text. This sample lesson is designed to be merely *one of several lessons* designed to teach students to summarize text independently.

- For the most part, the sample lesson plans *are not designed to be taught in one class period.* Students might need several opportunities for guided practice before moving on to independent practice. Then, after students are able to apply what they learn independently, they will need cumulative practice throughout the year.

- Most of the lessons are presented as scripts that include the exact wording of teacher instruction and student responses; detailed lesson scripts are included to provide a full illustration of the instructional approaches. *Teachers should not read these scripts as they are teaching, but use them as guides to plan their own instruction.* Obviously, student responses will vary and will not follow the scripted formats.

- The Daily Review component of each sample lesson describes a review of objectives and content that may have been covered on the previous day. This is not meant to dictate what should be taught on the day before the lesson but rather *provides an example of a quick review.* Of course, teachers need to review the specific material that they taught in the previous lesson and merely use the sample Daily Review as a guide.

Your goal is to arm your students with a toolkit of effective skills and strategies that they will eventually be able to apply independently with a variety of texts. The process of teaching new skills or strategies should be cumulative. This is why planning is so important. We hope that Section III of this book will provide you with valuable knowledge and with examples of lessons based on research with struggling readers and our knowledge of best practices in the field.

Chapter 7

Comprehension

Most struggling middle school readers have deficits in reading comprehension. **Comprehension,** the ability to gain meaning from text, is the ultimate goal of reading. To provide appropriate instruction, it is helpful to be familiar with the characteristics and needs of struggling readers in the area of comprehension. Table 7.1 lists some of these characteristics.

Comprehension strategies are employed before, during, and after reading. Effective readers typically employ strategies to understand what they are reading. Struggling readers, however, need explicit instruction on how to use strategies to assist them in understanding what they read as well as ample practice in using these strategies with a variety of texts. Table 7.2 lists some of these strategies.

The comprehension lessons described in this book are organized in the following manner:

Before, During, and After Reading	Previewing Text and Question Generation Generating Level 1 (Right-There) Questions Generating Level 2 (Putting It Together) Questions Generating Level 3 (Making Connections) Questions
During Reading	Mental Imagery Log Main Idea Strategy Identifying Text Structures and Using Graphic Organizers
After Reading	Summarizing Text Wrap-Up/Main Idea Log

Table 7.1. Characteristics of struggling versus effective readers

Struggling readers	Effective readers
Have difficulty gaining meaning from text; often focus on one sentence or section of text at a time and fail to connect ideas in that section to other text ideas or to their background knowledge	Continuously monitor reading for understanding, linking the content with their prior knowledge and making connections across the text to form an integrated, cohesive mental model of the meaning of the text
Have limited knowledge of strategies for gaining information from text	Use a variety of effective reading strategies before, during, and after reading
Need to be continually reminded that understanding and enjoyment are the primary goals of reading; even when a student is working on word recognition or fluency, the main goal is comprehension	Set a purpose for reading and adjust their rate and strategies depending on their reading goals, the text, and the content

Adaped with permission from The University of Texas Center for Reading and Language Arts. (2003b). *Special education reading project (SERP) secondary institute—Effective instruction for secondary struggling readers: Research-based practices.* Austin, TX: Author.

Table 7.2.   Strategies used by effective readers

Before reading	During reading	After reading
Establish purpose for reading	Identify main ideas and supporting details; paraphrase key ideas	Summarize key ideas from the text
Activate background knowledge	Make inferences that explain cause-and-effect, temporal, and spatial relationships across the text to create a cohesive mental model of the meaning of the text	Make inferences and critically evaluate ideas from the text; integrate new ideas from the text with prior knowledge to extend, validate, or change previous understandings
Make informed predictions based on inferences about the text content	Make informed predictions based on inferences and verify previous predictions	Verify predictions
Generate questions about the text	Generate questions about the text and monitor their understanding of the answers to the questions	Summarize what was learned to respond to the questions
Evaluate text structure and make predictions based on knowledge of text structures	Use text structure as a framework for comprehension	
	Monitor comprehension for understanding and reread or use "fix-up" strategies when they do not understand	
	Monitor understanding of words and use vocabulary strategies such as recognition of affixes and roots and informed use of context clues when they encounter unfamiliar words	

Adapted with permission from The University of Texas Center for Reading and Language Arts. (2003b). *Special education reading project (SERP) secondary institute— Effective instruction for secondary struggling readers: Research-based practices.* Austin, TX: Author.

Before-, During-, and After-Reading Comprehension

Previewing Text and Question Generation

INTRODUCTION

The question-generation routine has two parts—previewing the text before reading and generating different kinds of questions during and after reading. When students preview text and learn to ask questions about what they read, they understand and learn more from text. In particular, students benefit when, prior to reading, teachers 1) preteach key words featured in the text and 2) identify the most important idea in the reading. For most text, this means identifying key names, places, and/or concepts that are important to understanding the text and preteaching them.

Question generation is one of the strategies recommended by NICHD (2000) in its synthesis of the research on reading comprehension. Generating questions during reading has been found effective for improving the comprehension of students of all ability levels in Grades 4–9 and in college (Pressley et al., 1992; Rosenshine, Meister, & Chapman, 1996). Research also has demonstrated that approaches to reading comprehension that include question generation improve the achievement of students with learning disabilities (Klingner & Vaughn, 1996; Palinscar & Brown, 1989; Therrien, Wickstrom, & Jones, 2006) and that ELLs benefit from efforts to improve their ability to generate questions during reading (Garcia, 2003; Rivera, Moughamian, Lesaux, & Francis, 2008). English language learners who were taught to self-generate questions in their native language were able to transfer the strategy to reading in English and demonstrate improvements on standardized measures of comprehension administered in both languages (Muniz-Swicegood, 1994).

The question-generation lessons described in this chapter include four stages. In the first stage, students learn to preview text; the next three stages teach students to generate low-level literal questions and progress to generating higher-level questions. Taboada and Guthrie (2006) did a study in which they found that generating higher-level questions that required inferences from text enabled students to gain greater levels of understanding of concepts in expository text such as that found in content-area textbooks.

The next section provides an overview of the question-generation routine. This routine is most appropriate for narrative text such as literature and social studies text, which contains many proper nouns. It also can be applied to other expository text, such as science text, by selecting nouns that represent key concepts, or *big-idea words*. It is less applicable to math text unless students are reading biographies of mathematicians or some other extended text selection. The sample lessons in this section are based on a social studies unit on Texas history.

OVERVIEW OF THE INSTRUCTIONAL ROUTINE

1. Step 1: Preteach key proper nouns or critical concept nouns (big-idea words): Students may be unfamiliar with key words that are presented in a reading selection. Sometimes, not knowing key names, events, places, or other proper nouns prevents students from adequately understanding and learning from text. You can assist them by taking a few minutes to preteach the key proper nouns or critical concept nouns that are truly essential for understanding a passage.

   What is a key proper noun? It is the name of a person, place, or thing that is essential for understanding the meaning of the selected text. A key proper noun is *not* a proper noun of low importance. If there are no key proper nouns in the text, this step can be eliminated; however, it may be useful to preteach key nouns that are *not* proper nouns if they are unfamiliar and if an understanding of these words is essential for comprehending the selection. These will be referred to as critical concept nouns, or big-idea words.

2. Step 2: Introduce the big idea: Students benefit from text for which they have an advance organizer that gives them some background on the most important thing they will be learning. Teachers assist students when they tell them the most important thing they want the students to understand and remember from the reading. Providing this information prior to reading or discussing text is useful.

3. Step 3: Previewing text: Students learn from previewing text when the purpose of the activity is to identify key ideas, link content to students' background knowledge, and connect text to previously read text and/or content. The role for students is to quickly review the material, state what they know, and make logical predictions about what they will learn. Teachers help students when they keep the previewing activity brief and to the point and when they confirm and extend correct responses and disconfirm incorrect responses or illogical predictions.

4. Step 4: Students asking and answering questions: Students with reading difficulties benefit from instruction that teaches them how to answer and develop questions. When students are provided with meaningful opportunities to ask and answer questions during and after reading, they become more cognizant of their understanding. Learning to ask and answer different types of questions is an adaptation of the Question-Answer-Relationship strategy (Raphael, 1986; Raphael & Au, 2005; Raphael & Pearson, 1985).

It is usually best to introduce one type of question at a time; model how to answer each question type; provide guided practice as you scaffold instruction, providing support and feedback to students so that they can ask and answer questions appropriately; and ask students to generate different types of questions, calling on their classmates to answer them.

OBJECTIVE

- Students will learn important proper nouns or critical concept nouns that are central to understanding a text passage.
- Students will learn to preview the text and to connect key concepts with what they already know.

MATERIALS

- Figure 7.1: Previewing Planning Sheet for preparing the lesson (photocopiable version in the Appendix)
- Figure 7.2: Multisyllable Word Reading Strategy poster for review activity (photocopiable version in the Appendix)
- Text passage or chapter
- Figure 7.3: Preview and Questioning Learning Log (photocopiable version in the Appendix)
- Overhead projector, SMART Board, chalkboard, or chart paper
- Dry-erase markers, chalk, or markers
- List of important proper nouns or critical concept nouns (a transparency of the learning log may be used)

PREPARATION

1. Read through the passage or chapter and select the important proper nouns. If there are no proper nouns in the passage, then select other nouns that are absolutely essential for understanding the passage (i.e., critical concept nouns, or big-idea words). Depending on the subject area you teach, the number of appropriate words you select may range from one to five.

Proper nouns and critical concept nouns are essential to understanding the meaning of the selected text. A general guideline is to identify one or two *who,* one or two *where,* and one or two *what* proper nouns. For example, in an excerpt from a social studies text, possible important proper nouns might include *Bering Strait, North Atlantic, Leanderthal Lady,* and *Beringia.*

Similarly, critical concept nouns, or big-idea words, represent concepts that are essential for understanding the text. This is *not* the same as preteaching all of the vocabulary words for the selection. Sample big-idea words from a health selection might include: *bacteria*, *pathogen*, *streptococcus*, and *cholera*.

Most important proper nouns or critical concept nouns selected for this lesson will be unfamiliar to many students; however, some of these words may be familiar to some students.

2. Identify the big idea of the passage. Ask yourself, "What is the most important idea that I want all students to understand and remember from this reading?" A Planning Sheet (Figure 7.1) is provided to organize the planning process.

Previewing Planning Sheet

1. **Preteach proper nouns or critical concept nouns.**

   Introduce, read, and define. Students write brief definitions in learning log.

   Who:

   Where:

   What:

2. **Preview text.**

   Introduce the big idea of the text selection.

   What is the most important idea that you want all students to understand and remember from this reading?

   Important key concepts, subheadings, bolded print, etc.

   Connections to prior learning:

Figure 7.1. Previewing Planning Sheet. (Adapted with permission from materials developed by the Teacher Quality Research Project through funding from the U.S. Department of Education's Institute of Education Sciences, grant contract number R305M050121A [*Enhancing the quality of expository text instruction and comprehension through content and case-situated professional development*; Simmons, D., Vaughn, S., & Edmonds, M., 2006].)

DAILY REVIEW

Quickly review a skill, strategy, or concept that was previously taught and that the students need to practice. The following is an example based on the sample lesson Teaching the Multisyllable Word Reading Strategy found in Chapter 10. As needed, refer to the multisyllable strategy poster, shown in Figure 7.2. This poster should be clearly visible in the room for student reference as they learn and apply the strategy.

Teacher: Before we start today's lesson, let's quickly review our strategy, or plan, for reading words with more than one syllable. What is the first thing you do when you come to a long word you don't know? Steven?

Student: Find the vowels in the word.

Teacher: Yes, you find the vowels because every syllable will have a vowel sound. What will you do next? Tamika?

Student: You look for parts you know—especially at the beginning or end of the word.

Teacher: Exactly right. What is the next step? Juana?

Student: Read the parts. Then you put the parts together to read the word.

Teacher: Yes. But sometimes the word doesn't sound quite right. Then what do you do? Marcus?

Student: You have to play with it to make it sound right.

Teacher: Yes. Good memory. Sometimes, this step is hard. Let's try reading a word that you might need to work with so that it will sound like a real word.

Display the word dedicate *on the chalkboard, overhead, or SMART Board.*

Teacher: I see a closed syllable, *ded*, followed by an open syllable, *i* (pronounce as /ī/), and then a silent *e* syllable, *cate*. If I put them together, I would say /ded/-/ī/-/kāt/. That doesn't sound quite right. Work with your partner to change the /ī/ sound, and tell your partner the real word.

Multisyllable Word Reading Strategy

1. Find the vowels.

2. Look for word parts you know.

3. Read each word part.

4. Read the parts quickly.

5. Make it sound like a real word.

Figure 7.2. Multisyllable Word Reading Strategy. (From Archer, A.L., Gleason, M.M., & Vachon, V. [2005a]. *REWARDS: Multisyllabic word reading strategies.* Longmont, CO: Sopris West; adapted by permission.)

Give partners about 15 seconds.

What's the word? Everyone?

Students: Dedicate.

Teacher: Yes, *dedicate*. Remember, when you read a word with more than one syllable, sometimes the vowels don't follow the rules. Try other vowel sounds until it sounds like a real word.

STATE OBJECTIVE AND/OR PURPOSE

1.   Introduce the strategy.

Teacher: Today, we will begin to learn a new strategy that will help you understand and remember the important ideas you read. Often, you are asked to answer questions about what you read. You'll be able to answer more questions correctly if you learn how to ask yourself questions as you read and after you read. We're going to take several days to learn how to ask ourselves different kinds of questions when we are reading. First, let me tell you about the whole strategy. Then we'll learn the first step.

2.   Provide an overview of the question-generation routine.

Teacher: The first step is *previewing*. You preview a text *before* reading. We will be working on the previewing step today. Previewing has two parts: 1) identifying important proper nouns or big-idea words, and 2) predicting what we will learn by thinking of what we already know about the big idea of the passage.

The next step is called *Ask the question*. We will practice asking and answering different types of questions about what we read, just like teachers do.

3.   Introduce the rationale for preteaching important proper nouns or big-idea words.

Teacher: Textbooks are filled with lots of information. Sometimes, there are important words that are hard to pronounce or that we haven't heard of before. If we don't know these words, it can be difficult to understand what we read. Some of these words are proper nouns—proper nouns are names of people, places, or things. I'm going to teach you a few of the important proper nouns you will see in the passage before we start reading. When you know these proper nouns, it makes reading easier.

MODEL AND TEACH

Genre: Expository or narrative

Grouping: Whole class or small group

Note: This sample lesson, based on social studies text, will focus on preteaching proper nouns. Modify the lesson if you are preteaching critical concept nouns (i.e., big-idea words) instead of proper nouns.

1.   Present and discuss between one and five preselected important proper nouns or big-idea words. Write each word and a brief definition on the chalkboard, chart paper, or transparency (you may use a transparency of the student learning log for this; see Figure 7.3). Definitions should be short and easily understandable to students.

   • Sample introduction of the important proper noun *Leanderthal Lady*

   • The Leanderthal Lady is a skeleton of a woman who lived 9,500 years ago. Workers discovered the skeleton near Leander, Texas, not too long ago.

   • Definition to write on chart: *Leanderthal Lady—9,500-year-old skeleton found near Leander, Texas.*

Preview and Questioning Learning Log

Name: _____ Partner's name: _____ Date: _____

Chapter or selection name: _____

Unfamiliar Proper Nouns or Big-Idea Words	
1.	☐ Person ☐ Place ☐ Thing/event
2.	☐ Person ☐ Place ☐ Thing/event
3.	☐ Person ☐ Place ☐ Thing/event
4.	☐ Person ☐ Place ☐ Thing/event

What is the topic (or "big idea") of the selection?

What do I already know about the topic?

Make a prediction: What will I learn about the topic?

**Generate three questions about the important ideas
(use *who, what, when, where, why,* and *how*).**

Level ___ 1.	
Answer:	*Provide the evidence! How do you know that?*
Level ___ 2.	
Answer:	*Provide the evidence! How do you know that?*
Level ___ 3.	
Answer:	*Provide the evidence! How do you know that?*

Figure 7.3. Preview and Questioning Learning Log. (Adapted with permission from materials developed by the Teacher Quality Research Project through funding from the U.S. Department of Education's Institute of Education Sciences, grant contract number R305M050121A [*Enhancing the quality of expository text instruction and comprehension through content and case-situated professional development;* Simmons, D., Vaughn, S., & Edmonds, M., 2006].)

- Teach the other proper nouns in the same way. Then, read through the list chorally with students so they become familiar with reading the new words.

- Have the students record the important proper nouns and their definitions in their learning logs.

2. Introduce the big idea (the topic of the selection). Give the students a brief summary of the selected passage.

Teacher: Today, we will learn about how the earliest people got to Texas. Many people believe they may have been hunters who followed herds from Asia into North America.

3. Introduce the method for previewing. Model for students how to preview the passage by doing a **think-aloud**. During your preview, you should tell students the big idea of the text first. Then, go through previewing procedures to make connections to the big idea and to prior learning. As you model using a think-aloud process, be sure to focus on the reasons for your predictions.

Note: Previewing should be brief and focused on connecting the big idea and prior learning to headings and visuals such as illustrations, maps, and diagrams. As a rule, you should not spend more than 10 minutes in any lesson on previewing.

The following is a sample think-aloud for a passage about early Texans:

Teacher: When I look at this passage, the first thing I see is the title—*First Trail to Texas*. After reading the title and subheadings and browsing the chapter, I know that the big idea is that the earliest Texans may have been hunters who followed herds from Asia to North America. So, I think we are going to learn about the path they followed to get here. There also is a map with lines from Asia to North America to South America. Maybe they will tell us where other people went too. I also see a picture of elephant-like animals, and it says, "The first Americans hunted mammoths and other large mammals." These must be mammoths, and maybe these are the animals that the people followed to Texas so they could hunt them. Earlier, we read about the Leanderthal Lady, whose remains are thought to be around 10,000 years old, so I think we will learn that the earliest Texans came here 10,000 years ago or maybe much earlier.

GUIDED PRACTICE

Grouping: Whole class or small group

Using a different brief selection (such as a section of a chapter), preteach important proper nouns or critical concept nouns (big-idea words), and provide students with the overall big idea in no more than one or two sentences. Then, have students preview the passage with you. Ask students what they notice about headings and visuals. Connect their responses to the big idea and their prior learning. Finally, create a prediction statement together by asking the following questions:

- "What do you think you will learn about _____ (the big idea)?"
- "Why do you think you will learn that?"

INDEPENDENT PRACTICE

Grouping: Partners

Using a different brief selection, preteach important proper nouns or critical concept nouns, and provide students with the overall big idea of the passage in no more than one or two sentences. Then, have students work in pairs to preview the chapter and think aloud to make connections to the big idea and to prior learning. Circulate through the room to monitor and scaffold. Ask students to state the reasons for their predictions.

Ask the following questions:

- "What do you think you will learn about _____ (the big idea)?"
- "Why do you think you will learn that?"

Ask some pairs to share their predictions and to tell why they are making those predictions (based on headings, illustrations, diagrams, and so forth).

GENERALIZATION

Ask students for examples of situations in which previewing text would be helpful as they prepare to read. Emphasize the fact that they can preview text in all of their classes by taking a few minutes to read the title and headings and examine the illustrations and then to think about what they may learn from the passage.

MONITOR STUDENT LEARNING

Each time students read an unfamiliar passage, have them first use the previewing routine in pairs or small groups. Circulate through the room to monitor the students' ability to accurately connect information from headings and visual materials to previously learned material to make valid predictions. Ask questions that require students to tell the reasons for their predictions.

PERIODIC AND/OR MULTIPLE OPPORTUNITIES TO PRACTICE

Use the previewing routine each time students read unfamiliar text. Once students become skilled at making valid predictions, turn the process over to them but continue to preteach important proper nouns or big-idea words and to remind students to preview. Occasionally, return to previewing in partners so that you can monitor the process.

Before-, During-, and After-Reading Comprehension

Generating Level 1 (Right-There) Questions

OBJECTIVE

Students will increase literal comprehension of text by generating "right-there" questions.

MATERIALS

- Text passage or chapter
- Overhead projector, SMART Board, chalkboard, or chart paper
- Dry-erase markers, chalk, or markers
- Figure 7.3: Preview and Questioning Learning Log (photocopiable version in the Appendix)
- (Optional) Transparency of Figure 7.3: Preview and Questioning Learning Log
- Figure 7.4: Planning Sheet: Level 1 questions (photocopiable version in the Appendix)
- Figure 7.5: Level 1: Right-There Question Cards (one per student). See the Appendix for a photocopiable version that can be used to copy four cards at a time, front and back. We suggest that the three different types of question cards be copied on different colored cardstock. In this example, the Level 1 Question Cards are red. You may want to create your own versions of the cards with questions that are relevant to your content.

    Note: In the sample lesson, the teacher distributes all three kinds of Question Cards at one time, as a way to introduce questioning. If you choose to do this, you will also need:
- Figure 7.6: Level 2: Putting-It-Together Question Cards (one per student, copied front and back on white cardstock using the photocopiable versions in the Appendix; you may want to create your own versions of the cards with questions that are relevant to your content)
- Figure 7.7: Level 3: Making Connections Question Cards (one per student, copied front and back on blue cardstock using the photocopiable version in the Appendix; you may want to create your own versions of the cards with questions that are relevant to your content)

PREPARATION

For detailed directions on planning for Previewing Text, see the section on Preparation for the Sample Lesson earlier in this chapter. A Planning Sheet (Figure 7.4) is provided to organize the planning process.

1. Read through the passage or chapter and select the important proper nouns or critical-concept "big idea words." Depending on the subject area you teach, the number of appropriate words to select may range from one to five.

2. Identify the big idea of the passage. Ask yourself, "What is the most important idea that I want all students to understand and remember from this reading?"

Planning Sheet

LEVEL 1 QUESTIONS

1.   **Preteach proper nouns or critical concept nouns.**

     Introduce, read, and define. Students write brief definition in learning log.

     Who:

     Where:

     What:

2.   **Preview text.**

     Introduce the big idea of the text selection.

     What is the most important idea that you want all students to understand and remember from this reading?

     Important key concepts, subheadings, bolded print, etc.

     Connections to prior learning:

3.   **Model Level 1 questions.**

     Questions to use as examples:

Figure 7.4.   Planning Sheet: Level 1 questions. (Adapted with permission from materials developed by the Teacher Quality Research Project through funding from the U.S. Department of Education's Institute of Education Sciences, grant contract number R305M050121A [*Enhancing the quality of expository text instruction and comprehension through content and case-situated professional development*; Simmons, D., Vaughn, S., & Edmonds, M., 2006].)

3.   Identify several Level 1 questions that can be answered using the text. Level 1 questions are literal comprehension questions. They can be answered using information taken directly from the text, so they are "right there" in the text. For example, Level 1 right-there questions for a social studies passage might include the following:
     •   How long ago did the Mound Builders move to the Caddoan Mounds?
     •   Who were the Caddo people descendants of?

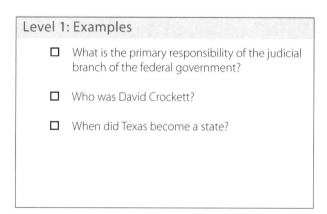

Right-There Question Cards (Front)

Level 1: Right-There Questions

☐ Questions can be answered in one word or one sentence.

☐ Answers can be found word-for-word in the text.

➢ Who?   ➢ Where?

➢ What?   ➢ Why?

➢ When?   ➢ How?

Right-There Question Cards (Back)

Level 1: Examples

☐ What is the primary responsibility of the judicial branch of the federal government?

☐ Who was David Crockett?

☐ When did Texas become a state?

Figure 7.5. Level 1: Right-There Question Cards, front and back (photocopy on red card stock). (Adapted with permission from materials developed by the Teacher Quality Research Project through funding from the U.S. Department of Education's Institute of Education Sciences, grant contract number R305M050121A [*Enhancing the quality of expository text instruction and comprehension through content and case-situated professional development*; Simmons, D., Vaughn, S., & Edmonds, M., 2006].)

- What kind of work did the Caddo do?
- What did the Caddo trade?
- In what shape did the Caddo make their houses?
- What materials did the Caddo use to make their houses?

DAILY REVIEW

1. Preteach important proper nouns or critical concept nouns and provide brief definitions. Review reasons for preteaching important proper nouns or big-idea words. Write each word and a brief definition on the chalkboard, chart paper, or transparency (you may use a transparency of the Preview and Questioning Learning Log for this; see Figure 7.3). Remember that definitions should be short and easily understandable to students. Have students copy important proper nouns and/or concept nouns and definitions in their Learning Logs. Then, read chorally the list of important proper nouns and/or concept nouns.

Putting-It-Together Question Cards (Front)

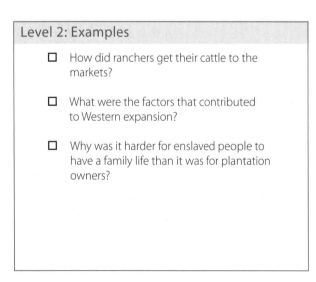

Level 2: Putting It Together

☐ Questions can be answered by looking in the text.

☐ Answers require one or more sentences.

☐ To answer the questions, you have to look in more than one place and put information together.

➢ Who?   ➢ Where?

➢ What?   ➢ Why?

➢ When?   ➢ How?

Putting-It-Together Question Cards (Back)

Level 2: Examples

☐ How did ranchers get their cattle to the markets?

☐ What were the factors that contributed to Western expansion?

☐ Why was it harder for enslaved people to have a family life than it was for plantation owners?

Figure 7.6.   Level 2: Putting-It-Together Question Cards, front and back (photocopy on white card stock). (Adapted with permission from materials developed by the Teacher Quality Research Project through funding from the U.S. Department of Education's Institute of Education Sciences, grant contract number R305M050121A [*Enhancing the quality of expository text instruction and comprehension through content and case-situated professional development*; Simmons, D., Vaughn, S., & Edmonds, M., 2006].)

2. Preview the passage, and present the big idea of the passage. Remind students how to preview a passage. Students should look for key concepts by reading the title, bold print, and subheadings. They should look at the pictures or other information that stands out. Students should then connect the key concepts to the big idea and to what they already know and say how they made the connection. Assist students in making connections and correct misinformation.

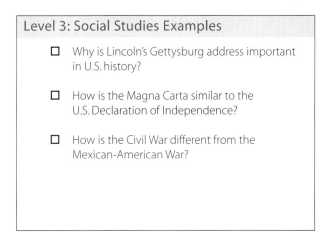

Making-Connections Question Cards (Front)

Level 3: Making Connections

☐ Questions cannot be answered by using text alone.

☐ Answers require you to think about what you just read, what you already know, and how it fits together.

➤ How is _____ like (similar to) _____?

➤ How is _____ different from _____?

➤ How is _____ related to _____?

Making-Connections Question Cards (Back)

Level 3: Social Studies Examples

☐ Why is Lincoln's Gettysburg address important in U.S. history?

☐ How is the Magna Carta similar to the U.S. Declaration of Independence?

☐ How is the Civil War different from the Mexican-American War?

Figure 7.7. Level 3: Making-Connections Question Cards, front and back (photocopy on blue card stock). (Adapted with permission from materials developed by the Teacher Quality Research Project through funding from the U.S. Department of Education's Institute of Education Sciences, grant contract number R305M050121A [*Enhancing the quality of expository text instruction and comprehension through content and case-situated professional development*; Simmons, D., Vaughn, S., & Edmonds, M., 2006].)

Note: Previewing occurs only *once* for a passage or reading. If students will be reading the same passage over the course of 2 or more days, do the following:

• On Day 1, introduce the important proper nouns or big-idea words, then have students write them in their learning logs and read through the list. Introduce the big idea and then preview the text.

• On subsequent days of reading the same passage, have students review the list of important proper nouns (e.g., read chorally, read with partners), and tell them the big idea of the passage. It is not necessary to do the entire prediction activity again.

STATE OBJECTIVE AND/OR PURPOSE

Tell students that today they will learn how to ask themselves questions that can be answered using ideas found right there in the text.

Teacher: Teachers ask questions to see whether students understand what they read. There are several types of questions, and understanding the different types will make it easier to find the answers. Some questions require you to find facts about what you read whereas others require you to draw conclusions or make inferences. There are two reasons why it is important to create and answer questions when you read. First, creating and answering questions helps you understand what you read, and second, it helps you remember important information about what you read.

MODEL AND TEACH

Model how to ask and answer "right-there" questions.

Distribute Question Cards for Level 1, Level 2, and Level 3 questions.

Teacher: Questions usually start with *who, what, when, where, why*, or *how*. When teachers create questions, they try to use lots of different question stems to make sure students understand different kinds of information. In the next few classes, you will be learning how to ask and answer three kinds of questions. I have given you a set of Question Cards. If you look on your Question Cards, you will see the different question types: Right-there, putting-it-together, and making-connections.

1. Introduce the Level 1, "right-there" question type.

    Teacher: Look at your red Question Cards. Today, we are going to learn about the first type of question. We call this a *right-there* question because the information needed to answer it can be found in one place, word-for-word in the text. Right-there questions usually can be answered in one word or one sentence. Answering right-there questions is usually easy and requires little thinking or effort, except that you must locate the answer in the text.

2. Use a short passage from your text to model how to create a right-there question. Give students the passage or have it on the overhead projector or a SMART Board. Preteach any difficult vocabulary words. After reading the passage out loud to students, model creating right-there questions. Consider the following example:

    Teacher: Let's see, I need to make up a question that I can find in one place in the passage. The first sentence says, "More than 1,200 years ago, Mound Builders migrated, or moved, south into the Piney Woods region to the site of the Caddoan Mounds." There is a lot of information in that sentence. One fact is that the Mound Builders moved to the Caddoan Mounds more than 1,200 years ago. I think I can turn that fact into a question. 1,200 years ago is a "when question," so I'll start with that. When did the Mound Builders move to the Caddoan Mounds? Let me check the answer. More than 1,200 years ago. Okay. That looks like a right-there question because I can easily find the answer in one place, word-for-word, in my reading. The Mound Builders moved to the Caddoan Mounds more than 1,200 years ago. Now I'll make up some more right-there questions, and you see whether you can find the answers in your reading.

3. If students have difficulty writing right-there questions, it may be helpful to have them first recognize right-there questions. You might provide them with several questions and model with a think-aloud, deciding whether each is a right-there question.

GUIDED PRACTICE

Grouping: Whole class or small group

Practice creating and answering right-there questions with your class. Remind students to look at their Question Cards to remember what a right-there question is. It might be helpful to stick with a short section or paragraph during initial modeling and guided practice.

Provide more guided practice in whole-class or small-group formats. Some students may need additional guided practice over several days to master the process of generating right-there questions.

INDEPENDENT PRACTICE

Grouping: Partners

Using a different brief selection, preteach important proper nouns or critical concept nouns and provide students with the overall big idea of the passage in no more than one or two sentences. Then, have students work in pairs to quickly preview the passage.

Next, have students work in pairs to generate right-there questions about the selection. Have students write their questions in their Learning Logs. They also should record their answers to the questions along with evidence supporting each answer. Circulate and provide feedback and scaffolding as needed. Ask pairs to share their right-there questions and to tell where in the text the answer to each question can be found.

GENERALIZATION

Ask students for examples of situations in which asking themselves right-there questions might help them understand and remember what they read. Emphasize the fact that they can preview text and ask themselves right-there questions in all of their classes, either while they are reading a text or after reading.

MONITOR STUDENT LEARNING

Each time students read an unfamiliar passage, have them use the previewing routine and generate right-there questions during and after reading, in pairs or small groups. Circulate through the room to monitor students' responses. Ask questions that require students to tell the reasons for their predictions and to show where they found the answers to the right-there questions they generated.

PERIODIC AND/OR MULTIPLE OPPORTUNITIES TO PRACTICE

Use the previewing and question-generation routine each time students read unfamiliar text. Once students become skilled at making valid predictions and generating right-there questions, turn the process over to them but continue to preteach important proper nouns or big-idea words and to remind students to preview and generate questions. Occasionally, return to previewing and question generation in pairs so that you can monitor the process.

Before-, During-, and After-Reading Comprehension

Generating Level 2 (Putting-It-Together) Questions

OBJECTIVE

Students will increase literal and inferential comprehension of text by generating putting-it-together questions.

MATERIALS

- Text passage or chapter
- Overhead projector, SMART Board, chalkboard, or chart paper
- Dry-erase markers, chalk, or markers
- Figure 7.3: Preview and Questioning Learning Log (photocopiable version in the Appendix)
- (Optional) Transparency of Figure 7.3: Preview and Questioning Learning Log
- Figure 7.8: Level 2 questions Planning Sheet (photocopiable version in the Appendix)
- Figure 7.6: Level 2: Putting-It-Together Question Cards (one per student, copied front and back on white cardstock using the photocopiable version in the Appendix; you may want to create your own version of the cards with questions that are relevant to your content)

PREPARATION

Read the passage and identify the following:

- Between three and five important proper nouns or key concept nouns
- The big idea
- Several Level 2, putting-it-together questions. Level 2 questions can be answered using ideas found in different places in the same text or in a different text. Example putting-it-together questions include the following:
  - What are adobe villages?
  - Why were the Jumano called pueblo people?
  - Why did the Jumano have to irrigate their crops?

Planning Sheet

LEVEL 2 QUESTIONS

1. **Preteach proper nouns or critical concept nouns.**

    Introduce, read, and define. Students write brief definition in learning log.

    Who:

    Where:

    What:

2. **Preview text.**

    Introduce the big idea of the text selection.

    What is the most important idea that you want all students to understand and remember from this reading?

    Important key concepts, subheadings, bolded print, and so forth:

    Connections to prior learning:

3. **Model Level 2 questions.**

    Questions to use as examples:

Figure 7.8. Planning Sheet: Level 2 questions. (Adapted with permission from materials developed by the Teacher Quality Research Project through funding from the U.S. Department of Education's Institute of Education Sciences, grant contract number R305M050121A [*Enhancing the quality of expository text instruction and comprehension through content and case-situated professional development*; Simmons, D., Vaughn, S., & Edmonds, M., 2006].)

DAILY REVIEW

Preteach important proper nouns or critical concept nouns and preview the reading.

1. Introduce between one and five new important proper nouns or big-idea words and provide brief definitions. Review reasons for preteaching important proper nouns. Read the list with the class. Record the words and definitions using an overhead projector with a transparency of the Learning Log for this lesson, a SMART Board, a chalkboard, or a chart tablet.

2. Have students copy important proper nouns or critical concept nouns and definitions in their Learning Logs.

3. Present the big idea. Remind students how to preview a passage. Students should look for key concepts by reading the title, bold print, and subheadings. They should look at the pictures or other information that stands out. Students should then connect the key concepts to what they already know and to the big idea and say how they made the connection. Assist students in making connections and correct misinformation.

4. Go through the preview as a whole-class activity. Call on students to say the key concepts and to make connections to what they already know and what they expect to learn. Validate all students' ideas while making sure that information is accurate. List only accurate connections and information on the chart paper, SMART Board, chalkboard, or transparency.

5. Ask a few students to generate Level 1, right-there questions about the first one or two paragraphs of the reading.

STATE OBJECTIVE AND/OR PURPOSE

Tell students that today they will learn more about generating questions.

> **Teacher:** Why do we ask questions when we read?

Answers might include the following: "To check what we know about what we read," "to test our understanding," and "to help us remember important information about what we read."

MODEL AND TEACH

1. Model creating putting-it-together questions. Distribute Level 2 Question Cards.

> **Teacher:** Remember that you can ask several types of questions and that understanding the different types will make it easier to find the answers. Some questions require you to find facts about what you read, whereas others require you to draw conclusions or make inferences. Last week, we worked on asking and answering right-there questions—the kinds of questions for which you can find the answer, word for word, in just one place in your reading.

2. Introduce the Level 2, putting-it-together question type.

> **Teacher:** This week we are going to learn about putting-it-together questions. Teachers like these questions because to find the answer, you have to put information together. That is, you usually have to use information from more than one place in your reading and put that information together to write an answer. Putting-it-together questions usually take a sentence or more to answer. Not only are putting-it-together questions a little more difficult to answer than right-there questions, but they also can be harder to ask.

3. Model the process of generating Level 2 questions using a think-aloud.

> **Teacher:** This passage is about the Jumano people. It says that different groups lived in adobe vil-
> lages. And then it says the Spanish called all these groups Pueblo. Later, it says the Jumano
> people are called Pueblo Jumano. So I can combine that information to make a question.
> Why were Jumano people called Pueblo Jumano? They were called Pueblo Jumano be-
> cause at that time, the Spanish called all the groups that lived in adobe villages Pueblo.
> I have to know that the Jumano lived in adobe villages and that the Spanish called the
> groups of people that lived in adobe villages Pueblo. So I had to put information together
> from different parts of the passage to answer that question. Let's try some more.

4. Model this process several times.

GUIDED PRACTICE

Grouping: Whole class or small groups

1. Ask students several more putting-it-together questions and talk about the process you are using to generate these questions (i.e., finding ideas in two parts of the text that can go together and combining them
to answer one question).

2. Read two or three paragraphs to students, and as a class or small group, have students practice forming
Level 2 questions. Have students give the answers to the questions they generate and tell where in the
text the information to answer the questions can be found.

3. Give feedback and continue to model how to create and answer these questions as needed.

Students likely will need quite a lot of practice generating Level 2 questions. Do not go on to Level 3
questions until students are successful and comfortable with Level 2 questions.

INDEPENDENT PRACTICE

Grouping: Partners

Using a different brief selection, preteach important proper nouns and provide students with the overall big
idea of the passage in no more than one or two sentences. Then, have students work in pairs to quickly preview the passage.

Next, have students work in pairs to generate putting-it-together questions about the selection. Have
students write their questions in their Learning Logs along with the answers and evidence (i.e., where the
answers are found).

Circulate and provide feedback and scaffolding as needed. Be prepared to model again if necessary. If
several students are confused, stop the independent practice and return to modeling and additional guided
practice. Ask pairs to share their putting-it-together questions and to tell where in the text the answer to each
question can be found.

GENERALIZATION

Ask students for examples of situations in which asking themselves putting-it-together questions might help
them understand and remember what they read. Emphasize the fact that they can preview text and ask
themselves putting-it-together questions in all of their classes.

MONITOR STUDENT LEARNING

Each time students read an unfamiliar passage, have them use the previewing routine and generate both Level 1 and Level 2 questions in pairs or small groups. Circulate through the room to monitor students' responses. Ask questions that require students to tell the reasons for their predictions and to show where they found the answers to the Level 1 and Level 2 questions they generated.

PERIODIC AND/OR MULTIPLE OPPORTUNITIES TO PRACTICE

Use the previewing and question-generation routine each time students read unfamiliar text. Once students become skilled at making valid predictions and generating Level 1 and Level 2 questions, turn the process over to them; however, continue to preteach important proper nouns or big-idea words and to remind students to preview and generate questions. Occasionally, return to previewing and question generation in pairs so that you can monitor the process.

Before-, During-, and After-Reading Comprehension

Generating Level 3 (Making-Connections) Questions

OBJECTIVE

Students will increase inferential comprehension of text by generating making-connections questions.

MATERIALS

- Text passage or chapter
- Overhead projector, SMART Board, chalkboard, or chart paper
- Dry-erase markers, chalk, or markers
- Figure 7.3: Preview and Questioning Learning Log (photocopiable version in the Appendix)
- (Optional) Transparency of Figure 7.3: Preview and Questioning Learning Log
- Figure 7.9: Planning Sheet: Level 3 questions (photocopiable version in the Appendix)
- Figure 7.7: Level 3: Making Connections Question Cards (one per student, copied front and back on blue cardstock using the photocopiable version in the Appendix; you may want to create your own version of the cards with questions that are relevant to your content)

PREPARATION

Read the passage and identify the following:
- Important proper nouns or critical concept nouns
- The big idea
- Several Level 3, making-connections questions. Level 3 questions require students to use information from the text along with background knowledge and/or prior learning to make inferences. Example Level 3 questions for a social studies passage include the following:
  - What are some of the reasons that Patrisia Gonzales might not have had many friends in school?
  - How do you think Patrisia Gonzales' family influenced her decision to teach others about Native American life?
  - Give an example of what Patrisia Gonzales might mean when she tells kids, "Open your hearts to all the endless possibilities that life might want to give you. And never give up on living a happy life."
  - How is the biography of Patrisia Gonzales related to the other passages we have read in this chapter?
  - How is the life of Patrisia Gonzales the same as or different from [another biography you have read]?

Planning Sheet

LEVEL 3 QUESTIONS

1. **Preteach proper nouns or critical concept nouns.**

   Introduce, read, and define. Students write brief definition in learning log.

   Who:

   Where:

   What:

2. **Preview text.**

   Introduce the big idea of the text selection.

   What is the most important idea that you want all students to understand and remember from this reading?

   Important key concepts, subheadings, bolded print, and so forth:

   Connections to prior learning:

3. **Model Level 3 questions.**

   Questions to use as examples:

Figure 7.9.   Planning Sheet: Level 3 Questions. (Adapted with permission from materials developed by the Teacher Quality Research Project through funding from the U.S. Department of Education's Institute of Education Sciences, grant contract number R305M050121A [*Enhancing the quality of expository text instruction and comprehension through content and case-situated professional development*; Simmons, D., Vaughn, S., & Edmonds, M., 2006].)

DAILY REVIEW

Grouping: Whole class; distribute Levels 1, 2, and 3 Question Cards.

Preteach important proper nouns or critical concept nouns and preview the reading:

1. Introduce between one and five new important proper nouns or critical concept nouns and provide brief definitions. Review reasons for preteaching important proper nouns or big-idea words. Read the list with class. Record the words and their definitions.

2. Have students copy important proper nouns and/or critical concept nouns and definitions in their Learning Logs.

3. Present the big idea.

4. Go through the preview as a whole-class activity. Call on students to say the key concepts and to make connections. Validate all students' ideas while making sure that information is accurate. Ask students to provide reasons for their predictions. List only accurate connections and information on the chart paper, chalkboard, or transparency.

5. Read the first two paragraphs of the selection to the students or have them read the paragraphs orally with partners, and have students generate one or two Level 1 and/or Level 2 questions. Ask some students to share their questions with the class and to provide the answers to the questions with an explanation of where in the text the answers are located.

STATE OBJECTIVE AND/OR PURPOSE

Tell students that today they will learn more about generating questions.

Teacher: Why do we ask questions when we read?

Answers might include the following: "To check what we know about what we read," "to test our understanding," and "to help us remember important information about what we read."

Teacher: Remember that you can ask several types of questions and that understanding the different types will make it easier to find the answers. Some questions require you to find facts about what you read, while others require you to draw conclusions or make inferences. Last week, we worked on asking and answering putting-it-together questions, the kinds of questions that you can answer by combining information from more than one place in your reading. Today, we will learn how to form and answer Level 3 making-connections questions. When you answer making-connections questions, you use information you already know along with information from the reading. Teachers ask many making-connections questions because good readers connect what they are reading with information they already know.

MODEL AND TEACH

1. Introduce the Level 3, making-connections question type.

   Teacher: Making-connections questions are different from right-there and putting-it-together questions because you cannot answer them only by looking in the passage. Look at your blue Question Cards. To answer a making-connections question, you need to think about what you just read and make connections to what you already know. Level 3 questions often start with the following question stems:

- How is this like...?
- How is this different from...?
- How is this related to...?

Note: The goal for Level 3 questions is to make extensions and/or connections to the text. Students should try to "stay with the text" and integrate the text with their prior learning instead of answering questions "away from the text" without any connection to what they are reading.

2. Read a short passage with your class.

3. Model how to create a making-connections question.

   After reading the passage with students, discuss a few important ideas from the passage. Then, model Level 3 questions.

   Teacher: This passage about Patrisia Gonzales talks about a woman who is alive today and who is part Kickapoo, part Comanche, and part Mexican. To write a Level 3 question, I have to ask about something that is related to what I've read but that I have to think about a little bit more. One question I have about this passage is, "How is this passage related to the other passages in the 'People of the Mountains and Plains' lesson?" To answer this question, we have to think about what we've already read and relate it to what we learned today. So, we've read about different groups that lived in the mountains and plains areas of Texas a long time ago. Today we are reading about Patrisia Gonzales, who is a descendant of several of these groups. I think this passage is related to the other passages in this lesson because the authors want us to know that there are people living today who are related to those same groups of people who lived in Texas a long time ago. Let's try to create some more Level 3, making-connections questions.

   Ask students several more making-connections questions and talk about the process you are using to generate these questions (i.e., connecting ideas in the text with ideas they have already learned or already know about).

4. Because Level 3 questions are the most difficult to generate and to answer, be sure to provide students with many models of this process and to return to modeling as often as needed.

GUIDED PRACTICE

Grouping: Whole class or small groups

1. Read two or three paragraphs to students, and as a class or small group, have students practice forming Level 3 questions. Have students provide answers to their questions and explain how they used information from the text as well as background information to do so. Remind students that their questions may begin with the following stems:

   - "How is this like...?"
   - "How is this different from...?"
   - "How is this related to...?"

2. Give feedback and continue to model how to create and answer these questions as needed.

   Students likely will need quite a lot of practice generating Level 3 questions. Do not go on to independent practice until students are successful and comfortable with Level 3 questions.

INDEPENDENT PRACTICE

Grouping: Partners

Using a different brief selection, preteach important proper nouns and provide students with the overall big idea of the passage in no more than one or two sentences. Then, have students work in pairs to quickly preview the passage.

Next, have students work in pairs to generate making-connections questions about the selection. Have students write their questions in their Learning Logs along with answers and evidence supporting the answers.

Circulate and provide feedback and scaffolding as needed. Be prepared to model again if necessary. If several students are confused, stop the independent practice and return to modeling and additional guided practice.

Ask pairs to share their making-connections questions and explain how they used information in the text as well as background information to answer each question.

GENERALIZATION

Ask students for examples of situations in which asking themselves making-connections questions might help them understand and remember what they read. Emphasize the fact that they can preview text and ask themselves making-connections questions during and after reading in all of their classes.

MONITOR STUDENT LEARNING

Each time students read an unfamiliar passage, have them use the previewing routine and generate Level 1, 2, and 3 questions in pairs or small groups. Circulate through the room to monitor students' responses. Ask students to share the reasons for their predictions, show where they found the answers to their Level 1 and Level 2 questions, and explain how they combined information in the text with background knowledge to answer their Level 3 questions. Provide more modeling and guided practice as needed.

PERIODIC AND/OR MULTIPLE OPPORTUNITIES TO PRACTICE

Use the previewing and question-generation routine each time students read unfamiliar text. Once students become skilled at making valid predictions and generating all three levels of questions, turn the process over to them. Continue to preteach important proper nouns or big-idea words and to remind students to preview and generate questions. Occasionally, return to previewing and question generation in pairs so that you can monitor the process.

‖‖‖ # During Reading
Mental Imagery Log

OBJECTIVE

Students will create mental images as they read and describe their mental images with words or illustrations.

MATERIALS

- Overhead transparency of short passage, or a copy to be projected on a SMART Board
- Overhead transparency or copy of Figure 7.10: Mental Imagery Log (photocopiable version in the Appendix)
- Blank Mental Imagery Logs (student copies)
- Several copies of a short passage or chapter

DAILY REVIEW

Teacher: Yesterday we began reading _____. Who or what was the story about? Good. Can anyone remember _____?

STATE OBJECTIVE AND/OR PURPOSE

Teacher: When I say the word *mental*, to what part of the body am I referring?

Accept responses.

That's right, the head—more specifically, the mind. Today I am going to teach you a strategy that will help you understand what you are reading. We are going to make pictures in our minds called *mental images*. Forming mental images, or pictures, while you are reading will help you better understand and remember what you read.

MODEL AND TEACH

Genre: Narrative or expository (works best to introduce with narrative text)
Grouping: Whole class

Introduce Mental Imagery

First, review the five senses with students: touch, taste, smell, sight, and hearing. Then, tell students to close their eyes. Circulate around the room.

Teacher: I want you to form a picture of a dog in your mind. Think about how the dog in your mind looks, smells, feels, and sounds. What color is your dog, Shelly? What kind of tail does your dog have, Jim? What does your dog smell like, Jose?

Mental Imagery Log

Title:	
Paragraph 1	Paragraph 5
Paragraph 2	Paragraph 6
Paragraph 3	Paragraph 7
Paragraph 4	Paragraph 8

Figure 7.10. Mental Imagery Log. (Adapted with permission from The University of Texas Center for Reading and Language Arts. [2003a]. *Meeting the needs of struggling readers: A resource for secondary English language arts teachers.* Austin, TX: Author; based on McNeil, J.D. [1992]. *Reading comprehension: New directions for classroom practices* [3rd ed.]. New York: Harper Collins; Wood, K.D., & Harmon, J.M. [2001]. *Strategies for integrating reading and writing in middle and high school classrooms.* Westerville, OH: National Middle School Association; and Gambrell, L.B., & Bales, R.J. [1986]. Mental imagery and the comprehension-monitoring of fourth- and fifth-grade poor readers. *Reading Research Quarterly, 21,* 454–464.)

Continue the same steps with other familiar objects such as shoes, cars, a room, and so forth. Then, read a sentence to your students and ask them to make pictures of the sentence in their minds. Ask students what words in the sentence help them build the mental image.

Teacher: Listen to this sentence. While I read it, make a picture of the sentence in your mind. "With a screech of its wheels, the bright red car sped around the corner." What word tells you that the car is moving quickly?

Students: Sped.

Teacher: That's right—*sped*. So now our mental image is moving. We are making movies in our minds. What do you see, Joe? What do you hear, Maria? Do you smell anything, Lisa? What kind of car do you see, James?

Model Mental Imagery

Model the process of completing a Mental Imagery Log (see Figure 7.10).

1. Project a short passage on the overhead or SMART Board.

2. Read the passage to the class. Ask students to make movies in their minds as they listen and follow along.

3. Tell the students that you are going to teach them to write a description or draw a picture of their mental images after reading each paragraph.

4. Reread the passage one paragraph at a time, and ask students to listen to the words and form a mental image or make a movie in their minds. Allow students to close their eyes while you read.

5. After reading each paragraph, stop and "think aloud" as you complete the Mental Imagery Log at the overhead projector or SMART Board.

Teacher: While I was reading that paragraph, I saw the ship with its sails up, cargo in place, and pots of food still dangling over cold fires. But all of the people were gone. So, on my Mental Imagery Log, I can write, "The ship looked occupied, but the people were gone."

Write the sentence on the Mental Imagery Log transparency while you are saying it.

Teacher: Or, I can draw a picture. The words that really help me make a picture in my mind are "pots full of food dangling over a cold fire."

Underline these words in the paragraph.

Teacher: This image really captures how the people seemed to have just disappeared. So, I will draw a picture of a large pot with food hanging over a fire that has gone out.

Sketch the picture on the Mental Imagery Log transparency.

6. Repeat steps 4 and 5 for several paragraphs.

GUIDED PRACTICE

Basic Lesson

Grouping: Partners or small groups

1. Give each group a blank Mental Imagery Log and a brief passage or chapter.

2. Have students begin reading the passage or chapter with a partner. Have partners take turns reading one paragraph at a time.

3. After reading each paragraph, ask partners to stop and share their mental images.

4. Have partners help each other identify and underline any words that helped form their mental images.

5. Ask partners to decide whether they are going to write a sentence describing their images or draw a picture. Then, have the students write a sentence or draw a picture in the appropriate space on the log.

During group practice, circulate around the room and listen. Remind students to make movies in their minds while they are reading.

Lesson Variation

Grouping: Whole class

1. Give students five different colors of highlighters or map pencils.

2. Choose a short passage that is very descriptive in nature.

3. Give each student a copy of the passage, and project your copy on an overhead or SMART Board.

4. Ask students to listen for descriptive words while you read the passage aloud.

5. Reread the passage together and highlight sensory words or phrases together. For example, highlight anything that describes sound with blue, smell with yellow, and so forth.

Most students love to see their writing projected. If a student writes an especially descriptive paragraph, make an overhead transparency or a copy to be projected and use his or her writing for this exercise. If a student has illegible handwriting, type the paragraph before projecting it.

INDEPENDENT PRACTICE

Grouping: Individuals

For independent practice, students will be expected to complete a Mental Imagery Log on their own. This should not occur on the same day as teacher modeling and guided practice. Students most likely will need several opportunities for guided practice before they are ready for independent practice. They will then need several opportunities to practice independently. This is true with teaching any strategy or skill. Students must be given opportunities to practice often so that the strategy or skill becomes a habit. One way to conduct independent practice for this strategy is as follows:

1. Give each student a copy of a passage or chapter and a blank Mental Imagery Log.

2. Read the first paragraph to the class while the students follow along. Before you read, remind the students to make movies in their minds as they follow along.

3. Ask students to write a sentence or draw a picture in the appropriate space on their logs. Reluctant readers are usually reluctant writers. Set a timer for an exact time, even if it is only 2 minutes, and ask students to write or draw continuously until the timer rings and then promptly stop. Gradually, increase the amount of time that students are asked to write continuously. If students are drawing pictures in response to the text, transition them to writing about their mental images in future lessons.

4. When students are finished writing, ask for a volunteer to share his or her response. Project the blank log on the overhead or SMART Board and fill it in with students' shared responses. Ask students to share which words from the text helped them form their mental images.

5. Continue this process, one paragraph at a time, until the passage or chapter is complete. Depending on the level of the text, you might continue reading each paragraph to the class or you might ask students to read one paragraph at a time silently.

GENERALIZATION

Teacher: Can anyone think of where the mental imagery strategy might be useful outside of this class?

Student: When we read stories in English class?

Teacher: Definitely. What story are you reading in English class right now?

Student: We're reading *To Kill a Mockingbird*. We're reading the courtroom scene.

Teacher: Oh, I love that book. So what should you be picturing in your mind as you read about the trial?

Student: We should picture the courtroom with the judge and lawyers and all the townspeople watching the trial. We should also picture the jury.

Teacher: That's exactly right. So when you go to English class today, pay attention as you are reading and make movies in your minds. Tomorrow, I am going to ask you whether making mental images helped you understand what you read in English class.

MONITOR STUDENT LEARNING

Check for appropriate responses on Mental Imagery Logs.

PERIODIC REVIEW AND MULTIPLE OPPORTUNITIES TO PRACTICE

Prepare by reading the text in advance and marking places conducive to creating a mental image. While reading with the class, stop at these places and ask students to make mental images. Ask questions about the images. Ask for words in the text that helped students form their images.

Periodically, remind students to make movies in their minds while they read. Have students write descriptions or draw pictures of their mental images *and* give evidence from the text to support their images. Asking students to provide evidence is very important. Periodically, or each day for a period of time, have students complete Mental Imagery Logs in pairs or individually for paragraphs in assigned reading.

During Reading
Main Idea Strategy

TERMS TO KNOW

detail   A specific, minor piece of information related to the topic

main idea What the text is mostly about

topic   The subject addressed by the author

The "Get the Gist" strategy (Klingner, Vaughn, & Schumm, 1998; Vaughn, Klingner, & Schumm, 1996) was developed as a way to help students understand the concept of main idea. It teaches students to pay attention to the most relevant information in the text and guides them to developing a main idea statement based on the following information:

- Who or what the paragraph is about (the topic of the paragraph, which will usually be the subject of the main idea statement).

- The most important information about the *who* or *what*.

Students are taught to combine the above elements into a main idea statement with 10 words or less, eliminating nonessential details.

OBJECTIVE

The students will determine the topic, main idea, and important details of a paragraph.

MATERIALS

- Copies of a short passage or chapter
- Blank Main Idea Form overhead transparency or copy of the form for SMART Board
- Transparencies or copies of pictures depicting easily identifiable characters executing simple actions (e.g., a dog jumping for a Frisbee; a boy dribbling a basketball)
- Figure 7.11: Main Idea Forms for students (photocopiable version in the Appendix)

DAILY REVIEW

Spend 3–5 minutes on vocabulary review.

1. Show the previous day's words and definitions, an example of which is shown in Table 7.3, on a transparency or chart. Read each word to the students, and have students repeat each one.

2. Briefly review the meaning of each word. Note that these are student-friendly definitions that are easy for students to understand.

3. Ask students questions to promote deep understanding of the words. Have students discuss each question with a partner; then call on partners to respond. Always ask students to give reasons for their answers.

Main Idea Form

| | Name(s): _____ Date: _____ |
| | Title or topic of the selection _____ |

Paragraph	Who or what is the paragraph about?	Most important information about the *who* or *what*	Key details

Figure 7.11.   Main Idea Form. (From Klingner, J.K., Vaughn, S., Dimino, J., Schumm, J.S., & Bryant, D. [2001]. *Collaborative strategic reading: Strategies for improving comprehension.* Longmont, CO: Sopris West; adapted by permission.)

Table 7.3. Vocabulary review

feisty	Strong and not afraid to argue
pact	A sworn agreement
desolate	Lonely and sad
dominant	More powerful or important than other things or people
anonymous	Sent or made by someone who does not want to be named
motive	The reason someone does something

These questions can have more than one correct answer. The important thing is that the student's reasoning reflects the true meaning of the vocabulary words.

Teacher: When might a *pact* be a *motive* for a crime? (Potential answer: If someone has made a sworn agreement, he or she might commit a crime to keep his or her promise.)

Why might a *feisty* person be *desolate?* (Potential answer: If a person is really strong and not afraid of arguing with people, he or she might not have a lot of friends. He or she might feel very lonely sometimes.)

Why might a *dominant* person give an *anonymous* gift? (Potential answer: Sometimes powerful or important people might not want anyone to know when they give someone a gift. They might want it to be a secret so they don't have a lot of publicity. Maybe if it were public that they did something nice, then others would think they were "soft" or not as powerful.)

STATE OBJECTIVE AND/OR PURPOSE

Teacher: Today, I am going to show you a strategy, or plan of action, that will help you determine the main idea of each paragraph as you read. It is important to be able to identify main ideas so you can monitor your understanding as you are reading.

MODEL AND TEACH

Genre: Expository

Grouping: Whole class

1. Define the main idea through the "Get the Gist" strategy.

   Teacher: The name of the strategy you will be learning today is "Get the Gist." If you get the gist of something you read or hear or see on television, then you understand the most important ideas. The "Get the Gist" strategy is a step-by-step way to help you find the most important ideas in paragraphs you read. The strategy has three parts: 1) Ask yourself, "Who or what is the paragraph about?" 2) Ask yourself, "What is the most important information about the *who* or *what?*" and 3) Say it in a main idea statement with 10 words or less.

   One way to introduce this strategy to students is to teach it without text.

2. Project a picture of an animal doing something. No words are necessary—just a character involved in some sort of action. For instance, you might project a picture of a dog jumping to catch a Frisbee in his mouth. Perhaps there are surrounding trees, flowers, and sunshine. Now, ask the students to look at the picture.

   Teacher: In one or two words, tell me who or what this picture is about.

   Students: A dog.

Teacher: What is the most important thing about the dog?

Students: He's jumping to catch a Frisbee.

Some students may mention the flowers, or the trees, or that it is a sunny day. If this happens, ask questions to guide students to see the difference between the most important idea and nonessential details.

Teacher: Is the sunny day the most important thing about the picture? If we just looked at this picture, would we say, "This is a picture of a dog on a sunny day" or would we say, "This is a picture of a dog jumping to catch a Frisbee"?

Now that the students have identified who or what the picture is about and the most important information about the *who* or the *what*, ask them to count on their fingers to come up with a main idea statement that has 10 words or less. Consider the following examples:

- "The dog is jumping to catch a Frisbee." (8 words)
- "The dog is catching a Frisbee in his mouth." (9 words)
- "The dog leaps to catch a Frisbee." (7 words)

3. Repeat this process with other pictures, if needed, until students clearly understand the concept of main idea and the "Get the Gist" strategy.

4. Give students a copy of a short passage.

- Project a blank Main Idea Form (see Figure 7.11). Figure 7.12 is a sample of a partially completed Main Idea Form. The sample lesson is from a science passage about hurricanes.
- Preview the passage: Look at the illustrations, title, headings, and bold words.
- Write the title or topic of the selection on the line provided.
- Prior knowledge: Ask students to think about what they already know about the topic. Accept responses.
- Read the first paragraph with the students.
- Reread the paragraph one or two sentences at a time. Think aloud as you identify who or what the paragraph is about and the most important thing about the *who* or *what*. Be sure to include in the think aloud the *process* of deciding what is the most important thing and *why*. Record these answers in the appropriate spaces on the Main Idea Form.
- Think aloud the process of identifying important details in the passage. Ask yourself and answer questions such as, "Is this detail important?" and model using complete sentences such as, "The important information in this sentence is…" and, "This detail is not important because…" Then, record important details in the appropriate column.
- Think aloud to illustrate how you make sure that all of the important details are related to the main idea.
- After reading an additional paragraph, show students sample main idea statements, including some that are correct and some that are incorrect. Discuss each statement and determine whether it is an accurate statement of the main idea.

GUIDED PRACTICE

Grouping: Partners

1. Give partners a blank Main Idea Form.

Main Idea Form

Name(s): _____		Date: _____	
Title or topic of the selection _What are hurricanes?_____			

Paragraph	Who or what is the paragraph about?	Most important information about the *who* or *what*	Key details
1	Hurricanes	Large tropical storms with heavy winds	• Winds more than 74 mph • Large areas of rain • Produce tornadoes • Cause flooding
2	Hurricanes	Form over warm ocean water	• Water must be over 79 degrees F • If winds are less than 74 mph, they are called tropical storms
3	Hurricanes	Have calm centers with very powerful winds around them	• Center is called the eye • Eye is 10–30 miles wide • Wind around eye can gust to 186 mph

Figure 7.12.   Sample partially completed Main Idea Form. (From Klingner, J.K., Vaughn, S., Dimino, J., Schumm, J.S., & Bryant, D. [2001]. *Collaborative strategic reading: Strategies for improving comprehension.* Longmont, CO: Sopris West; adapted by permission.)

2. Working with a partner, have students read the next paragraph and use the "Get the Gist" strategy. Ask students to work with their partners to come up with a main idea statement that includes the following:

    *   Who or what the paragraph is about

    *   The most important thing about the *who* or the *what* stated in 10 words or less

3. Share main idea statements with the class. Think aloud with the class to modify any statements that are inaccurate or incomplete. Also, emphasize that all of the main idea statements do not have to be exactly the same to be correct.

4. Ask students to record important details that relate to the main idea.

5. Circulate around the room and be available to clarify and check for accurate details. Continue to ask questions such as, "What are the most important details?"

6. At the overhead or SMART Board, ask partners to share the important details and tell why they think the details they selected are important.

INDEPENDENT PRACTICE

Grouping: Partners, then individual

Provide an additional short passage or the next few paragraphs in a chapter and have students use a Main Idea Form to develop a main idea statement and record key details. Initially, have students work with a partner. Once students are more proficient, ask them to use this strategy independently.

GENERALIZATION

Teacher: Think about your other classes. Raise your hand if you can think of a way to use the "Get the Gist" strategy in another class.

Student: We could use the strategy in science class.

Teacher: How would that look?

Student: Well, we could find the main idea of each paragraph as we read the chapter.

Teacher: That's right. Do you have to have a Main Idea Form to do that?

Student: Well, we could draw our own form, or we could just come up with a main idea statement for each paragraph and write down the important details.

Teacher: Good thinking. Does anyone have a science textbook? Let's quickly look at a chapter together and see how we could take notes using the "Get the Gist" strategy.

MONITOR STUDENT LEARNING

Check accuracy of main idea statements and key details.

*   Does the main idea statement encompass the significant details of the paragraph?

*   Are the details accurate?

*   Did students select key details that relate directly to the main idea?

PERIODIC REVIEW AND MULTIPLE OPPORTUNITIES TO PRACTICE

Students determine the main idea of an entire passage or chapter. This is particularly important in narrative text because reading comprehension tests often ask students to identify a correct main idea statement for multiple paragraphs or an entire passage.

- Have students write the main idea statements for each paragraph in the passage.
- Use these statements to determine the main idea of the entire passage.

Students also may use the main idea statements of each paragraph to write a summary of the entire passage or chapter (see page 113 for a sample lesson). Students also may extend the main idea strategy to complete a Main Idea Log (see Figure 7.13; photocopiable version in the Appendix) or some other note-taking form.

Main Idea Log

Title of passage: _____

Identify three or four important ideas from the passage:

1. _____
2. _____
3. _____
4. _____

Write the main idea of the entire passage (10 words or less):

_____

_____

Generate three questions about the important ideas:
(Who? What? When? Where? Why? How?)

1. _____
2. _____
3. _____

Create one question about the passage that might be on a test:

_____

_____

Figure 7.13. Main Idea Log. (Reprinted with permissions from The University of Texas Center for Reading and Language Arts. [2003b]. *Special education reading project [SERP] secondary institute—Effective instruction for secondary struggling readers: Research-based practices.* Austin, TX: Author.)

During Reading
Identifying Text Structures and Using Graphic Organizers

TEXT STRUCTURES

Good readers use text structure as a context for comprehension. Text structure refers to the organization of text. It is important that students are aware of and are able to recognize different types of text structures. When students identify text structures, they are more likely to activate background knowledge, preview the text efficiently, and understand the purpose of the text. The explicit teaching of text structures and how to recognize them is particularly important for students with learning disabilities and for ELLs (Dickson, Simmons, & Kame'enui, 1998). Understanding the relationships among the ideas presented in text alleviates some of the complexity of information-dense expository text. Teachers can support students' understanding of text by using graphic organizers to illustrate how text is organized.

The two broad categories of text that older readers will encounter are *narrative text* and *expository text*. Saenz and Fuchs (2002) found that secondary students with learning disabilities must be taught the distinctions between expository and narrative text structures. This likely is true for other struggling readers as well. It is important to explicitly teach the purpose, characteristics, and key terms related to each type of text. Explain to students how recognizing text structure will help them better understand, or comprehend, what they read.

Narrative text structure commonly is found in English language arts and social studies textbooks, particularly in biographies. Sometimes, other content-area textbooks provide biographies of leaders as well (e.g., famous mathematicians or scientists). Figure 7.14 (photocopiable version in the Appendix) describes key elements of narrative text.

Expository texts can have several different text structures; and within one text, the text structure can change multiple times. This can present particular challenges to middle school readers. Figure 7.15 (photocopiable version in the Appendix) illustrates elements of expository text. It is helpful to teach students explicitly how to recognize different text structures. Focus on one structure at a time, and add more as students master each one.

As they attempt to identify expository text structures, it can be helpful for students to locate signal words commonly associated with different text structures. A list of signal words commonly associated with each text structure is included in Figure 7.16 (photocopiable version in the Appendix).

Signal words can help students think about the relationships between ideas, but signal words should be only one piece of information that is used to determine the text structure. Some signal words can indicate more than one text structure. For example, the phrase "for this reason" may signal a cause-and-effect structure or a position-reason structure. It is important that students learn to *focus on what the author is trying to communicate about the information in the text* rather than relying only on signal words. Figure 7.17 (photocopiable version in the Appendix) illustrates the connection between the author's purpose and the text structure typically associated with it.

As mentioned above, sometimes one passage may contain several different text structures. When there are multiple text structures in a single passage or when it is difficult to identify a text structure, teachers find it helpful to return to the primary focus of the passage or of the lesson. Teachers may ask themselves questions such as, "What is it I want students to know and be able to do as a result of reading the text?" and, "What is the organizational pattern inherent in that primary focus?" For example, if a section of science text describes an activity in which students determine what will happen as a result of mixing certain chemicals, then the overarching structure may be cause and effect. If, however, the focus is on comparing mixtures and solutions, the overarching structure may be compare and/or contrast. If the text describes an activity in which students

Elements of Narrative Text

Examples	Fiction Autobiographies Legends	Historical fiction Biographies Folktales	Science fiction Fantasies Myths	Plays Mysteries
Purpose	To entertain or inform			

Characteristics	Follow a familiar story structure:
	    Beginning: Introduction of setting, characters, and conflict
	    Middle: Progression of plot, which includes rising action, climax, and falling action
	    End: Resolution or solution to the problem			

Narrative Terms (student-friendly definitions)	Exposition	Introduction of setting, characters, background information, and conflict
	Setting	Time and place
	Characters	People, animals, or other entities in the text
	Conflict	Problem
	Internal conflict	A character's struggle within him- or herself
	External conflict	A character's struggle with another character
	Rising action	Events leading up to the climax; trying to solve the problem
	Climax	Emotional high point of the story; conflict is addressed
	Falling action	Consequences or events caused by the climax
	Resolution	Final outcome

Figure 7.14. Elements of Narrative Text. (Adapted with permission from The University of Texas Center for Reading and Language Arts. [2003b]. *Special education reading project [SERP] secondary institute—Effective instruction for secondary struggling readers: Research-based practices.* Austin, TX: Author.)

combine substances and then determine whether this results in mixtures or solutions, then the overarching structure is probably description and/or categorization.

USING GRAPHIC ORGANIZERS TO HELP STUDENTS ORGANIZE INFORMATION

Graphic organizers help students understand what they read by connecting prior knowledge to new learning (Schwartz, Ellsworth, Graham, & Knight, 1998) and making the relationships within and between concepts clear and visual. Such organizers can be used before, during, and after reading to help students connect new information to prior knowledge, compare and contrast, sequence events, identify important information in the text, see part-to-whole relationships, and categorize information (Schwartz et al., 1998). Kim, Vaughn, Wanzek, and Wei (2004) examined the research on using graphic organizers with students with learning difficulties and concluded that "Across the board, when the students were taught to use graphic organizers, large effect sizes were demonstrated on researcher-developed reading comprehension post-tests" (p. 114).

Several premade graphic organizers can work well with different types of text. These are often provided with textbooks, but teachers should ensure they correspond to the primary focus of the lesson and align with the text structure(s) of the passage for which they will be applied. We provide several examples below. It is also relatively easy to design effective graphic organizers that align with the specific content of a text.

The steps to designing a graphic organizer are simple but require that teachers have a strong grasp of the concepts they plan to teach and what they expect their students to learn.

Elements of Expository Text

Examples	Newspapers	Textbooks	Magazine articles	Brochures	Catalogs
Purpose	To inform				
Characteristics	Titles Headings Tables Diagrams		Subheadings Graphics	Boldface words	Charts
Organization	One expository passage may be organized using several different text structures.				
Types of organization	Cause–effect		How or why an event happened; what resulted from an event		
	Chronology or sequence		The order of events or steps in a process		
	Compare and contrast		How two or more things are alike and different		
	Description		How something looks, moves, works, and so forth; how things with various characteristics fit into categories; a definition or characterization		
	Problem–solution		What's wrong and how to fix it		
	Position–reason		Why a point or idea should be supported or what's wrong with an idea		

Figure 7.15. Elements of Expository Text. (Adapted with permission from The University of Texas Center for Reading and Language Arts. [2003b]. *Special education reading project [SERP] secondary institute—Effective instruction for secondary struggling readers: Research-based practices.* Austin, TX: Author.)

HOW TO DESIGN A GRAPHIC ORGANIZER

1. Read the text and list or outline the most important concepts, or big ideas, that students need to learn.
2. Identify the overarching text structure of the passage or of a section of the passage.
3. Organize the key concepts in a way that shows how they are related to one another. Your goal is to present the key concepts visually for students.
4. Provide relevant background information, such as the relationship to previous lessons. Look for ways to connect to students' prior knowledge.
5. Add any terms, phrases, or ideas that clarify the relationships.
6. Check that the major relationships within and between concepts are clear and presented as simply as possible.
7. Provide blank space for students to fill in appropriate information. Students should be actively engaged in completing the organizer.

It is not necessary to add any peripheral information or "busywork" for students. It is important that the graphic organizer shows only the essential information that students need to learn. Figure 7.18 shows a graphic organizer that was created specifically for a science lesson.

SAMPLE GRAPHIC ORGANIZERS

Several types of graphic organizers work well for different purposes. Samples of the following types are included in the Appendix.

Signal Words

Cause–effect		
How or why an event happened; what resulted from an event		
Accordingly	For this reason	Next
As a result of	Hence	Resulting from
Because	How	Since
Begins with	If…then	So that
Consequently	In order to	Therefore
Due to	Is caused by	Thus
Effects of	It follows	When…then
Finally	Leads/led to	Whether

Chronological order or temporal sequencing		
The order of events or steps in a process		
After	Following	On (date)
Afterward	Formerly	Preceding
Around	Immediately	Previously
As soon as	In front of	Second
At last	In the middle	Shortly
Before	Initially	Soon
Between	Last	Then
During	Later	Third
Eventually	Meanwhile	To begin with
Ever since	Next	Until
Finally	Not long after	When
First	Now	While

Compare and contrast		
How two or more things are alike and different		
Although	Even though	Nevertheless
And	However	On the contrary
As opposed to	In common	On the other hand
As well as	In comparison	Opposite
Better	In contrast	Otherwise
Both	In the same way	Same
But	Instead of	Similar to
Compared with	Just as/like	Similarly
Despite	Less	Still
Different from	Likewise	Whereas
Either	More than	Yet

Figure 7.16. Signal Words. (Unpublished supplemental material created by Deborah Reed in 2004 and produced for SEDL. Reprinted with permission.)

Description		
How something looks, moves, works, and so forth; a definition or characterization		
Above	Down	Near
Across	For example	On top of
Along	For instance	Onto
Appears to be	Furthermore	Outside
As in	Generally	Over
Behind	Identify	Refers to
Below	In addition	Such as
Beside	In back of	To illustrate
Between	In front of	To the right/left
Consists of	Including	Typically
Describe	Looks like	Under

Problem–solution		
What's wrong and how to fix it		
Answer	Problem	The problem facing
Challenge	Puzzle	The task was
Clarification	Question	Theory
Difficulty	Reply	This had to be accomplished
Dilemma	Resolution	To fix the problem
How to resolve the issue	Response	To overcome this
Lies	Riddle	Trouble
Obstacles	Solution	Unknown
One solution was	Solved by	What to do
Overcomes	The challenge was	What was discovered
Predicament		

Position–reason		
Why a point or idea should be supported; what's wrong with an idea		
Accordingly	It is contended	Therefore
As illustrated by	It is evident that	Thesis
Because	It will be argued that	This contradicts the fact that
Consequently	Must take into account	This must be counterbalanced by
For instance	Since	This view is supported by
For this reason	The claim is limited due to	Turn more attention to
In conclusion	The implication is	What is critical
In order for	The position is	What is more central is
It can be established	The strengths of	

Figure 7.16. *(continued)*

Identifying Text Structure

If the author wants you to know…	The text structure will be…
How or why an event happened; what resulted from an event	Cause–effect
The order of events or steps in a process	Chronological order or sequencing
How two or more things are alike and different	Compare and contrast
How something looks, moves, works, and so forth; a definition or characterization	Description
What's wrong and how to fix it	Problem–solution
Why a point or idea should be supported; what's wrong with an idea	Position–reason

Figure 7.17. Identifying Text Structure. (Unpublished supplemental material created by Deborah Reed in 2004 and produced for SEDL. Reprinted with permission.)

Story Map

A story map is a graphic organizer designed for narrative text. Story maps may include elements such as exposition or introduction, conflict or problem, rising action, climax, falling action, and the resolution. Story maps also may contain a description of the characters and setting. Figure 7.19 (photocopiable version in the Appendix) is a sample Story Map.

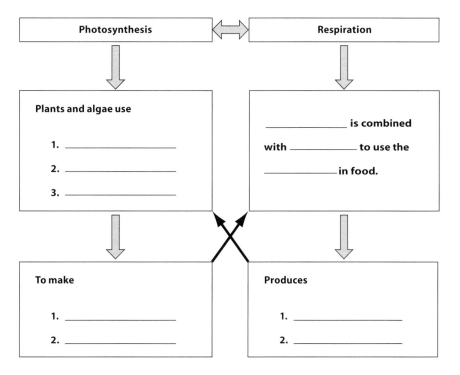

Figure 7.18. Teacher-developed graphic organizer.

Story Map

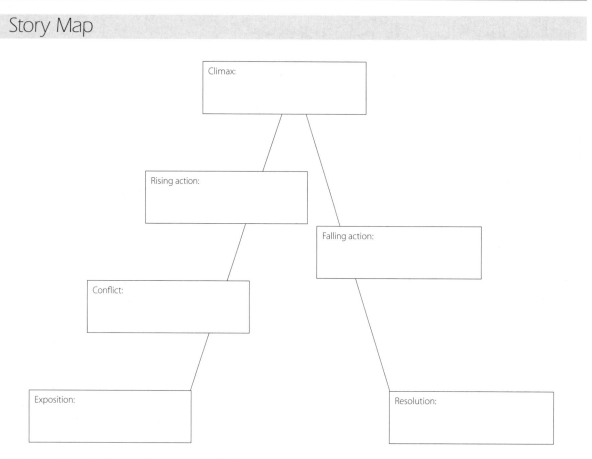

Figure 7.19.   Sample Story Map. (Adapted with permission from The University of Texas Center for Reading and Language Arts. [2003b]. *Special education reading project [SERP] secondary institute—Effective instruction for secondary struggling readers: Research-based practices.* Austin, TX: Author.)

Main Idea Web

A main idea web is a simple graphic organizer that can be used with paragraphs, sections of a chapter, or entire textbook chapters. Figure 7.20 (photocopiable version in the Appendix) is a sample Main Idea Web.

Partially Completed Outline

Students can complete this type of organizer either individually or in pairs while they are taking notes, as they read the text. Figure 7.21 illustrates a portion of a partially completed outline designed for a specific science text.

Graphic Organizers Based on Specific Expository Text Structures

Text structures can be represented by a variety of graphic organizers. Teachers may choose to have students complete only one of these organizers to represent a single overarching text structure, or the organizers can be combined or used sequentially to represent more than one important text structure within a lesson.

In the following section, we provide examples of graphic organizers that may be used with various text structures. In some cases, more than one graphic organizer is provided for the same text structure. When selecting graphic organizers to accompany a text, it is important to consider which diagram most clearly represents the relationships between the ideas in that text. In some cases, figures illustrate partially complete

Main Idea Web

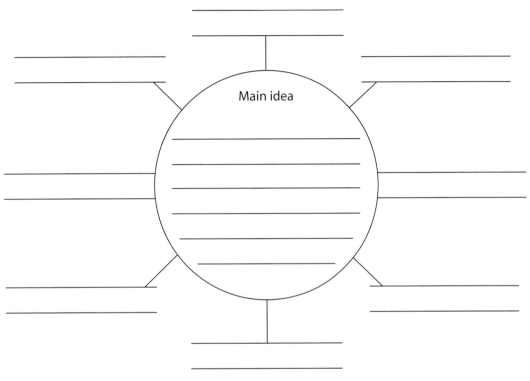

Main idea

Figure 7.20. Main Idea Web.

LIFE IN THE OCEAN

I. Things the oceans provide for organisms

    A. _____

        1. Allows easy _____

        2. Ocean organisms use less _____ to move around.

    B. _____

    C. _____ for life processes.

    D. _____ outside the parents' bodies.

    E. _____ (p. 317)

    F. _____ (p. 317)

Figure 7.21. Sample partially completed outline.

examples. Reproducible blank graphic organizers corresponding to each example can be found in the Appendix. There are many sources of other formats of graphic organizers on the Internet and in books published for teachers. These can be helpful; however, it is critical that teachers preread the text used in instruction and consider how well each organizer will work to represent relationships between important ideas in the text. It is not good practice to quickly select a generic graphic organizer for a lesson without thoughtfully considering how it will support students' understanding of the text.

- Cause and effect: Used to illustrate how or why an event happened or what resulted from an event (See Figures 7.22 and 7.23; photocopiable versions in the Appendix.)
- Chronology or sequence: Used to illustrate the order of events or steps in a process (See Figures 7.24, 7.25, and 7.26; photocopiable versions of Figures 7.24 and 7.25 in the Appendix.)
- Compare and contrast: Used to illustrate how two or more things are alike and different (See Figure 7.27; photocopiable version in the Appendix.)
- Description or categorization: Used to illustrate how something looks, moves, works, and so forth; may be used to illustrate a definition or characterization (See Figures 7.28, 7.29, and 7.30; photocopiable versions of Figures 7.28 and 7.29 in the Appendix.)
- Problem–solution: Used to illustrate a problem and how to fix it (See Figures 7.31 and 7.32; photocopiable versions in the Appendix.)
- Position–reason: Used to illustrate why a point or idea should be supported or what is wrong with an idea (See Figure 7.33; photocopiable version in the Appendix.)

Cause–Effect Herringbone

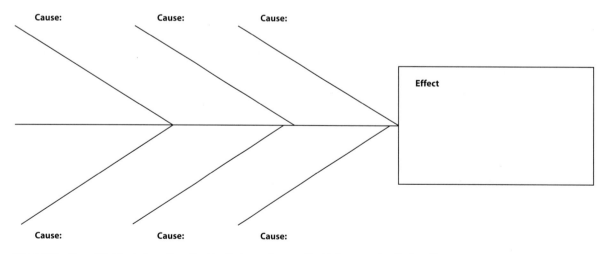

Figure 7.22. Cause–Effect Herringbone. (From "Teaching Students to Construct Graphic Representations," by Beau Fly Jones, Jean Pierce & Barbara Hunter, 1988, *Educational Leadership* 46[4], pp. 20–25. © 1988 by ASCD. Reprinted with permission. Learn more about ASCD at www.ascd.org.)

Cause–Effect Semantic Map

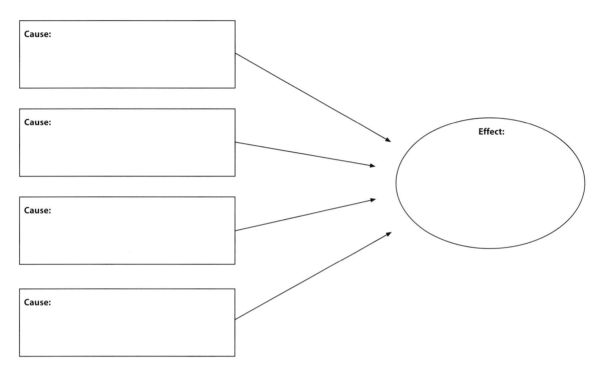

Figure 7.23. Cause–Effect Semantic Map.

HOW TO USE A GRAPHIC ORGANIZER

Graphic organizers can be used in many ways to support students' understanding of text structures and comprehension of text before, during, and after reading. It can be effective to have pairs of students work together to complete a graphic organizer, as long as both students contribute actively to the process.

Before reading:

- Provide a partially completed graphic organizer, and have pairs of students take no more than 1–2 minutes to use the organizer as a guide for a discussion of their prior knowledge related to the topic and/or their predictions about what they will learn in the text.
- Have pairs of students use the graphic organizer as a guide to preview the chapter or text. Space may be provided within the organizer for students to record one or two sentences predicting what they will learn. Writing down their predictions makes it easier to verify whether they were correct or incorrect.

During reading:

- Have students fill in important information as they read the text, either individually or in pairs.
- As they complete the graphic organizer, have students confirm and/or modify their predictions about the text. Provide space for this activity within the organizer.

Chronological Ordering or Sequencing

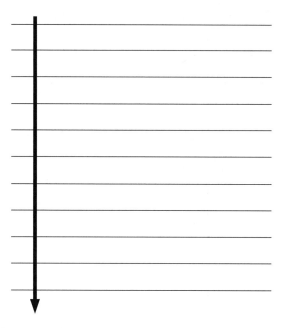

Figure 7.24.   Chronological Ordering or Sequencing graphic organizer.

Temporal Sequencing

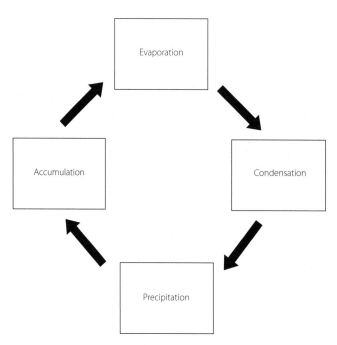

Figure 7.25.   Temporal Sequencing example.

Figure 7.26. Chronological ordering or sequencing example.

Compare and Contrast Graphic Organizer

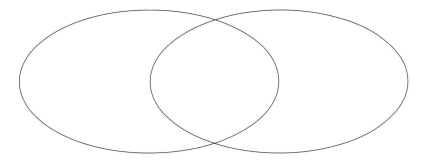

Figure 7.27. Compare and Contrast Graphic Organizer.

Description (Web)

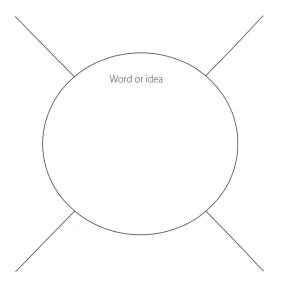

Figure 7.28. Description graphic organizer (web).

Description (Chart)

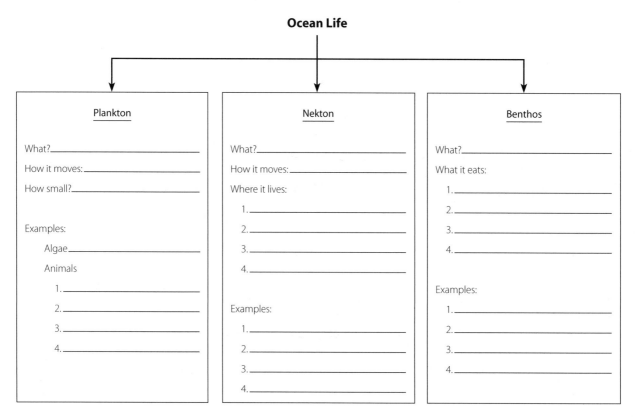

Figure 7.29. Description graphic organizer: Example 1 (chart).

Ocean Life

Plankton	Nekton	Benthos

Plankton

What?_____

How it moves:_____

How small?_____

Examples:

   Algae_____

   Animals

     1._____

     2._____

     3._____

     4._____

Nekton

What?_____

How it moves:_____

Where it lives:

   1._____

   2._____

   3._____

   4._____

Examples:

   1._____

   2._____

   3._____

   4._____

Benthos

What?_____

What it eats:

   1._____

   2._____

   3._____

   4._____

Examples:

   1._____

   2._____

   3._____

   4._____

Figure 7.30. Description graphic organizer: Example 2 (chart).

Problem–Solution Graphic Organizer

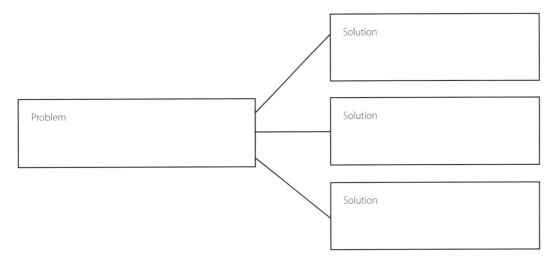

Figure 7.31. Problem–Solution Graphic Organizer.

Problem–Solution–Result

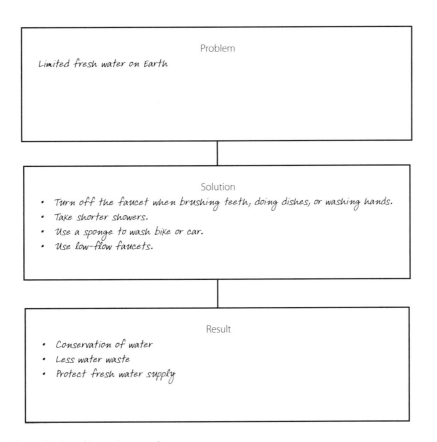

Figure 7.32. Problem–Solution–Result graphic organizer example.

Position–Reason

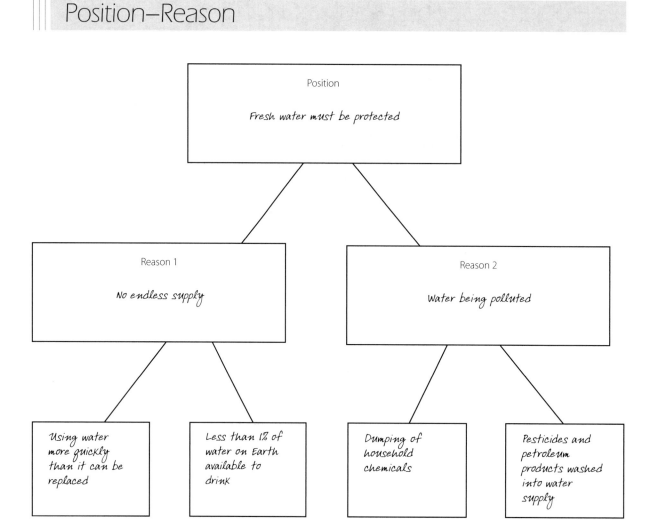

Figure 7.33.   Position–Reason graphic organizer example.

After reading:

- Have students write a summary of the text using the graphic organizer as a guide.
- Have students use the graphic organizer to "teach" the content orally to a peer. Within small groups, you can assign different students to orally summarize the content of different text sections for the group, using the organizer as a guide.
- Have students write study guide or test questions based on the graphic organizer.
- Blank graphic organizers can be provided to students to use as guides as they plan various types of writing assignments related to text they are reading. For example, students can use a position-reason organizer to plan a persuasive piece related to a controversial topic that was the focus of a recently read text, or they can use a chronology graphic organizer to plan an overview of a person's major life events described in a biography.

SAMPLE LESSON ||| # After Reading
Summarizing Text

OBJECTIVE

Students will write a summary that is concise and includes the most important information from an entire passage.

Note: Students should have already learned to write main idea statements before they are taught to write summaries. (See the sample lesson on Main Idea Strategy beginning on p. 91.) This sample lesson should be one of a series of lessons on writing summaries. It is not intended to be the only instruction students receive on this strategy. Also please note that this lesson would not be taught in a single class period, but would extend over several days.

MATERIALS

- Text (expository or narrative); expository for introductory lessons
- Figure 7.34: How to Write a Summary (photocopiable version in the Appendix)
- Transparency of a chapter with main idea statements (ideally from a recent lesson on the Main Idea Strategy)

DAILY REVIEW

Review the "Get the Gist" strategy with students (see p. 91; Klingner et al., 1998; Vaughn et al., 1996; Vaughn & Klingner, 1999).

Teacher: Yesterday, we read Chapter 6 and found the main ideas of several paragraphs. How did we find the main idea of each paragraph…Joel?

Accept responses. Students should recall that after reading each paragraph they decided who or what the paragraph was mainly about and what was the most important information about the who *or the* what. *Then, they came up with a main idea statement in 10 words or less.*

STATE OBJECTIVE AND/OR PURPOSE

Teacher: Today, we are going to use our main idea statements to write a summary of an entire passage. A summary is a shortened version of something, and it contains only the most important points. Summarizing will help you in all reading because the overall goal of any reading is to understand the most important points in the text. Summarizing is a skill you will be expected to use throughout your life. You may be asked to give a summary of a phone conversation or a summary of what was discussed in a meeting. You can impress your friends, your teacher, your parents, and maybe someday even your boss with good summarizing skills.

MODEL AND TEACH

Genre: Expository
Grouping: Whole class

Introduce Summarizing

One way to introduce students to summarizing is through a movie clip.

1. If possible, show your students an appropriate scene or segment from a popular movie.

2. Tell students that you are going to show them several written summaries of the scene and that you want them to pick the best summary. Remind students that a good summary will be a shortened version of the scene and will include only the most important information.

3. Show students several correct examples and incorrect examples of good summaries of the scene. Correct examples should be short summaries that include only the most important points. Incorrect examples can be lengthy and/or include information that is either irrelevant or too general.

4. Discuss each summary with the class and identify whether each example is a good or weak summary of the scene. Elicit discussion to clarify the reasons that one of the sample summaries is better than others.

Model Summarizing

Display Figure 7.34 (see Appendix) as a poster and refer to it as you model each step of the summarizing strategy.

Point to Figure 7.34 and tell students that it shows a strategy, or step-by-step plan, for writing a strong summary and that they will learn to complete each step of the plan. Display all of the main idea statements from the first section of the textbook chapter (in this scenario, Chapter 6). Tell the students that you will demonstrate how to write a summary for this section of the text. Indicate Step 1 and say, "Step 1 is LIST the main ideas for each paragraph in the passage. We completed Step 1 of the Summarizing Strategy yesterday in class. Let's review the statements we wrote. Catherine, will you read the first statement?"

Call on individual students to read a main idea statement until you have read through them all.

Teacher: Step 2 asks us to UNDERLINE the main idea statements that include the most important ideas from the passage.

Provide a think-aloud model of the process. Read each main idea statement and talk about your thought processes as you decide which main ideas to keep, which to leave out, and why. As you model these decisions, remind students that only the most important information goes in the summary. Be sure to explain why you think some ideas are more important than others.

How to Write a Summary

Summary: A shortened version of something that includes only the most important ideas

Step 1:	**List** the main ideas for each paragraph in the passage.
Step 2:	**Underline** the main idea statements that include the most important ideas from the passage.
Step 3:	**Combine** any ideas that could go into one sentence.
Step 4:	**Number** the ideas in a logical order.
Step 5:	**Write** your summary in one paragraph.
Step 6:	**Edit** your summary.

Figure 7.34.   How to Write a Summary. (From Archer, A.L., Gleason, M.M., & Vachon, V. [2005b]. *REWARDS Plus: Reading strategies applied to social studies passages.* Longmont, CO: Sopris West; adapted by permission.)

Now that I have identified only those main idea statements that contain the most important information, Step 3 asks us to COMBINE any ideas that could go into one sentence.

Think aloud as you read the statements and identify some that could be combined into a single sentence. Discuss these decisions with the students.

Step 4 says we should NUMBER the ideas in a logical order. We need to read the main idea statements and decide how to put them in order so that they make sense.

Think aloud through the process of ordering the remaining main idea statements.

Once we have underlined the important statements, combined the ones that go together, and numbered all the remaining ideas in an order that makes sense, we are ready to write our summary. The summary should be only one paragraph long.

Continue to think aloud as you write on an overhead transparency a summary that is several sentences in length, is a shortened version of the passage, and contains the most important information from the passage.

The last step is to EDIT the summary. When we edit something we have written, we check for correct capital letters, punctuation, spelling, and, most of all, whether what we have written makes sense.

Model checking capitalization, punctuation, and spelling one at a time. Finally, be sure to read the entire summary to model the process of checking to be sure it makes sense. It can be helpful to quickly model actually editing your summary to improve its clarity (e.g., improving word choice or further combining parallel sentences or phrases).

GUIDED PRACTICE

Grouping: Small groups or partners

1. Direct students to look at the next section of the textbook chapter you used to review the main idea strategy (Chapter 6 in this scenario). Project the main idea statements for the textbook selection on the overhead or SMART Board. Pass out one copy of the same main idea statements to each group or pair of students. Give students 2–3 minutes to read all of the main idea statements with their partners or small groups.

2. Give students 1–2 minutes to think about and discuss the section as a whole with their partners or small groups. Then, call on individual students to share their thoughts on the big ideas of the section. Next, ask students to discuss, select, and underline the main idea statements that are most closely related to those big ideas. Give them 2–3 minutes, and then ask for volunteers to share which statements they excluded and why. Based on their responses and the class discussion, underline the important statements.

3. Give students 2–3 minutes to decide whether any of the statements can be combined into one sentence and to write out the combined sentences. Again, ask volunteers to share, lead the class in discussion of the decisions, and note which statements can be combined.

4. Give students 3–4 minutes to number the statements to put them into a logical order. Again, ask volunteers to share, lead the class in discussion of the decisions, and number the statements on the projected form.

5. Give students 5–7 minutes to use the statements to develop and write out a summary of Section 2 of the textbook chapter (e.g., Chapter 6). Then, ask for volunteers to share their summaries. Discuss the quality of each summary by asking, "Is this a shortened version of the section?" and, "Does this summary include the most important information from the section?" If needed, discuss ways to modify the summaries.

6. Give students 3–4 minutes to edit their summaries. Remind them first to check capital letters, then punctuation, then spelling, and, finally, to read their summaries to be sure that they make sense.

INDEPENDENT PRACTICE

Grouping: Partners

Pass out individual copies of Figure 7.34 and tell students that they will work in pairs to summarize a section of text. Ask pairs to read a short passage or chapter one paragraph at a time, taking turns reading paragraphs aloud to each other. Ask them to stop after each paragraph to apply the main idea strategy and write a main idea statement for each paragraph. Remind them to discuss who or what the paragraph was mainly about and the most important information about the *who* or the *what,* then to state the main idea of the paragraph in 10 words or less.

Circulate around the room to monitor independent practice and be available for assistance. After students have written main idea statements, review steps 1–6 of the summarizing strategy, shown in Figure 7.34, and ask students to work through each step with their partners.

Again circulate around the room as students work. Depending on the length of the chapter or passage, students will probably need 30–60 minutes to complete steps 1–6. Once all pairs have written a summary, ask volunteers to share their summaries. Discuss and evaluate each summary.

Even though this is independent practice, it is essential that you circulate around the room while groups are working to check for understanding and to provide guidance and additional modeling as needed.

GENERALIZATION

Teacher: How can you use your summarization skills outside of this class?

Student: Our English tests always ask us to choose the best summary.

Teacher: That's right. Many tests will ask you either to choose the best summary or to write a summary yourself. Why do you think teachers want to know whether you can identify or write a summary?

Student: Because teachers want to know whether we understand the most important information.

Teacher: Exactly. Summarizing indicates that you probably understand the most important ideas from your reading.

MONITOR STUDENT LEARNING

Check that students have appropriately excluded any main idea statements that are irrelevant or redundant. In addition, check for accurate and concise summaries that are a shortened version of the reading and include the important ideas or information from the entire passage or chapter.

PERIODIC REVIEW AND MULTIPLE OPPORTUNITIES TO PRACTICE

Chapter Summary

Grouping: Pairs, small groups, or individuals

1. Rather than having students read an entire chapter, assign each student, pair, or group of students a section of a chapter to read and summarize.

2. Return to whole group and, one section at a time and in consecutive order, have students read their section's summary.

3. Write down the summary for each section.

Choosing a Summary

Grouping: Pairs, small groups, or individuals

1. After reading a passage or chapter, show students several correct examples and incorrect examples of summaries.

2. Ask students to choose the best summary.

3. Ask students to share their responses. Discuss why each option is either a correct example or an incorrect example of a summary.

Completing a Summary

Grouping: Pairs or individuals

1. Write a summary of a passage or chapter but leave out one sentence (see Figure 7.35 for an example).

2. Give students three or four sentence choices to complete the summary, with only one sentence being correct.

3. Ask students to choose the best sentence to complete the summary and discuss why the other sentences are incorrect.

Summary of "The Princess and the Pea,"
by Hans Christian Andersen

Once upon a time, there was a prince who wanted to marry a princess. He searched and searched, but it was very difficult to find a real princess. During a storm, the old king heard a knock at the city gate and found a girl standing soaking wet in the rain. She said that she was a real princess, but she certainly didn't look like one! The old queen decided to test this girl. She put a single pea underneath 20 mattresses that the princess had to lie upon all night.

Now they all knew that this girl was a real princess because only a true princess could be that sensitive. She and the prince were married, and the pea was put in a museum.

Which sentence best completes the summary?

    a.   No ordinary person could feel a pea under all those mattresses.
    b.   The next morning, the princess said she didn't sleep at all because she was lying on something hard.
    c.   The mattresses were decorated with gold-and-purple-laced pillows.
    d.   The queen also stacked 20 blankets on top of the 20 mattresses.

Figure 7.35.   Example of completing a summary.

SAMPLE LESSON ||| # After Reading
Wrap-Up/Main Idea Log

OBJECTIVE

Students will complete a Main Idea Log by identifying important information, developing a main idea statement, generating questions, and writing possible test questions based on the information in the text.

MATERIALS

- Textbook chapter or short passage
- Overhead projector or SMART Board
- Transparency or copy of Figure 7.13: Main Idea Log (photocopiable version in the Appendix)
- Several blank Main Idea Logs (student copies)

DAILY REVIEW

Teacher: We have been practicing writing main idea statements. About how many words should be in a main idea statement…Yeimi? That's right, 10. Who can tell me the two components of a main idea? That's right, who or what the paragraph is about and the most important information about the *who* or *what*.

STATE OBJECTIVE AND/OR PURPOSE

Teacher: Today, we are going to learn how to complete a Main Idea Log. Completing a Main Idea Log will help you organize and remember the important information when you read. You can also use this log as a study guide. When you complete a Main Idea Log you will be combining several strategies we have learned. The difference is that, this time, you will be finding the main idea of the entire passage, instead of just one paragraph at a time. You will practice previewing the text, finding important information, writing the main idea of a passage in 10 words or less, generating questions, and making up test questions.

MODEL AND TEACH

Genre: Expository

Grouping: Whole class

1. Provide an instructional-level passage to students. (See "Assessing Reading Fluency" in Chapter 3 to learn how to determine whether a text is at a student's frustration, instructional, or independent reading level.)
2. Preview the text: To determine the topic of the article or chapter, direct students to look at the following:
   - Title and subtitles
   - Headings and subheadings
   - Boldface words

- Illustrations
- Charts
- Graphs
- Maps
- Diagrams

3. Prior knowledge: Ask questions about what students already know about the topic of the passage. Keep this prereading activity brief.

4. Read the passage aloud with the students. There are several ways to read a passage with your class:

   - Last word: Modeling fluent reading, the teacher reads the passage aloud and stops at the last word of every sentence. Then, the students chorally read the last word of each sentence. All students are encouraged to follow along with a pencil or finger. It sounds like this:

     Teacher: Boomerangs have been around for thousands of…

     Students: …years.

     Teacher: Many peoples, including the ancient Egyptians and the Hopi Indians in the Southwestern United States, used throwing sticks that were similar to…

     Students: …boomerangs.

   - Choral reading (echo reading): The teacher reads a sentence or two, and then students read the same sentences chorally. This way the students have heard a model of fluent reading before they read the sentences.

   - Choral reading (alternating): The teacher reads one or two sentences. Then, students read the next one or two sentences chorally *without* the teacher. Continue to alternate teacher reading and students reading chorally.

   - Highlighted sections: Highlight sentences or groups of sentences like you would lines in a play. Students follow along and read their highlighted section at the appropriate time.

5. Project a blank Main Idea Log on an overhead or using a SMART Board. Tell the students that you will demonstrate how to complete a Main Idea Log.

6. Think aloud as you complete the form. Talk about your thought processes as you identify three or four important ideas from the entire passage. Demonstrate using headings, boldface words, and other text features to help you locate important ideas. Show how you decide which are the important ideas and which are less important. Record the ideas in the first section.

7. Using the important information, create a main idea statement for the selection with 10 words or less. Record the statement in the next section. Emphasize that the main idea is concise (10 words or less) and that, unlike previous assignments, this main idea statement will be about the entire passage.

8. Generate three questions about the entire passage using question starters: who, what, when, where, why, and how. Record them in the third section. Relate these questions to the three question types students learn to generate in the question-generation lessons found at the beginning of this chapter: right-there questions, putting-it-together questions, and making-connections questions. Model writing one of each type of question.

9. Create at least one question about the passage that students might see on a test. Record it in the final section.

GUIDED PRACTICE

Grouping: Small groups

1. Provide students with a second instructional-level passage.
2. Ask students to preview the passage and identify the topic.
3. Allow small groups 1–2 minutes to discuss their prior knowledge of the topic.
4. Read the passage with the students.
5. Place a second blank Main Idea Log on an overhead or project it on a SMART Board.
6. One section at a time, lead students through each section of the log, using the steps below. Set a timer for each step to keep the process moving.

    a. Allow small groups 3–5 minutes to find important ideas. Ask each group to share one important idea from the passage. Record four of these on the projected log.

    b. Allow small groups 3–5 minutes to formulate a main idea statement for the entire passage. Ask each group to share its statement. Discuss the accuracy of the statements: Are they concise? Are they about the entire passage? Record one example on the projected log.

    c. Allow small groups 5–7 minutes to generate questions. Encourage students to include at least one "putting it together" question and one "making connections" question. Ask each group to share one question. Record examples on the projected log.

    d. Allow small groups 3–5 minutes to formulate a test question. Ask each group to share its question. Ask students in each group why they think their question would be a good test question. Record an example on the projected log.

INDEPENDENT PRACTICE

Grouping: Partners

1. Provide an independent-level passage to partners or small groups.
2. Ask partners to preview the passage and identify the topic.
3. Direct partners to tell each other one thing they already know about the topic.
4. Have students read the passage aloud to each other, alternating paragraphs.
5. Instruct partners to complete the Main Idea Log.
6. Circulate around the room and check for accurate responses.
7. Ask partners to share either a main idea statement or a possible test question with the class.

GENERALIZATION

Teacher: How could you use the Main Idea Log in your other classes?

Student: We could use it to study for science or social studies tests.

Teacher: How would that work?

Student: We could come up with our own test questions.

Teacher: That's right. What else?

Student: As we are reading the chapter, we could write down the most important ideas from the passage and come up with the main idea of the entire chapter. Then we could use our Main Idea Logs to quiz our friends.

Teacher: That's a great idea! I know you have a social studies test on Friday over Chapter 12. Tomorrow we will complete a Main Idea Log for the chapter together. Then you can use it to help you study for the test. Please bring your social studies books to reading class tomorrow.

MONITOR STUDENT LEARNING

Check Main Idea Logs for the following:

- Important information that is related to the entire text
- Use of important information to develop the main idea statement
- Questions that relate to the important information

PERIODIC REVIEW AND/OR MULTIPLE OPPORTUNITIES TO PRACTICE

Main Idea Logs

Periodically, have students complete a Main Idea Log with an instructional-level passage (guided practice) or an independent-level passage (independent practice).

Main Idea Logs Using Science and Social Studies Text

Choose an interesting chapter in your students' grade-level science or social studies text. Have students work in partners to complete a Main Idea Log using the science or social studies chapter as the text.

Student-Generated Questions

1. After reading a passage, chapter, or story, ask partners or small groups to generate questions and make a quiz over the text.
2. Collect all quizzes.
3. Have each group take a quiz made up by another group in the class.
4. Discuss questions and answers.

Chapter 8

Vocabulary

TERMS TO KNOW

academic words	Words that students will see and use often in academic settings; words that appear often in academic texts, tests, or other school contexts, including words that appear frequently in directions for activities (e.g., *evaluate, categories, calculate*)
affix	A word part that is added to a word and modifies its meaning; a prefix or a suffix
base word	A word that can stand alone and to which affixes can be added (e.g., *spell* in *misspelled*)
common words	Most basic words used in everyday conversation (e.g., *run, house, door*)
content-specific words	Highly specialized words related to a specific discipline and not frequently encountered outside that discipline
context clues	Surrounding words or phrases in text that provide a reader with information about the meanings of unfamiliar words
criteria chart	A list of standards that define and clarify a task or assignment
prefix	A word part that is added to the beginning of a base word or root and modifies its meaning
root	A unit of meaning that cannot stand alone but that can be used to form words with related meanings (e.g., *spect* in *spectacle, inspection,* and *spectator*)
rubric	A scoring guide in which the standards from the criteria chart are assigned a point value
semantic mapping	Instructional procedure in which a graphic organizer is used to link words and clarify the relationships among them
semantic feature analysis	Instructional procedure in which words are categorized in a grid according to predetermined criteria
suffix	A word part that is added to the end of a base word or root and modifies its meaning

vocabulary   Words a student is able to recognize and use orally or in print

word consciousness   Awareness of and curiosity about words, their meanings, and their usage

Comprehension, or understanding, is the ultimate goal of reading. The goal of instruction in **vocabulary**, word recognition, and fluency, then, is to improve reading comprehension. This and the next two chapters include lessons designed to improve vocabulary, word recognition, and fluency. These skills are important and necessary because of their relationship to the ultimate goal: comprehension. The lessons in this chapter will focus on instruction designed to support the development of reading vocabulary. We define reading vocabulary as words in print that a student recognizes and understands.

Many of the approaches commonly implemented to teach vocabulary are not effective in building the level of word knowledge students need to comprehend text they read in middle and high school classes. One mistake that even good teachers make is assuming that students' use of **context clues** is sufficient to provide them with word meanings, and that vocabulary does not need to be directly taught. Many older struggling readers have impoverished vocabularies, and heavy reliance on context clues is simply not adequate. Some other common approaches that research has shown are *not* very effective for building students' word knowledge are:

- Having students copy definitions from a dictionary
- Providing students with definitions for long lists of vocabulary words to memorize for a quiz
- Quickly "going over" the vocabulary words listed in the teacher's edition of a textbook before students read a passage silently

The lessons in this chapter are designed to provide examples of more elaborated vocabulary instruction designed to build deep understanding of word meanings and to enable students to use the words in meaningful ways. This type of elaborated vocabulary instruction is particularly important for ELLs (Stahl, 1999).

In order to design effective vocabulary instruction for all students, it is important to know the following:

- How to identify common, academic, and content-specific words
- How to choose words to teach
- How to plan for instruction

WORD TYPES

In their book *Bringing Words to Life*, Beck, McKeown, and Kucan (2002) suggested that a literate person's vocabulary consists of three tiers—or levels—of words. The first level, which we will call **common words**, includes the most basic words such as *gate, eat, right, walk,* and so forth. These words, especially in upper grades and with native English speakers, do not normally require explicit instruction. The third level includes **content-specific** words that are rarely encountered outside of specific subject areas. Content-specific words such as *neptunium* or *sonata* are best taught when students need to know the words to understand what they are reading, studying, or discussing in a specialized lesson in a content area or elective class.

The second level of words consists of **academic words**, or words that students will see, hear, and use often in a variety of academic settings (e.g., *coincidence, synthesize, selec-*

tion, neutral, fortunate). Academic words are particularly important for comprehending textbook material, literature, and academic lectures and conversations, and they are found frequently in the questions and answer choices on standardized tests of reading comprehension. Academic vocabulary should be prioritized in vocabulary instruction. Table 8.1 provides definitions and examples of each of the three levels of words, along with guidelines for teaching words at each level.

CHOOSING WORDS TO TEACH

When faced with providing vocabulary instruction, teachers may be overwhelmed by the sheer number of words that students need to learn. Teachers can make instructional time more efficient by choosing the best words to teach. The general principle for selecting words to teach directly is to look for words that can have the biggest impact on students' ability to read and comprehend academic text—both the text they are about to read in your class and other texts they encounter across subject areas. With this in mind, choose:

- Words students *must know* in order to understand the main ideas of the text they are about to read; include carefully chosen content-specific words if they represent key concepts in the passage and are not well-defined and elaborated within the text itself.

- Words students *are likely to use and encounter frequently*

- Words many students *are unlikely to know* or that *can be confusing* to students

Table 8.1. Which words should I teach?

Three Levels of Vocabulary Words			
Type	Definition	Examples	Instruction
Common words	Basic words used often in everyday conversation	house go happy drink phone gate afraid	These words do not need to be explicitly taught, especially in upper grades with native English speakers. Some English language learners may need brief explanations of some common words.
Academic words	More complex, frequently occurring words in academic settings	coincidence neutral fortunately synthesize plead represent environment collaborate extend adapt	Teach these words. Students will see and use these words often in academic texts.
Content-specific words	Highly specialized words that are related to a specific discipline	pogrom quagmire locution polyglot neptunium sonata isosceles nova	Teach these words when a specific lesson requires knowledge of the word and underlying concept.

In *Narrowing the Language Gap: The Case for Explicit Vocabulary Instruction*, Feldman and Kinsella (2005) suggest that teachers provide instruction in the following categories of words:

1. Big-idea words: These are the words that are critical for understanding the *important ideas* in the text that will be read. Teachers can waste valuable time teaching words that are unfamiliar to students, but that are not critical to their understanding of the text. Feldman and Kinsella (2005) refer to this as "lexical accessorizing [or]…spending an inordinate amount of time explicating words peripheral to the central themes and issues, yet intriguing to the teacher or a small cadre of precocious students" (p. 9). Similarly, many textbook editions feature vocabulary lists full of rare and unusual words that are indeed unfamiliar to students but are also unlikely ever to be used or encountered frequently by students (Lehr, Osborn, & Hiebert, 2004). Effective teachers preview the text that students are going to read and teach academic and content-specific words that students must understand to comprehend the text.

2. Multiple-meaning words: It may be particularly important to teach multiple-meaning words, especially words that have different meanings in different subject areas. A sound *wave* in science is different from a *wave* of fear in literature, and these concepts may confuse students if not addressed directly. Multiple-meaning words can be particularly confusing for ELLs. Even simple words such as *run* can confuse ELLs when the word is used to mean very different things in different sentences (e.g., a *run* on a bank versus a *run* in a stocking). In general, it is important to teach words that students are not likely to learn outside of school but that students will encounter again in academic settings. Table 8.2 provides a helpful checklist for planning vocabulary instruction.

EXPLICITLY TEACHING WORD MEANINGS

The meanings of some words selected using the procedures above may be most effectively taught through brief explanations in the context of reading the text, especially if they are well defined within the text or are composed of meaningful word parts (e.g., prefixes, suffixes, roots) that students know. In contrast, important academic words that students are likely to encounter frequently should be taught directly through an elaborated instruc-

Table 8.2. Guide to word selection for vocabulary instruction

Guide to word selection for vocabulary instruction
PREVIEW the text.
IDENTIFY:
(You may not be able to directly teach all of these words.)
Academic words that students are likely to use and encounter frequently in various settings; especially consider words that can be used to generate many other words (e.g., *consider, considerate, reconsider, inconsiderate*)
Words students must understand to comprehend the text, including *critical concept-specific, or big-idea words*
Words that many students are *unlikely to know*
Words that may be confusing to students, such as multiple-meaning words or words that sound similar to other words students have heard
ELIMINATE:
Words that are adequately defined in context; discuss these words while reading instead of preteaching them
Words likely to be in students' background knowledge. Discuss these words during the activation of prior knowledge part of the lesson.
Words whose meanings students' may be able to determine based on their knowledge of prefixes, suffixes, and root or base words (e.g., *misused*); discuss the meanings of these words and their parts before or during reading, as necessary

Sources: Beck, McKeown, and Kucan (2002); Feldman and Kinsella (2005); and Lehr, Osborn, and Hiebert (2004).

tional format that is likely to result in deep understanding. The procedure recommended by Beck and colleagues (2002) and other experts included the following steps:

1. Show students the word, pronounce it, and have students repeat it after you.

2. Provide a simple definition of the word, often called a "student-friendly" definition. Providing a formal dictionary definition is less effective than giving students a definition they can readily grasp. If the word represents a concept students know well, simply provide one or more common words that are synonyms for the vocabulary word. For example, students know what it is to be *very hungry*, so they can easily understand the concept underlying the word *ravenous*. In this case, it is sufficient to simply say that ravenous is another word for very hungry. If the word represents a concept that is more complex or unfamiliar to the students, it will be important to provide a more complete definition, perhaps using a graphic organizer like the Frayer Model described later in this chapter.

3. Use the word in a sentence that demonstrates its meaning in context.

4. Provide examples and nonexamples of the word (or have students generate them, using a process described later in this chapter).

5. Provide opportunities for students to link the new word to their prior knowledge (see semantic mapping and semantic feature analysis lessons later in this chapter) and to use the word in speaking and writing (see, e.g., the sample writing assignments later in this chapter).

6. Provide multiple contacts with the word. Students may need many encounters with a new word in an instructional setting to develop a deep understanding of the word and to have ready access to the word in speaking and writing.

It is obvious that teachers cannot provide this level of intensive instruction for every word that students need to learn. Therefore, it is important that teachers thoughtfully consider which words will be most useful to their students.

The remainder of this chapter includes vocabulary lessons designed to empower students with knowledge of words and their meanings, the ability to understand and use the words they learn, a curiosity about the words around them, and word-learning strategies to help them infer the meanings of unfamiliar words as they read. The goal is to give students ownership of their own vocabularies.

The vocabulary lessons are organized in the following manner:

Word knowledge	Semantic mapping
	Semantic feature analysis
	Generating examples and nonexamples of words
Word consciousness	Prepared participation
	Possible sentences
Word learning	The word part strategy
	Using context clues
	The "Outside-In" strategy

WORD KNOWLEDGE

Semantic mapping (Heimlich & Pittelman, 1986; Reyes & Bos, 1998; Scanlon, Duran, Reyes, & Gallego, 1992; Schifini, 1994; Stahl & Vancil, 1986), semantic feature analysis (Anders & Bos, 1986; Bos & Anders, 1992; Reyes & Bos, 1998), and generating examples and nonexamples of words (Baumann & Kame'enui, 2003; Blachowicz & Fisher, 2000; Stahl & Fairbanks, 1986) are research-based instructional practices designed to teach word meanings. **Semantic mapping** is an instructional routine in which students learn to use web-type graphic organizers to link words to each other and illustrate the relationships among them. In **semantic feature analysis,** concepts represented by vocabulary words are classified using a grid according to their properties. Research suggests that knowledge is stored in categories and that words are linked in memory to other words, or concepts, based on their relationships to each other (Anderson, 1980; Rumelhart, 1980), so a student's ability to retain new word meanings is directly related to the student's ability to associate the new word with his or her prior knowledge. Therefore, it is important to activate a student's background knowledge and demonstrate how words are connected to each other when introducing a new word or concept. This approach helps improve retention of new word meanings.

English language learners, in particular, benefit from instruction showing relationships between words—especially synonyms, antonyms, and word family associations (Echevarria, Vogt, & Short, 2004; Grognet, Jameson, Franco, & Derrcki-Mescua, 2000). It is also helpful to give examples of a new word in different parts of speech (e.g. *enthusiasm, enthusiastic, enthusiastically*) and to provide a meaningful sentence for each word.

Semantic mapping, semantic feature analysis, and the generation of examples and nonexamples of words are effective for the following reasons:

- They are flexible and require minimal preparation time.
- They activate students' prior knowledge of words and concepts.
- They help students understand the relationships between words.
- They may improve students' recall of word meanings.

WORD CONSCIOUSNESS

Word consciousness refers to a student's interest in and awareness of words (Graves, Juel, & Graves, 1998). A word-conscious student is interested in learning new words and knows a lot of words. This kind of student loves to use words, pursues the discovery of interesting words, and understands that words can be used to communicate precisely and clearly (Graves et al., 1998). Teachers can encourage students to be word-conscious by modeling their own love of words. Teachers can model their interest in words by pointing out unique or intriguing words during in-class reading. Teachers can also model the use of precise words by explaining to students their own word choices. For example, a teacher may start the day by telling students that during the storms the previous night the winds were howling. Then the teacher could explain that *howling* is a good word to use when describing how strong winds sound because the word *howling* makes us think of the sound of a howling animal. In addition to modeling a love of words and the use of effective words, it is important to praise students for their use of clever or precise words in their speaking or writing (Graves et al., 1998).

Further suggestions for promoting word consciousness include the following (Texas Reading Initiative, 2000):

- Guide students to understand the difference between the ways words are used in written language and conversation.

- Have students keep a journal of effective written language, including well-written descriptions, figurative language, or dialogue.

- Write a dull version of a particularly well-written paragraph or chapter, and read both versions to the class. Discuss the differences and what makes language effective and exciting.

- Incorporate word plays such as palindromes, puns, jokes, and riddles into your instructional routines (Stahl, 1999).

WORD LEARNING

Teachers cannot directly teach students every single word they need to know. They can, however, teach some words directly and then equip students with independent word-learning tools—ways to figure out word meanings on their own as they read. Teaching students how to recognize and analyze meaningful word parts such as prefixes, suffixes, and roots is one such independent word-learning tool. Another way to teach independent word learning is through instruction in the use of context clues to infer the meanings of unknown words. Research on teaching word learning to middle school students suggests that combining word-part–clue and context-clue strategies is a powerful way to increase students' ability to discover word meanings independently (Anderson & Nagy, 1992; Baumann, Font, Edwards, & Boland, 2005; Sternberg, 1987). The use of word parts and context clues may be taught separately but eventually should be combined so that students can use the two strategies in tandem to infer the meanings of unknown words. Having flexible access to both strategies also allows students to select the best approach when they do not recognize meaningful word parts in a word or when context is not supportive.

Word Knowledge
Semantic Mapping

INTRODUCTION

The following sample lesson is based on the short story "The Ghost of the Lagoon" by Armstrong Sperry. Semantic mapping can be used with simple or advanced concepts and is equally effective with both narrative and expository text. A key to effective use of semantic mapping is to encourage students to discuss their reasoning as they contribute to the maps. Stahl and Vancil (1986) described a study in which they examined reading comprehension after sixth grade students participated in 1) just semantic mapping without discussion, 2) just discussion of words' relationships without completing the semantic mapping graphic organizer, or 3) both. The students who completed semantic maps in the context of rich discussion had the best outcomes.

OBJECTIVE

The students will associate new word meanings with prior knowledge through the use of a semantic map.

MATERIALS

- Text (narrative or expository)
- Overhead projector, SMART Board, chalkboard, or chart paper
- Dry-erase markers, chalk, or markers

PREPARATION

Preview the text, looking for academic words—challenging words that students are likely to see and use often in academic settings. Also identify content-specific words that students must know to understand the text. Table 8.3 provides a sample word list for "The Ghost of the Lagoon," by Armstrong Sperry.

Table 8.3. Sample word list for "The Ghost of the Lagoon"

"The Ghost of the Lagoon," by Armstrong Sperry
Target words
Island
Harpoon
Phosphorus
Lagoon
Risk
Expedition
Reef
Native
Canoe

Source: Sperry (1984).

DAILY REVIEW

Teacher: Yesterday, we talked about people we know or have read about who are brave. Who is one person we talked about, Philip? Why was he or she brave?

Accept and briefly discuss responses.

What is one thing a brave person might do? Can anyone think of another word for *brave?*

STATE OBJECTIVE AND PURPOSE

Teacher: Today, we are going to create a semantic map. Researchers tell us that knowledge is stored in your brain in categories or groups. Words in your memory are linked to other words based on their relationships. So, if you can connect a new word with a word you already know, you will be better able to remember the new word. I'm going to show you how to go through this process today by developing a semantic map. First, I want to introduce you to our story.

We will read *The Ghost of the Lagoon,* by Armstrong Sperry. This is a story about a courageous boy, Mako, who lives on the island of Bora Bora. An island is a piece of land surrounded by what? Yes, water. What are some bodies of water that could surround an island?

Accept responses. When a student gives the answer "sea," write SEA *on the board (or overhead or SMART Board) or just tell the students that in this story the island is in the sea.*

MODEL AND TEACH

Genre: Narrative or expository

Grouping: Whole class

1.   Ask students to brainstorm or think of words related to the sea. List all of the words on one half of the board. Write down all appropriate student responses.

Ask questions to lead students to say target words from the story. For example, if you want students to add *risk* to the list, you might ask, "Sara, you said the sea could be dangerous. What is another word for *danger*?" If you want to add *harpoon*, you might ask, "Does anyone know the name of a spear used to kill sea animals?" Some target words may be unknown to students. Add unfamiliar words to the list and give a brief student-friendly definition for each. Figure 8.1 shows what the board might look like at this point.

SEA | water   ocean   island   shark   whale   fish   beach   shells
       | dangerous   starfish   blue   boat   ship   waves   surfing   reef
       | nature   risk   coral   algae   adventure
       | Harpoon—*spearlike weapon used to kill fish*
       | Phosphorus—*glowing substance*
       | Lagoon—*shallow water separated from the sea by coral reefs or sandbars*

Figure 8.1.   Sample semantic map: Phase 1.

2. Draw a circle with the topic in the middle.

3. Read through the list of brainstormed words and model how to come up with categories to group the words. Think aloud.

> **Teacher:** I see the words *starfish*, *sharks*, *whales*, *coral*, and *algae*. What do these words have in common? They are not all animals, but they are all living. We could have a sea life category.

4. Ask students to come up with categories. Encourage active discussion among students throughout this activity. Write each category in a circle or rectangle and connect it to the topic. Figure 8.2 shows a sample of this phase of a semantic map.

5. If students have difficulty generating categories, you may need to think aloud and model how to come up with categories several times. You may also need to start with just a few words at a time. Consider the following example:

> **Teacher:** Let's look at a few words together. Would *shark* and *beach* be in the same category? Well, a shark lives in the sea near a beach, but they are not really in the same category. How about *shark* and *starfish*? Yes, both sharks and starfish are animals that live in the sea. So, raise your hand if you can think of a category that both shark and starfish would belong to? Yes, sea animals or sea life would be a good category. Look at our list of words, and raise your hand if you see any other words that would fit into this category.

GUIDED PRACTICE

Grouping: Partners

1. Assign partners.

2. Have pairs copy the map. Then, ask pairs to generate any remaining category titles and to categorize the brainstormed words. Encourage students to discuss their reasons for putting words into various categories.

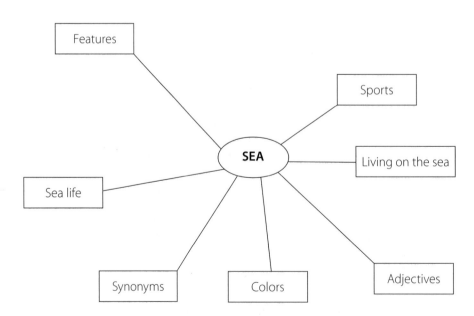

Figure 8.2.   Sample semantic map: Phase 2. (*Source:* Heimlich & Pittelman, 1986.)

3. Ask students to come up with additional words for each category.

4. Circulate around the room and be available for guidance and feedback. Check in with each pair of students to check for understanding. Be prepared to model again if needed.

5. Ask pairs to add a blank category to their map to fill in after they read the story or chapter. As you circulate around the classroom, ask leading questions to guide student responses. For example, if you hear one pair of students talking about features of the sea, ask them, "Which one of our new words is a feature with shallow water?"

6. Return to the map on the board and whole-class grouping.

7. Ask for student responses to each category and write appropriate responses on a master map. Allow students to add words to their maps based on class discussion and the master map. Figure 8.3 shows a sample master map with the target vocabulary words in bold.

READ SELECTION

Grouping: Partners, small group, or whole class

Read the selection "The Ghost of the Lagoon." Remind students to be aware of target words in the reading and to look for other categories they might want to add to their maps.

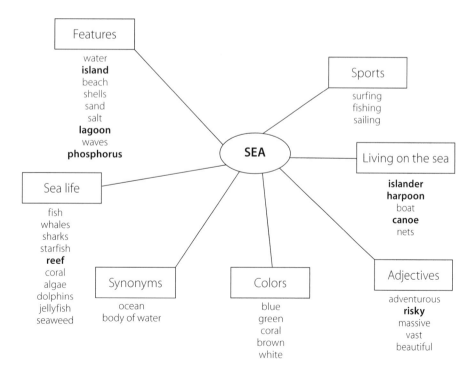

Figure 8.3. Sample semantic map: Phase 3. (*Source:* Heimlich & Pittelman, 1986.)

AFTER READING

Grouping: Partners

1. When the class is finished reading the selection, return to the master map.

2. Discuss the concepts included in the reading. Add new concepts learned during reading such as *expedition* and *native*.

3. Ask students whether they discovered any other categories, or groups of things with common characteristics, in the reading. If needed, think aloud for the class.

   Teacher: Mako was brave several times during the story. So, we could have a category labeled Brave Actions. Now, find a word in the story that is a brave action.

   Call on students and write responses under the category Brave Actions.

4. Continue to ask students for examples of new categories.

5. Have students work with partners to fill in examples under each new category.

6. When students are finished, ask for responses and discuss. See Figure 8.4 for an example of a completed map with additional categories brainstormed after reading.

INDEPENDENT PRACTICE

1. Before reading a passage or selection, preview the text for challenging words that students will use and see often (see procedure at the beginning of this lesson).

2. Tell students the topic of the reading passage or selection, and lead students to brainstorm a list of words related to the topic. Discuss background knowledge of the topic and help students make connections between what they already know and what they will learn while reading.

3. Working in small groups or pairs, ask students to create a semantic map by categorizing the brainstormed list of words. This includes generating logical category titles and placing words in appropriate categories. Encourage them to provide their reasons for the categories they generate and for placing words in different categories.

4. Return to whole group and discuss the students' maps.

GENERALIZATION

Teacher: Can anyone think of a way you might use a semantic map in your other classes?

Student: Sometimes our social studies teacher gives us lots of new words to learn.

Teacher: How could a semantic map help you understand your social studies reading?

Student: We could put all the new words in a semantic map.

Teacher: What would that look like? What would be the first step? Think about our *Ghost of the Lagoon* map.

Student: We wrote a word in the middle first.

Teacher: That's right. The word in the middle represents the topic of the reading—one word that tells what the reading is about. What are you reading about in social studies right now?

Student: We're reading about Martin Luther King Jr. and Rosa Parks.

Teacher: Good. So, the topic of your semantic map could be *civil rights*. Let's quickly brainstorm some words related to civil rights so you can get an idea of how this might look in social studies.

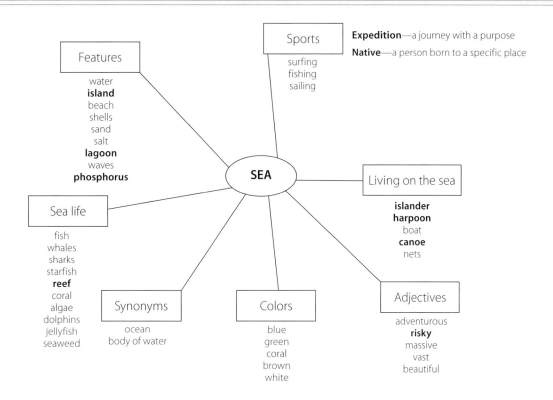

Categories added after reading:

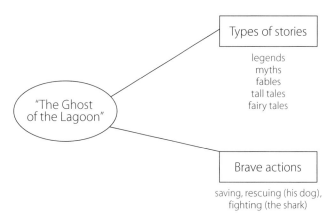

Figure 8.4.   Completed sample semantic map. (*Source:* Heimlich & Pittelman, 1986.)

MONITOR STUDENT LEARNING

Check maps for completion and check that words are accurately matched with categories. Give students a list of the target vocabulary words along with a few other words from the map. Ask students to write a story that includes 10–12 of the words on the list. Check that students are able to use the words correctly in their writing. Figure 8.5 shows a sample vocabulary writing assignment.

| **Name of selection:** |
| "The Ghost of the Lagoon" |

| **Directions:** |
| Look at the words in the vocabulary word list below. Write a story that includes 10–12 words from the list. Underline each word in your story. Be sure your story has a setting, characters, a problem, attempts to solve the problem, and has a resolution, or solution, to the problem. |

| **Vocabulary word list:** |
| island, lagoon, risk, expedition, native, canoe, phosphorus, harpoon, shark, beach, sea, adventure, massive, waves, coral reef |

| **Your story:** |
| |

Figure 8.5.   Sample vocabulary writing assignment.

Helpful Habit

Struggling readers are usually struggling writers. To encourage your students to write creatively, do not penalize students for every writing error. Make a **criteria chart** with students for this assignment, such as the one in Figure 8.6. Make it clear that they only will be penalized for spelling errors that they make in the words on the list and in frequently occurring words for which they are responsible, such as *what, who,* and *they*. A list of these everyday words may be posted in the room or in students' folders. Tell the students that you expect them to practice spelling the vocabulary words on the new list correctly. Develop a **rubric** (see Figure 8.7 for an example) based on the criteria chart that can be used to grade students' writing.

PERIODIC REVIEW AND MULTIPLE OPPORTUNITIES TO PRACTICE

When introducing a new concept, follow the semantic mapping procedure. Semantic mapping helps students understand the connections between words by organizing them visually on a map. This is an excellent instructional activity for use in content areas.

Criteria for writing assignment

- The story has a beginning, middle, and end and includes a setting, characters, a problem, attempts to solve the problem, and has a resolution, or solution.
- The story uses 10–12 of the words on the list (vocabulary words).
- The vocabulary words are underlined in the story.
- The vocabulary words are spelled correctly.
- All sentences start with a capital letter and end with a period, question mark, or exclamation point.
- The story is interesting and fun to read.
- The vocabulary words and our everyday words are used correctly.

Figure 8.6.   Sample criteria chart for vocabulary writing assignment.

Rubric for writing assignment		
The story has a beginning, middle, and an end and includes basic story elements (setting, characters, problem, attempts to solve problem, solution).		20 pts
Each sentence starts with a capital letter and ends with a period, question mark, or exclamation point.		15 pts
Vocabulary words		
	10–12 included	10 pts
	Underlined	10 pts
	Spelled correctly	10 pts
	Used correctly	25 pts
	Everyday words spelled correctly	10 pts
	TOTAL	100 pts

Figure 8.7. Sample rubric for vocabulary writing assignment.

‖ # Word Knowledge
Semantic Feature Analysis

INTRODUCTION

Semantic feature analysis is very similar to semantic mapping in that it draws upon students' prior knowledge, teaches the relationships between words in a visual way, and incorporates discussion as a key element. Instead of a map, semantic feature analysis uses a grid to organize connections between words. The grid is based on a subject or concept. Down the left side of the grid, the teacher writes several words related to the concept. Across the top, the teacher writes several features or characteristics that each word may or may not exhibit.

Discussion is a key element in the effectiveness of this strategy. Encourage students to talk about *how* they decided whether a certain feature applies to a word. The following sample lesson is based on a typical textbook chapter about the digestive system.

OBJECTIVE

The students will complete a Semantic Feature Analysis Grid by drawing from prior knowledge to discuss and identify important features and/or characteristics of words.

MATERIALS

- Textbook chapter or passage
- Overhead projector, SMART Board, chalkboard, or chart paper
- Transparency of a blank Semantic Feature Analysis Grid or copy for SMART Board (photocopiable version in the Appendix)
- Blank Semantic Feature Analysis Grids—a teacher copy and student copies (one for each pair and/or group)

PREPARATION

Preview the chapter, looking for academic words—challenging words that students are likely to see and use often. Identify content-specific words that students must know to comprehend the text. See Table 8.4 for a sample word list from a chapter on the digestive system.

DAILY REVIEW

Teacher: Yesterday, we read Chapter 4: The Digestive System. Who can remember an organ in our digestive system and its important function?

Accept responses and briefly review the main ideas of the chapter.

Table 8.4.   Sample word list from a chapter on the digestive system

Digestion	The process of breaking down food in the body
Mouth	Opening where food is taken in
Saliva	Clear liquid in the mouth that moistens food and starts the digestion process
Esophagus	Tube through which food moves from the mouth to the stomach
Liver	Organ that makes bile and filters blood
Stomach	Organ between the esophagus and small intestine where food is partially digested
Pancreas	Organ near the stomach that produces enzymes that help digest food
Enzyme	A substance made by the body that causes a chemical reaction in the body
Mucus	A clear, slimy substance that coats and protects the linings of the nose and throat
Peristalsis	Muscle contractions in the esophagus and intestines that push food and waste through the body
Small intestine	Section of intestine between the stomach and the large intestine where most chemical digestion takes place
Large intestine	Part of the digestive system that absorbs water and forms waste to be eliminated from the body

STATE OBJECTIVE OR PURPOSE

Teacher: Today, we are going to complete a Semantic Feature Analysis Grid using some of the words we learned while reading the chapter. I know this is a long title, but it is easy to remember when you know what the title means. *Semantic* means the "meaning of words," a *feature* is "a characteristic," and *analysis* (or *analyze*) means "to study or examine." So, we are going to analyze or examine the words we learned by looking at their features, or characteristics. This will help you understand more fully the words and concepts in our reading.

*It may be helpful to point to the words of the title—*Semantic, Feature, *and* Analysis—*as you explain the meaning.*

MODEL AND TEACH

Genre: Expository or narrative

Grouping: Whole class

Teacher: Before we look at the words from our chapter, I want to show you how a Semantic Feature Analysis Grid works. I'll demonstrate with a simple concept you have all studied before—mammals. Raise your hand if you can give me an example of a mammal.

Accept responses and write the examples down the left side of the grid.

See Figure 8.8 for an example of what the grid may look like with the names of mammals listed down the left side.

Teacher: Now, across the top, we are going to write features, or characteristics, that any or all mammals have. For example, I know that all mammals have hair. I also know that mammals are vertebrates and that some mammals live on land whereas others live at sea. So, I will write these features across the top. Raise your hand if you can give me another characteristic of mammals.

Accept and guide responses as necessary. Ask guiding questions such as "What do mammals eat?" or, "How do mammals move around?"

Examples										
Bear										
Bat										
Lion										
Seal										
Kangaroo										
Whale										
Ferret										
Human										

Figure 8.8.   Creating a Semantic Feature Analysis Grid (concept: mammals): Step 1.

See Figure 8.9 for an example of what your grid may look like with the animal characteristics listed across the top.

Teacher: Now, I am going to look at each animal and place a plus sign if the animal exhibits the feature, a minus sign if the animal does not exhibit the feature, and a question mark if I'm not sure (Stahl, 1999). Watch as I think through the first mammal on our list. The first mammal is a bear. I know that bears have hair and are vertebrates. I also know they live on land, not in the sea. Bears definitely don't fly. I know that bears eat meat, but they also eat plants and berries, so I am going to put a plus sign under *Omnivore*. Bears don't have pouches, so they are not marsupials. But they do produce milk to feed their young.

See Figure 8.10 for an example of a Semantic Feature Analysis Grid with plus and minus signs.

Call on students individually to come up and complete the grid for one animal at a time. Discuss answers with the whole class.

Figure 8.11 shows a finished grid.

GUIDED PRACTICE

Grouping: Whole class, sitting with partners

Note: This sample uses a chapter from a health or science textbook but can be adapted to any subject matter.

Ask students to open their textbooks to the chapter on the digestive system.

Teacher: We are going to complete a grid for the concept *the digestive system*. Skim through the chapter, and raise your hand if you can tell me a very important word we learned when

Examples	Has hair	Vertebrate	Lives on land (terrestrial)	Lives at sea (aquatic)	Able to fly	Herbivore (primary consumer)	Carnivore (secondary consumer)	Omnivore	Marsupial	Produces milk
Bear										
Bat										
Lion										
Seal										
Kangaroo										
Whale										
Ferret										
Human										

Figure 8.9. Creating a Semantic Feature Analysis Grid (concept: mammals): Step 2.

Examples	Has hair	Vertebrate	Lives on land (terrestrial)	Lives at sea (aquatic)	Able to fly	Herbivore (primary consumer)	Carnivore (secondary consumer)	Omnivore	Marsupial	Produces milk
Bear	+	+	+	−	−	−	−	+	−	+
Bat										
Lion										
Seal										
Kangaroo										
Whale										
Ferret										
Human										

Figure 8.10. Creating a Semantic Feature Analysis Grid (concept: mammals): Step 3.

Examples	Has hair	Vertebrate	Lives on land (terrestrial)	Lives at sea (aquatic)	Able to fly	Herbivore (primary consumer)	Carnivore (secondary consumer)	Omnivore	Marsupial	Produces milk
Bear	+	+	+	−	−	−	−	+	−	+
Bat	+	+	+	−	+	+	+	−	−	+
Lion	+	+	+	−	−	−	+	−	−	+
Seal	+	+	−	+	−	−	+	−	−	+
Kangaroo	+	+	+	−	−	+	−	−	+	+
Whale	+	+	−	+	−	−	+	−	−	+
Ferret	+	+	+	−	−	−	+	−	−	+
Human	+	+	+	−	−	−	−	+	−	+

Figure 8.11.   Creating a Semantic Feature Analysis Grid (concept: mammals): Completed example.

reading this chapter. Remember, important words or concepts are often bold, in italics, or found in illustrations. Also, don't forget to look at titles and headings.

Accept responses and then show students on an overhead or SMART Board Figure 8.12, the blank Semantic Feature Analysis Grid for the digestive system.

Teacher: Listen as I think through the first item on our list. Is *digestion* a process? Yes, I know that digestion is the process of breaking down food in the body. What should I put in this box…Lucia? That's right. I need to put a plus sign because digestion is a process.

Continue to think aloud through the rest of the features. Remember, discussion is a key element of this strategy.

Teacher: Now let's look at *mouth*. Working with your partner, put a plus sign if a mouth displays the feature, a minus sign if it does not display the feature, and a question mark in the square if you are not sure.

Allow students to look at their chapter, and give them 2–3 minutes to complete the row for mouth. *Circulate around the room and be available for guidance. Then, return to the overhead and ask for a volunteer to share his or her answers. Take time to discuss each answer with the class. Continue the process above for the next five or six terms.*

Figure 8.13 provides an example of a completed chart. Remember, your class chart may look a little different depending on the discussion with your students. For example, some students may say that mucus is a part of chemical digestion because it lines the stomach and protects it from being burned by the strong acids. Other students may say that mucus is not a part of chemical digestion because the substance itself

Examples	A process	An organ	A substance	Part of chemical digestion	Part of mechanical digestion	Breaks down starch	Breaks down protein	Breaks down fat
Digestion								
Mouth								
Saliva								
Esophagus								
Liver								
Stomach								
Pancreas								
Enzyme								
Mucus								
Peristalsis								
Small intestine								
Large intestine								

Figure 8.12. Sample Semantic Feature Analysis Grid (concept: the digestive system).

Examples	A process	An organ	A substance	Part of chemical digestion	Part of mechanical digestion	Breaks down starch	Breaks down protein	Breaks down fat
Digestion	+	−	−	+	+	+	+	+
Mouth	−	+	−	+	+	+	−	−
Saliva	−	−	+	+	+	+	−	−
Esophagus	−	+	−	−	?	−	−	−
Liver	−	+	−	+	−	−	−	+
Stomach	−	+	−	+	+	−	+	−
Pancreas	−	+	−	+	−	+	+	+
Enzyme	−	−	+	+	−	+	+	+
Mucus	−	−	+	−	+	−	−	−
Peristalsis	+	−	−	−	?	−	−	−
Small intestine	−	+	−	+	−	−	+	−
Large intestine	−	+	−	+	−	−	−	−

Figure 8.13. Completed Semantic Feature Analysis Grid (concept: the digestive system).

does not chemically break down food. Discussion is the key element of this type of activity. It is okay for students to disagree as long as they are presenting arguments based on accurate information.

INDEPENDENT PRACTICE

Grouping: Partners

1. If, after guiding your students through the first half of the terms on the grid, your students are ready to move on to independent practice, then allow them to continue working with their partners to complete the last half of the Semantic Feature Analysis Grid.

2. Continue to circulate around the room and be available for guidance as your students are working.

3. Return to the overhead and ask for volunteers to share their answers for each row. Discuss answers with the class.

4. If students think of any other key terms or features, have them fill in the blank row or column.

GENERALIZATION

Teacher: How could you use the Semantic Feature Analysis Grid in your other classes?

Student: We could use it to study words in our other classes.

Teacher: Think about your social studies class. How could the grid help you learn new words in social studies?

Student: We could work with a partner to make a grid using words related to the subject we are studying.

Teacher: That's right. When you put words you need to learn in this grid and discuss their characteristics, you are able to see the relationship between those words, which can help you remember what each word means. When learning new words, it always helps to think first about what you already know about the word. Using a Semantic Feature Analysis Grid can be helpful when reading new chapters in textbooks and novels. It allows you to keep track of and learn new words. It can also serve as a resource to go back to for a review of the words.

MONITOR STUDENT LEARNING

Check grids for completion and accuracy. Give students a list of the terms along with other key terms from the chapter. Ask students to use the terms in complete sentences. Figure 8.14 provides a sample format for the assignment.

The Semantic Feature Analysis Grid can be used with both narrative and expository text. Figures 8.15 and 8.16 are examples based on a novel and a social studies text, respectively.

Writing based on:

Chapter 4, Section 1

Directions:

Using words from the vocabulary list below, write 10 complete sentences. Each sentence must

- Begin with a capital letter and end with a period, question mark, or exclamation point
- Make sense
- Include two words from the vocabulary word list below

Vocabulary word list:

digestion, mouth, saliva, absorption, nutrients, esophagus, liver, bile, churning, function, stomach, pancreas, enzyme, starch, protein, fats, health, mucus, peristalsis, small intestine, large intestine, produce, lining, diameter

Your sentences:

Figure 8.14. Sample vocabulary writing assignment.

Subject: Characters in a novel Example: *Number the Stars,* by Lois Lowry (1989)									
Examples	Brave	Soothing	Belligerent	Unwavering	Jewish	Talented	Imaginative	Gentle	Threatening
Annemarie									
Ellen									
Kristi									
Mrs. Johansen									
Mr. Johansen									
Mr. and Mrs. Rosen									
German soldiers									

Figure 8.15. Semantic Feature Analysis Grid: Narrative text example. (*Source:* Lowry, 1989.)

Subject: Historical documents									
Examples	Lists grievances of colonists to express dissatisfaction with British rule	Gives government the authority to make, apply, and enforce rules and laws	Written after Constitution was sent to states for ratification	Document continues to be relevant in U.S. society today	Influenced the vote in favor of ratification and shaped future interpretations of the Constitution	Reflects values and principles of American democracy	Precedent for documents that followed	Expresses the right to freedom of assembly	Emphasizes government as a means to securing rights
Magna Carta (1215)									
English Bill of Rights (1689)									
Mayflower Compact (1620)									
Declaration of Independence (1776)									
Federalist Papers (1787)									
Anti-Federalist Writings (1787)									
U.S. Constitution (1787)									
Bill of Rights (1791)									

Figure 8.16.   Semantic Feature Analysis Grid: Expository text example.

Word Knowledge
Generating Examples and Nonexamples

INTRODUCTION

There are two good reasons for providing students with, or having them generate, examples and nonexamples of unfamiliar words. First, providing both examples and nonexamples can help clarify the meanings of words. Students who receive vocabulary instruction that provides more contextual information outperform students who receive only definitions of words (Baumann & Kame'enui, 2003; Blachowicz & Fisher, 2000; Stahl & Fairbanks, 1986). For example, you might read the following sentence in an article on reading acquisition: "In the logographic phase, beginners recognize nonphonemic characteristics." A straightforward definition for *logographic* is *representing words or ideas rather than sounds*. Even after hearing this definition, the meaning of the word probably is not perfectly clear. Providing examples and nonexamples of things that are logographic should help you have a sharper understanding of the term. An example of a logographic language is Chinese, and logos found in advertising materials are also logographic. English, Spanish, and Italian are not examples of logographic languages. Your background knowledge probably will help you understand that characters or symbols in logographic languages represent whole words or ideas rather than sounds, as is the case in alphabetic languages. Beginning readers recognize logos (such as the McDonald's arches) or whole words (such as Walmart) and connect them with ideas rather than using letter–sound relationships to read the words. This is referred to as the *logographic stage* in reading development.

The second reason to provide students with examples and nonexamples of words, or to have students generate examples and nonexamples, is that this can help them develop an understanding of the concepts underlying key content-specific words. For example, it is critical that students understand various science concepts such as *matter*, *energy*, and *reactions*. When students engage in generating examples and nonexamples of these key concept words, they develop a deeper understanding of the concepts themselves.

It is helpful to teach students to organize examples and nonexamples of words using a graphic organizer. One framework for organizing examples and nonexamples of words is a graphic organizer known as the Frayer Model (Frayer, Frederick, & Klausmeier, 1969). This lesson will focus on teaching students to use the Frayer Model while focusing on a science term—*amphibian*. Although this lesson is based on a science text, reading teachers may use the same process to help students learn to generate examples and nonexamples of words in any expository or narrative text. It can be important for reading teachers to teach lessons actually using students' content-area textbooks to encourage students to generalize what they are learning in the reading class to other classes throughout the day.

OBJECTIVE

Students will develop a deep understanding of key words by generating examples and nonexamples of words.

MATERIALS

- Text (narrative or expository)
- Overhead projector, SMART Board, chalkboard, or chart paper

- Dry-erase markers, chalk, or markers
- Two overhead transparencies of a blank Frayer Model graphic organizer or copies for a SMART Board (alternatively, they may be drawn on chart paper or on the board)
- Figure 8.17: Blank Frayer Model graphic organizers for students (photocopiable version in the Appendix)

Frayer Model

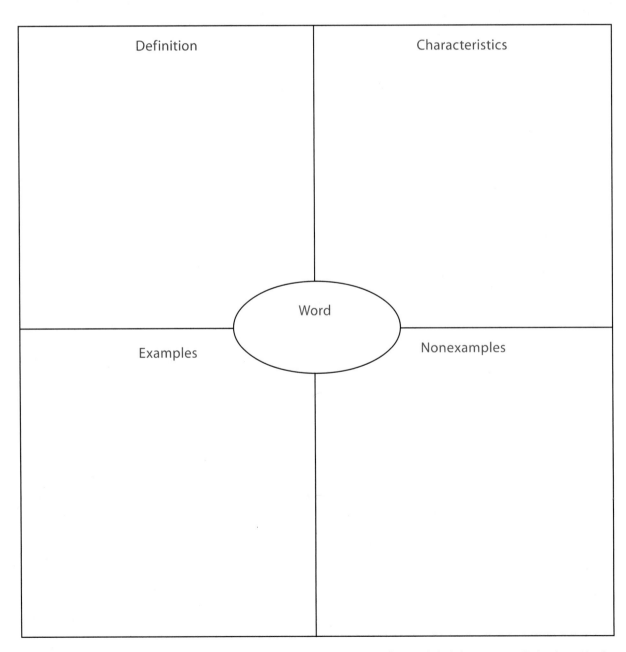

Figure 8.17.   Blank Frayer Model. (From Frayer, D.A., Frederick, W.C., & Klausmeier, H.G. [1969]. *A schema for testing the level of concept mastery [Technical report No. 16].* Madison, WI: University of Wisconsin Research and Development Center for Cognitive Learning; adapted by permission.)

PREPARATION

Preview text looking for academic words and key content-specific words that represent central concepts in the text. Identify one or two important words that represent key concepts in the text and that are good candidates for teaching students to generate examples and nonexamples of words. If it is difficult for you as the teacher to think of clear examples and nonexamples of a term, then that term is not a good choice to use when students are just learning the strategy.

DAILY REVIEW

Teacher: We have been working on reading, understanding, and learning from the textbooks you read in your science and social studies classes. From your science book, we learned that scientists classify animals as vertebrates or invertebrates according to whether the animals have a…what…Joseph? Yes, a backbone, or spine, running down their bodies. Yesterday, we learned that we can separate the vertebrates into classes, or smaller groups. What class of vertebrates lives in water and breathes with gills…Samantha? Yes, fish. Today you will read about another class of vertebrates.

STATE OBJECTIVE OR PURPOSE

Teacher: Today, we are going to learn to generate examples and nonexamples of important vocabulary words. Listing examples and nonexamples of words can help you have a better understanding of important words and can help you remember these words.

MODEL AND TEACH

Genre: Narrative or expository

Grouping: Whole class

1. Explain the concept of examples and nonexamples using a simple word.

    Teacher: I'll show what I mean by examples and nonexamples using a very simple word first. Let's think about the word *animals*. What are some examples of animals?

    Accept a few student responses. Don't allow more than a minute or so for this.

    Yes, dogs, snakes, goldfish, and tigers are all examples of animals. A nonexample would be a word that is *not* an example of an animal. That could be almost anything, couldn't it? After all, a boat is not an animal. Neither is a house. But, these nonexamples won't help us understand and remember what animals are. The trick is to come up with nonexamples that are related to the word but that are not examples of the word. A nonexample of an animal would be a bean plant. Plants are like animals because they are living things, but they are not examples of animals. Another nonexample of an animal is a bacteria. Bacteria are living things, but they are not animals. What are some other nonexamples of animals?

    Accept student responses and provide guidance as necessary.

2. Show students the blank Frayer Model graphic organizer shown in Figure 8.17. Tell them that they will be using it as a framework as they talk about definitions, characteristics, examples and nonexamples of

words. Point out that the target word will be placed in the center of the graphic organizer and that there are spaces to write a definition, characteristics, examples, and nonexamples of the word.

3. Distribute blank Frayer Model graphic organizers to students and ask them to copy the information as you model the process. Tell them that they will be completing several of these graphic organizers and that they should keep them to use as study guides.

4. Model completing the Frayer Model graphic organizer for the classification *amphibian*. Place the word *amphibian* in the center of the graphic organizer. Think aloud as you write a definition of the term, list characteristics of amphibians, list examples of amphibians, and list animals that are not amphibians in the space labeled *Nonexamples*.

> **Teacher:**   Yesterday, we learned about the class of vertebrates called amphibians. I'm going to put the word *amphibian* in the center of the diagram. We learned that a scientist would define an amphibian as an animal that lays eggs in the water but can live on land or in the water. I'll write that definition in the first box. That definition had some of the characteristics of amphibians in it, but I know some other characteristics of amphibians. They are cold-blooded vertebrates, they have a two-stage life cycle, they have moist skin, and they have no claws. I'll put those in the box labeled *Characteristics*. Now, I need some examples of amphibians. What are some examples you know of…Michael? Good, a frog is one example. A toad is also an amphibian, so I'll add that.

> *Accept answers from the class. Ask students to tell why their examples are classified as amphibians. If any suggested answers are not examples of amphibians, talk about why they are not.*

> Now, for nonexamples of amphibians, I could write the words *boat* and *story*, but those words wouldn't help me understand more about what an amphibian is, would they? I want to choose words that are related to the word *amphibian*, but are not amphibians. I'm going to write *crocodiles*, since a crocodile is a vertebrate but not an amphibian. Let's add three more nonexamples. Crystal, can you think of one?

Your completed graphic organizer may look something like Figure 8.18.

GUIDED PRACTICE

Grouping: Whole class or small group and pairs

1. Put a blank Frayer Model transparency on the overhead or project it on the SMART Board, and distribute blank copies to pairs of students.

2. Write the key content-specific word in the middle of your graphic organizer, and ask students to do the same.

3. Tell students that you will complete the graphic organizer together as they read the first part of the text. Before reading the text, provide clear "student-friendly" definitions of the key content-specific words and any other key vocabulary, and have students quickly preview the selection, examining illustrations, headings, subheadings, and so forth. Previewing should take no longer than 1–2 minutes. Ask students what they think they will learn in the selection. Allow no more than 2–3 minutes for this discussion.

4. Have students read the first part of the text with their partners. (See directions for partner reading on page 195.)

5. Once students have read the first section of the text, work as a class to complete any part of the Frayer Model graphic organizer that can be finished based on that section. Ask students to tell *why* the terms they identify are examples and nonexamples of the target word.

6. Read the next section of text, and continue to add to the graphic organizer as appropriate.

Frayer Model

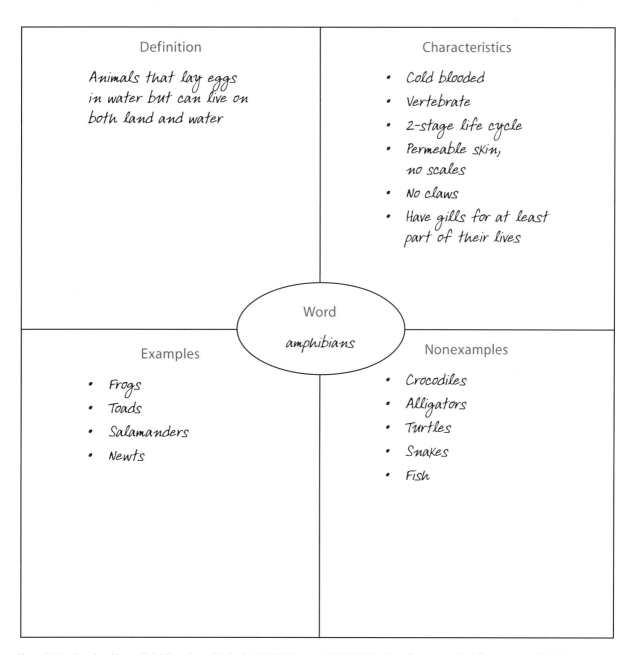

Definition	Characteristics
Animals that lay eggs in water but can live on both land and water	• Cold blooded • Vertebrate • 2-stage life cycle • Permeable skin, no scales • No claws • Have gills for at least part of their lives

Word

amphibians

Examples	Nonexamples
• Frogs • Toads • Salamanders • Newts	• Crocodiles • Alligators • Turtles • Snakes • Fish

Figure 8.18. Completed Frayer Model. (From Frayer, D.A., Frederick, W.C., & Klausmeier, H.G. [1969]. *A schema for testing the level of concept mastery [Technical report No. 16].* Madison, WI: University of Wisconsin Research and Development Center for Cognitive Learning; adapted by permission.)

INDEPENDENT PRACTICE

Grouping: Partners

Once students are comfortable with the process, have them continue to work in partners, reading and adding to their graphic organizers. Monitor student work carefully and provide scaffolding and feedback as needed.

GENERALIZATION

Teacher: How might writing down examples and nonexamples of words help you in your other classes?

Student: We can use them to study for our science or social studies tests.

Teacher: Yes, the Frayer Model graphic organizer can be helpful as a study guide. How might completing them help you understand what you are reading?

Student: If we don't really understand the important words, then we won't know what the book is trying to say.

Student: Yes, we can work together and do the examples and nonexamples of important words in social studies like *colonies*, which we are studying now. Then we might understand the book better and make better grades.

Teacher: That's a good idea. All of your teachers are getting together to talk about using these Frayer Models in different classes, so your other teachers may give you time to work on them when you read your textbooks. If not, you could do them during study hall or after school to help you study.

MONITOR STUDENT LEARNING

Check graphic organizers for completion and accuracy. Ask students to tell why they put certain words in the *Example* or *Nonexample* boxes.

PERIODIC REVIEW AND MULTIPLE OPPORTUNITIES TO PRACTICE

1. Review the use of the Frayer Model on subsequent days. Ask students questions about the target words they defined using the graphic organizers (e.g., "What are some examples of amphibians?"). If needed, allow students to refer to their completed Frayer Models to help them recall characteristics, examples, nonexamples, and definitions of target words. This helps illustrate to students that these models may be helpful study guides. Frequently, have students work in pairs to generate examples and nonexamples of key concept words before or after reading a text selection. This is especially helpful for expository text. Use students' science, math, or social studies textbooks for review and practice of the strategy.

2. On other days, ask students questions that require them to connect two unrelated vocabulary words (Beck et al., 2002). These may be words that were learned at different times, associated with different text. For example, you might ask the following:

   • Can an *amphibian* live in a *lagoon*? Why or why not?

   • How is *digestion* like an *expedition*?

   • How would you find the *diameter* of a *crustacean*?

   • Could an *adventurous* person be *renowned*?

   • When might a *courageous* person escape from a *dangerous* place?

   • Can you be *unaware* of an *audible* sound?

   • How is being *suspicious* different from being *thoughtful*?

   • Can *collaboration* be *compulsory*?

Always ask students to give reasons for their answers. There can be more than one correct answer to these questions. The important thing is that the students' reasoning reflects the true meanings of the vocabulary words.

3. Use vocabulary words often in the classroom in the course of normal conversation and provide many opportunities and encouragement to students to use vocabulary words, especially academic words.

||| # Word Consciousness
Prepared Participation

INTRODUCTION

The Prepared Participation activity, as described by Feldman and Kinsella (2005), gives students the opportunity to use vocabulary words during a classroom discussion as opposed to reading the words and hearing them used by the teacher. This practice works especially well with both ELLs and students with impoverished vocabularies. It can be used with novels (as seen in the example below), textbook chapters, or even short passages. Before planning this type of lesson, identify the topic of discussion as well as any academic words in the reading that are related to the topic.

Remember the previous discussion of how to choose words to teach. Preview the text and choose words that

- Students must know in order to understand what they read.
- Students are likely to use and encounter frequently in academic settings.

For example, in the novel *Holes*, by Louis Sachar (1998), one important topic is the issue of bullying. In Chapter 30 of *Holes*, some words related to bullying are *uneasy, astonished,* and the phrase *feeble attempt.* These words are used as examples in the following sample lesson.

OBJECTIVE

The student will use new vocabulary words in small-group and whole-class discussions.

MATERIALS

- Textbook or novel
- Overhead projector, SMART Board, chart paper, or chalkboard
- Dry-erase markers, chalk, or markers

DAILY REVIEW

Teacher: Yesterday we completed Part 1 of *Holes.* Can anyone tell me…? Who remembers…?

Quickly review the following:
- List of character names
- Setting locations
- Major plot events

STATE OBJECTIVE OR PURPOSE

Teacher: Bullying is a central idea in the book *Holes.* Today, we are going to have a class discussion about bullying. I am going to give you an opportunity to use some of our vocabulary words. First, we will prepare for our discussion, and then we will all participate in the discussion. Using new words in a discussion is an opportunity to practice and learn the new words. The more you actually use a word the more it becomes your own.

MODEL AND TEACH

Grouping: Whole class and pairs

1. List several words from the text to be read. Tell the students that the words are in the text. The following topic and sample words are from *Holes* by Louis Sachar (1998).

Topic:	*Bullying*: Teasing or picking on someone who does not deserve it
Related words:	• *Uneasy*: Feeling uncomfortable
	• *Feeble attempt*: A failed or weak try
	• *Astonished*: Surprised

2. Ask students to work with their partners to make a list of examples of bullying that they have seen or heard about.

3. Once the students write several examples, ask individual students to read and share items from their lists. Record several examples. Asking students to read exactly what they wrote will encourage them to be specific in their writing and will discourage students who like to share lengthy stories with the class but refuse to write anything down.

4. Give a few sentence starters and show students how to use their background knowledge about bullying to complete a sentence that includes one of their vocabulary words. Consider the following examples:

   • "One example of bullying I have seen at our school is. . . ."

   • "I was *astonished* when I saw. . . ."

5. Model the activity by thinking aloud.

   Teacher: We just wrote down several examples of bullying. One example that sticks out to me is the eighth-grader who was teasing the sixth-grader at the bus stop every day. So, if I wanted to complete the first sentence starter, I might write, *One example of bullying I have seen at our school is teasing at the bus stop.*

   Record on the board, overhead, or SMART Board.

   Or, I could write, *I was astonished when I saw the large eighth-grade boy picking on a much smaller sixth-grade boy at the bus stop right next to the school!*

   Record on board, overhead, or SMART Board.

   What does *astonished* mean...Jessica? That's right. *Astonished* means "surprised." So, I was surprised to see such a big kid picking on a smaller kid at the bus stop that was so near to school.

6. Give a few more sentence starters that use the target words and allow students a few minutes to work with their partners to complete more sentences. Consider the following examples:

   • "Once I made a *feeble attempt* to stop a bully by. . . ."

   • "Bullying makes me *uneasy* because. . . ."

7. Circulate around the room and check for understanding. Check that students' sentences are complete, make sense, and that vocabulary words are used appropriately. Ask several volunteers to share one of their sentences, and record a few examples using the board, overhead, or SMART Board.

INDEPENDENT PRACTICE

Grouping: Pairs

1. Explain that in few minutes you are going to have a class discussion about bullying and that you want each student to be armed with several sentences about their own experience in order to contribute to the discussion. Ask students to expand their current list by writing at least two additional sentences about bullying using sentence starters, vocabulary words, and their own experience as a guide. Circulate around the room and be available to guide as needed.

2. Have students rehearse their sentences with their partners.

3. Lead a structured discussion of the topic. Now that students have practiced reading their sentences, it is time to participate.

4. One at a time, allow students to read one of their rehearsed sentences to the class.

5. Ask questions to encourage students to elaborate on their sentences and comment on other students' sentences as appropriate.

GENERALIZATION

Teacher: How could you use this activity in your other classes?

Student: We could use it to practice our new vocabulary words.

Teacher: That's right. Remember, the more you use a word, the more it becomes your own. When I was in college, I used to write my new vocabulary words on index cards and keep the stack of cards in my backpack. I would try to use each of the words during normal conversation at least once each day.

Student: So we could do that, too. We could even keep track of how many times we use the word each day.

Student: Yeah, we could keep score.

Teacher: Or, we could keep a chart in the classroom of some important words we need to learn. When any of you use one of the words either in another class or while talking to your friends or family, we will keep track on the chart.

MONITOR STUDENT LEARNING

During the class discussion, listen and check for the following:

• Are students using topic word and related words correctly?

• Are students responding appropriately to each other's ideas during discussion?

PERIODIC REVIEW AND MULTIPLE OPPORTUNITIES TO PRACTICE

The Word Wizard activity (Beck & McKeown, 2001; Beck et al., 2002) involves giving students points or rewards for noticing or using their vocabulary words after initial instruction. This can be accomplished by adding tally marks next to students' names on a Word Wizard chart. Using Word Wizard in your classroom may help you incorporate frequent review and encourage word consciousness in your students. This is important because students are not likely to learn and use new words without thinking about and practicing the words after initial vocabulary instruction (Beck & McKeown, 2001).

Keep a list of vocabulary words posted on a word wall or chart. These may be words students used in the Prepared Participation activity. Add a tally next to a word each time a student uses the word correctly in class or each time a student notices or uses the word outside of class and can give the context in which the word was used. Reward the class with the highest tally marks at the end of each week or each month.

||| # Word Consciousness
Possible Sentences

INTRODUCTION

The Possible Sentences activity is designed to improve students' comprehension and retention of what they learn (Stahl & Kapinus, 1991). It taps into students' prior knowledge and asks them to make predictions about sentences they might read in a particular passage or chapter. This instructional activity was found to improve students' recall of word meanings and their passage comprehension (Stahl & Kapinus, 1991). It is easy to implement; works well with narrative, expository, and content-area text; and requires little preparation.

PREPARATION

- Preview the text, looking for academic words—challenging words that students are likely to see and use often.
- Choose between six and eight words that are related to the content of the text and might be difficult for students.
- Choose between four and six words that students likely know and can use to form logical sentences with the more difficult words.
- Write the 10–12 words on the board or overhead.

Table 8.5 shows a sample word list for a passage or chapter about Frederick Douglass.

OBJECTIVE

The students will use prior knowledge to make predictions about sentences they might read in a particular passage or chapter.

MATERIALS

- Chapter or passage
- Overhead projector, SMART Board, chart paper, or chalkboard
- Dry-erase markers, chalk, or markers

Table 8.5. Sample word list for a passage or chapter about Frederick Douglass

Renowned	Advocate	Freedom
Eloquence	Recruit	Brutality
Abolitionist	Slavery	Persuade
Emancipation	Escape	

DAILY REVIEW

Sample Review of Narrative Text

Teacher: We have been reading the novel *Amos Fortune*. Can anyone give me a word to describe Amos?

Accept responses.

How do we know that Amos is patient? Courageous?

Sample Review of Expository Text

Teacher: You have been studying the Civil War in your social studies class. Who can tell me one thing that you have learned about the Civil War?

Accept responses.

Who are some of the important people involved in this war?

Accept and discuss responses.

Repeat students' accurate responses. For example, if a student responds, "Abraham Lincoln," you would immediately say, "Yes, that is correct, Cyndi. Abraham Lincoln was an important Civil War figure." And then extend, "Can anyone tell me why Abraham Lincoln was important?"

STATE OBJECTIVE OR PURPOSE

Genre: Narrative or expository

Teacher: Today, we are going to read a passage (or chapter) about Frederick Douglass. Frederick Douglass was an important figure of the Civil War. He was born into slavery. During his lifetime, he escaped from slavery, became known worldwide as an advocate for freedom and the antislavery movement, worked for the national government, and had a personal relationship with Abraham Lincoln. Before we read about him, we will review some words included in the passage about him. We will use those words to generate a list of possible sentences that we might read in the chapter. Using your prior knowledge to make predictions about the ideas that will be discussed in the chapter will help you remember important words and understand what you read.

MODEL AND TEACH

Grouping: Whole class

- Refer to the 10–12 words written on the board or overhead. Read each word aloud and have students repeat words after you.
- Even struggling readers often like the challenge of reading a few words for the class. Once you have read each word and had the entire class repeat them, stop and ask for a volunteer to read the first row or first five words. Then, ask for another volunteer to read the final five words. Next, ask a volunteer to read the entire list and maybe a final volunteer to read the list starting with the last word and moving to the first. This takes only 2–3 minutes but helps the students solidify the pronunciations of the words. If students have difficulty pronouncing a word, model reading the word one syllable at a time, then reading the whole word, and have students do the same after you.

- Ask students to raise their hands if they know what any of the words mean.
- Accept responses and write students' definitions next to the word. Clarify or correct students' definitions through questioning. For example, a student might say that *escape* means "to run away." Ask follow-up questions to encourage the student to extend the definition.

> **Teacher:** Is escaping a special kind of running away? For example, if my dog was playing catch with me in the back yard and ran away from me each time I threw the ball, would I say he was escaping? Why not?

- If any words are undefined, you may provide a brief, student-friendly definition next to those words.

> **Teacher:** I am thinking about what I already know about slavery and the Civil War. We are about to read a passage (or chapter) about Frederick Douglass. I'm asking myself what type of sentences we might read. Using our preview words, I will predict some possible sentences we might find in our passage. Each sentence must contain at least two of our preview words. For example, I might think, "I see the word *abolish* in *abolitionist*. *Abolish* means 'to get rid of,' and the abolitionists worked to get rid of slavery." So I could write, Frederick Douglass supported the abolitionists, who fought to get rid of slavery.

GUIDED PRACTICE

Grouping: Whole class and partners

1. Brainstorm possible sentences.
   - Project Figure 8.19: Setup for possible sentences about Frederick Douglass, with the overhead projector or SMART Board.

Preview words
Slavery: Being forced to work for somebody else
Escape: To free oneself; get away from danger or harm
Renowned: Famous
Persuade: Make someone believe something
Brutality: Cruel behavior
Abolitionist: A person who wanted to get rid of slavery
Eloquence: Speaking with expression and persuasion
Freedom: Ability to live the way one chooses
Emancipation: The process of setting someone free
Recruit: To get a person to be involved in or work for a cause
Advocate: To support or speak in favor of something
Example possible sentence: Frederick Douglass supported the abolitionists who fought to get rid of slavery.

Figure 8.19.   Setup for possible sentences example.

- Ask students to work with their partners to think of and write another possible sentence they might read in the chapter or passage. In this way, students are essentially predicting ideas that will be emphasized in the passage. Remind the class that a possible sentence must make sense and include at least two preview words.

- Give students 2–3 minutes to think and write. Circulate around the room and be available for guidance and clarification.

- Return to the board and ask several students to share their sentence. Record all possible sentences. Do not discuss at this point whether the sentence is correct.

- Repeat the last three steps a few more times or until all preview words are used at least once.

2. Read the chapter or passage.

- With their partners, have students read the passage (or chapter) aloud to each other. Direct pairs to alternate reading one paragraph at a time.

- Once each paragraph has been read, ask the reader to tell his or her partner briefly what the paragraph was about.

- Circulate around the room, pausing at each pair of students to listen to their reading.

3. Discuss and revise possible sentences.

- Once students have read the passage (or chapter), return to the sentences on the board.

- Think-aloud: Model the thinking process for the students. Read a sentence and decide, based on the reading, whether the sentence makes sense. If it does, leave it alone. If it does not, think aloud ways to change the sentence to make it correct. For example, if the word *renowned* is used incorrectly in a possible sentence, you might say, "I'm going to look back at the chapter and see how the word *renowned* is used." Then, locate and read examples from the text. Discuss how to modify the sentence to make it make sense.

4. Partner practice: Ask students to work with a partner to read through and modify the remaining possible sentences.

INDEPENDENT PRACTICE

Grouping: Partners

Follow this procedure before reading a selection or a chapter:

1. Preview text for academic words.

2. Write target and known words on the board.

3. As a class, discuss the meaning of each word.

4. Ask students to work with their partners to generate a list of possible sentences using the procedures described above.

5. Record sentences on the board.

6. With their partners, have students read the selection or chapter.

7. With their partners, have students read each sentence and decide whether it is logical based on the word meaning and what was read in the selection or chapter. If a sentence does not make sense, ask students to change it.

8. Conduct a class discussion. Read through each possible sentence and discuss its accuracy.

GENERALIZATION

Teacher: Did thinking of possible sentences help you understand our reading about Frederick Douglass?

Student: Yes. It made me pay attention. When I saw one of the words we used in the possible sentences, I looked carefully because I wanted to see whether I used it correctly in the possible sentence.

Teacher: Good. Do you think you could make possible sentences in your other classes?

Student: Yes. We could make a list of the boldface words in the chapter before we start reading. Then, we could think of what types of sentences we might read in the chapter and make possible sentences with the boldface words.

Teacher: Very good thinking. When you make predictions about what you are going to read, it helps you to anticipate what you are going to learn and to understand the text better; and when you use the vocabulary words in your predictions, it helps you to learn the meanings of the new words.

MONITOR STUDENT LEARNING

Grouping: Whole group

Check students' revisions of possible sentences for accuracy and understanding of word meanings.

PERIODIC REVIEW AND MULTIPLE OPPORTUNITIES FOR PRACTICE

Have students generate additional sentences or a story using the vocabulary words. Assign points when a student uses one of the vocabulary words correctly during class discussion. Explain to students that they "own" their words when they can use them in writing or conversation.

Word Pairs

Using current and previously studied vocabulary words, make a chart like the one shown in Figure 8.20. Ask students to mark an X in the box or boxes that indicate the relationship of the words. For example, students may mark that *slavery* and *emancipation* are different. The beauty of this activity is the discussion of the relationships between the words. Discussion about relationships encourages deeper thinking about word meaning. Figure 8.21 shows what the completed chart might look like.

	Similar	Different	No relation
renowned unknown			
slavery emancipation			
abolitionist astonish			
eloquence persuade			
eloquence brutality			
feeble bully			

Figure 8.20. Sample word pairs chart: Uncompleted. (*Source:* Stahl & Kapinus, 2001.)

	Similar	Different	No relation
renowned unknown		x	
slavery emancipation		x	
abolitionist astonish			x
eloquence persuade	x		
eloquence brutality			x
feeble bully		x	

Figure 8.21. Sample word pairs chart: Completed. (*Source:* Stahl & Kapinus, 2001.)

||| # Word Learning
The Word-Part Strategy

INTRODUCTION

It is common for secondary teachers to assume that their older students already have a grasp on the parts that make up words, such as roots, prefixes, and suffixes. All too often, this assumption is wrong for struggling readers. Content and vocabulary become more complex as students get older, and this may frustrate or overwhelm struggling readers. Even more advanced readers can benefit from knowledge of Greek and Latin roots; therefore, it is important to teach students how to break complex words into smaller parts.

Teaching students to find and analyze meaningful word parts can help struggling readers do the following:

- Recognize words
- Decode words quickly and accurately
- Understand the meanings of words

Teaching Prefixes

Prefixes may be the easiest word parts to teach because their definitions tend to be more consistent. Whereas suffixes usually indicate a word's part of speech, prefixes usually have a concrete definition. Just 20 prefixes make up approximately 97% of prefixed words used in school English (White, Sowell, & Yanagihara, 1989). Figure 8.22 lists some of the most commonly used prefixes, organized according to their meanings (photocopiable version in the Appendix). Just teaching the prefixes on this list will improve students' vocabulary learning (Stahl, 1999; White et al., 1989). Prefix instruction should include abundant examples along with nonexamples and even silly words. It is important to provide nonexamples, or words that look like they have prefixes but that are not really prefixed words. Students must understand that identifying word parts is not always straightforward and does not always work as they expect it to. Giving—and generating—examples of silly words can help students understand how **affixes** work to change the meanings of words.

For instance, instruction of the prefix *re-* (meaning *again*) might include the following:

- Examples: *redo, rewrite, replay, reclaim, rewind, recycle*
- Nonexamples: *ready, reason, really, regular* (words that begin with *re-* but are not prefixed words)
- Silly words: *resleep* (to sleep again), *reswim* (to swim again), *redine* (to eat again) (Emphasize that these are not real words.)

Teaching Suffixes

Suffixes often are more difficult to teach than prefixes because their definitions are not as consistent or concrete. Some suffixes contribute to meaning (*-s* in *books* = more than one book), and others show parts of speech (*-ly* in *patiently* = adverb). Therefore, Stahl (1999) suggests that it is better for students to have a lot of experience using suffixed words rather than learning definitions for specific suffixes. See Figure 8.23 for a list of common suffixes organized by their functions or the parts of speech they represent (photocopiable version in the Appendix).

Common Prefixes

Recommended order	Prefixes and meanings	Example words	Notes[a]
1. Common prefixes that mean *not* or *the opposite of*	un-; non-; im-, in-, il-, ir-; dis- (not; the opposite of); de- (not; a reversal or removal)	unhappy, nonfiction, impossible, inactive, illegal, irregular, dishonest, decaffeinated	About half of all prefixed words contain just these prefixes.
2. Common prefixes that are related to time	re- (again); pre- (before); fore- (before)	repay, preview, forethought	Lists 1–2 cover about 70% of all prefixed words.
3. Common prefixes that are related to position	in-, im- (in; into); ex- (out); sub- (under); inter- (between); trans- (across); mid- (middle); tele- (far away)	input, imprison, export[b], subway, interstate, transatlantic, midnight, television	Lists 1–3 cover about 82% of all prefixed words.
4. Common prefixes that are related to quantity or quality	over- (too much); under- (too little); super- (above or better than normal); semi- (half)	overcooked, underpay, supermodel, semicircle	Lists 1–4 cover about 88% of all prefixed words.
5. Other common prefixes	en-, em- (cause to; in); mis- (wrongly); anti- (against)	enable, embed, misunderstand, antiwar	Lists 1–5 cover about 96% of all prefixed words.

[a]Estimates of word coverage from White, Sowell, & Yanagihara (1989).

[b]For most prefixes, we have provided examples of words in which the prefix is added to a base word (a word that can stand alone), as these are easier for students to understand when they are first learning the prefixes; however, in the case of the prefix *ex-* the example word is built from the prefix plus the Latin root *port* (i.e., ex*port* = *ex* + *port*, meaning *to carry*). This word may require a bit more explanation.

Figure 8.22. Recommended order of introduction for prefixes.

Common Suffixes

Recommended order	Suffixes	Example words	Notes[a]
1. Inflectional endings	-s, -es (plural of a noun); -ed (past tense of a verb); -ing (progressive tense of a verb)	frogs, boxes, sailed, jumping	About 65% of all suffixed words contain just these inflectional endings.
2. Noun suffixes	-er, -or (one who...); -tion, -sion, -ition; -ity, -ty; -ment; -ness (an abstract noun)	runner, actor, education, confession, activity, loyalty, payment, kindness	Lists 1–2 cover about 76% of all suffixed words.
3. Adjective (and one adverb) suffixes	-ly (usually an adverb, but can be an adjective); -able, ible (able to); -al, ial; -y; -ic	lovely (adjective)/ quickly (adverb); fixable, convertible, medical, racial, sleepy, poetic	Lists 1–3 cover about 88% of all suffixed words.
4. More adjective suffixes	-ous, -ious; -er (more than); -est (the most); -ive, -ative, -tive; -ful (full of) , -less (without)	dangerous, glorious, taller, strongest, active, talkative, beautiful, careless	Lists 1–4 cover about 93% of all suffixed words.

[a] Estimates of word coverage from White, Sowell, & Yanagihara (1989).

Figure 8.23. Recommended order of introduction of suffixes.

Teaching Roots and Base Words

Roots and base words contain the basic meanings of words. It is important that students understand this so that they are able to isolate roots and base words. When students are able to recognize and recall the meanings of common roots and base words, they are more able to determine the meanings of complex words.

The most common roots in the English language are Anglo-Saxon, Latin, and Greek. About 60% of all English words have Latin and Greek roots (Armbruster, Lehr, & Osborn, 2003). See Figure 8.24 for a list of Common Latin and Greek Roots (photocopiable version in the Appendix).

Common Latin and Greek Roots

Root	Origin	Meaning	Examples
aud	Latin	Hear	Auditorium, audition, audience, audible, audiovisual
astro	Greek	Stars or heavens	Astronaut, astronomy, asterisk, asteroid, astrology
bio	Greek	Life	Biology, biography, biochemistry, biome, biomass
cept	Latin	Take	Intercept, accept, reception
dict	Latin	Speak or tell	Dictation, dictate, predict, contradict, dictator
duct or duce	Latin	Lead	Conduct, induct, conductor, productive, seductive, deductive, inductive, produce, deduce
geo	Greek	Earth	Geography, geology, geometry, geophysics
graph	Greek	Write or draw	Autograph, biography, photograph, polygraph, graphic, graphite
ject	Latin	Throw	Eject, reject, projectile, inject
meter	Greek	Measure	Thermometer, barometer, centimeter, diameter
min	Latin	Little or small	Miniature, minimum, minimal
mit or mis	Latin	Send	Mission, transmit, missile, dismiss, submit
ped or pod	Latin	Foot or feet	Pedal, pedestal, pedestrian, tripod, podiatrist, hexapod
phon	Greek	Sound	Telephone, symphony, microphone, phonics, phoneme
port	Latin	Carry	Transport, portable, import, export, porter
rupt	Latin	Break	Disrupt, erupt, rupture, interrupt, bankrupt
scrib or script	Latin	Write	Scribble, scribe, inscribe, describe, prescribe, manuscript, prescription, script, transcript, scripture
spect	Latin	See or look	Inspect, suspect, respect, spectacle, spectator
struct	Latin	Build or form	Construct, destruct, instruct, structure
tele	Greek	From afar	Telephone, telegraph, teleport
tract	Latin	Pull	Traction, tractor, attract, subtract, extract
vers or vert	Latin	Turn or change	Reverse, inverse, convert, convertible, divert, vertigo

Figure 8.24. Common Latin and Greek Roots. (*Sources:* Diamond & Gutlohn, 2006; Ebbers, 2011; Stahl & Kapinus, 2001.)

If Latin and Greek roots are not taught directly to students, some struggling readers will look for familiar English words within a larger word and will not be able to isolate the root. For example, if a struggling reader with no knowledge of Latin roots is asked to find the root word of *incredible*, the student may conclude, "I see the word *red. Red* is the root." But, if a student is familiar with the Latin root *cred*, he or she may be able to deduce, "I see the prefix *in-* and the suffix *-ible*. The root *cred* means 'to believe'—and the prefix *in-* means 'not.' So *incredible* may mean 'not able to believe.'" This is, of course, the type of logical thinking students need to learn, but they will not do it automatically.

Teaching How Word Parts Work

It is important that students understand the function of meaningful word parts. Explain to the students that many words are made of parts that carry meaning. These word parts work together to alter, or change, a word's meaning. As an overall introduction to word parts, define the parts simply, as follows:

- **Prefix:** A word part that is attached to the beginning of a word
- **Suffix:** A word part that is attached to the end of a word
- **Root or base word:** The basic part of a word that carries meaning. A **base word** can stand alone (e.g., *depend* in *independent*). A **root** is a word part that carries meaning but cannot stand alone (e.g., *cred* in *incredible*).

It is important that students understand how word parts function together and not just focus on the definition of the terms *prefix, suffix,* and *root* (Stahl, 1999). Explain and give multiple examples of affixes being attached to the beginnings or ends of words. Then, discuss how the affixes change, or alter, the meanings of the words. Give your students multiple opportunities to manipulate word parts. Activities may include the following:

- Using a pocket chart, demonstrate how to manipulate word parts to make real words. Discuss how adding or removing an affix changes the meaning of a word.
- Write word parts on index cards, and have the students make real words with a partner or in small groups. Have students discuss how adding or removing an affix changes the meaning of each word.
- Give partners or small groups of students a stack of index cards containing prefixes, suffixes, and base words. Have partners or groups work together to make a complete list of real words with their stack of word parts.
- Have students use word-part cards to generate silly words, or "words" that are not real words but that illustrate how prefixes and suffixes can change the meaning of words. This is most effective for prefixes, as suffixes often change a word's part of speech rather than clearly altering the word's meaning.

Directly Teaching Word Parts

Directly teaching two components of the word-part strategy will enable students to better understand words independently as they are reading:

- Directly teach the most commonly used affixes and roots.
- Give students strategies for chunking, or breaking words apart.

The following sample lesson illustrates direct instruction in the Latin root *port,* meaning "to carry."

OBJECTIVE

Students will recognize the Latin root *port* in words and will learn and apply the meaning of that root.

MATERIALS

- Chalkboard, SMART Board, or overhead
- Pictures illustrating the words *aware* and *unaware* (optional)
- Small poster board or chart paper
- Pocket chart
- Index cards
- Pictures illustrating the words *port*, *transportation*, *portable*, *import*, *export*, and *porter*
- Word-Part Clue Evaluation Chart (photocopiable version in the Appendix)

DAILY REVIEW

In this example, the teacher reviews the meaning of the prefix *un-*. The students will encounter the word *unaware* in their reading selection on this day.

Write the target word on the board, overhead, or SMART Board. Have students copy the word into their notebooks.

Teacher: This word is *unaware*. What's the word?

Students: *Unaware.*

Teacher: Raise your hand if you see a familiar word within this word. Remember, if there is a prefix, cover it and see whether you recognize a word. If not, look for a suffix. If there is one, cover it and look for a familiar word.

When a student responds that he or she sees the word aware, *ask the student to come up and demonstrate how he or she found the word. The student should cover the prefix* un-, *leaving the word* aware *exposed.*

Teacher: What does it mean to be aware of something?

Accept responses.

That's right. *Aware* means to notice things and to know what is happening. Raise your hand if you remember what the prefix *un-* means? Correct, the prefix *un-* means 'not.' So, who can tell me what the word *unaware* means?

Accept responses. Students should be able to say that unaware means "not aware or not noticing what is going on." Give the students scenarios and/or show pictures of people being aware and unaware of their surroundings. Have students reply "aware" or "unaware" to each situation.

Sample scenarios might include the following:
Aware:

- A child looks both ways before crossing the street.
- A man carries an umbrella on a cloudy day.
- A student notices the words *pop quiz* on the board and takes out her notes to study.

Unaware:

- A mother talks on her cell phone while her child darts across a busy street.
- A man tells a joke about his boss while his boss is standing behind him.
- While a teacher helps a small group of students, another student throws a paper airplane while the principal is looking in the window. (The teacher is unaware of the paper airplane and the student is unaware of the principal.)

STATE OBJECTIVE OR PURPOSE

Teacher: You have learned that looking for word parts can help you read and understand the meanings of complicated words, and you know the meanings of several common prefixes. Today you will learn a common root. Most of the roots and base words in our language come from Anglo-Saxon, Greek, or Latin. When you can recognize some of these roots and know what they mean, it will unlock the meanings of many words you read. This should help you learn new vocabulary words more easily in all your subjects. Today, we'll learn a common Latin root—*port*.

Optional: If this is the first time you are introducing Latin or Greek roots, you may want to tell students the story about how the English language came to be built from parts of several other languages. This story is found in the Appendix. We suggest that teachers read this story themselves to increase their own background knowledge about the influences on English that came from other languages. This can help unlock mysteries such as why the long a sound in ballet is spelled with an "e-t."

MODEL AND TEACH

Grouping: Whole class or small group

Write port *at the top of a small piece of poster board or chart paper.*

Teacher: The Latin root *port* means "to carry."

Write the meaning "to carry" under the root port *on the poster board or chart paper.*

Teacher: Do you know some English words that have the root word *port* in them?

Call on individuals. Students may recognize that port *is an English word itself. Tell them that a port is a place where things are put on ships or taken off ships. Discuss the relationship between this idea and the meaning "to carry."*

Teacher: Yes, ships come to a port to unload the goods, or things, that are on them and to load up other things to take away to other places. We learned that the root *port* means "to carry." How is a port where ships come and go related to carrying something?

Accept responses.

Teacher: Yes, ships carry things across the water, and things are carried off and onto the ships at ports.

If students cannot generate words, ask questions or give clues to help them think of the words transport *or* transportation *or* portable *or* porter. *For example, you might prompt students by saying something such as the following:*

Teacher: I have a big CD player at my house. It is not something I can carry around very easily, but I have a little MP3 player that I can put in my pocket and listen to with headphones. When something is easy to carry around we say it is _____.

Simply tell students any words that they cannot easily generate themselves. Model using word parts as clues to the meanings of words containing the root port. *Give brief, simple definitions of the example words, and write these words on the poster board or chart paper:*

Write transport *on the poster or paper.*

Teacher: The word part *trans* means "across." Because *port* means "to carry," *transport* means "to carry something across something" or "to carry things from one place to another." You can transport furniture in a truck, and you can transport people in your car.

Write export *on the poster.*

Teacher: The word part *ex* can mean "out." *Export* means "to send out things that are made in one country to a different country." Many of the things we buy are made in China and exported to the United States.

Continue this process with the rest of the words on the list. Examples include the following:

- "Import: The prefix *im-* can mean 'into.' *Import* means 'to bring (or carry) things into one country from a different country.' We import many things from China."

- "Portable: The suffix *-able* means 'able to,' so if something is portable, we are able to carry it."

- "Porter: The ending *-er* can mean 'someone who.' A porter is someone who carries suitcases or other things. If you go to an airport, a porter may carry your suitcases."

Read the completed word list to the students and have them repeat each word after you. Then have the students read the list together. If necessary, have them read it again, starting from the last word and going to the first word. Then call on individuals to read the list.

Teacher: So, what does the word part *port* mean?

Students: To carry.

Note: Greek and Latin roots can be used to build a family of words with related meanings, but these words will not always have clear relationships with prefixes and suffixes. For example, the Latin root *aud* means "to hear." It is found in the words *auditorium, audience,* and *audiovisual.* When you teach Greek or Latin roots, be sure students understand that the roots may be found in long words, even if these long words do not have recognizable prefixes and suffixes.

GUIDED PRACTICE

Grouping: Whole class or small group

Use a pocket chart to provide students with the opportunity to practice word parts they have previously learned along with the newly learned root *port.* Form words in the pocket chart using index cards with previously learned prefixes, suffixes, base words, and roots written on them. Include a card with the new Latin root *port* on it. Have students read the words and tell the class the meaning of the word parts and of the words. Figure 8.25 shows some sample word-part cards.

INDEPENDENT PRACTICE

Grouping: Partners

Have students work with partners to complete Frayer Model graphic organizers for the words *portable* and *transport* or *transportation.* Assign one of these words to each pair of students. Have students use the definitions you provided for the words during the Model and Teach portion of the lesson, and generate examples and nonexamples of the words. Figure 8.26 shows a sample graphic organizer used for learning word parts.

pre	view		re	view		port	er

Figure 8.25. Sample word-part cards.

Frayer Model

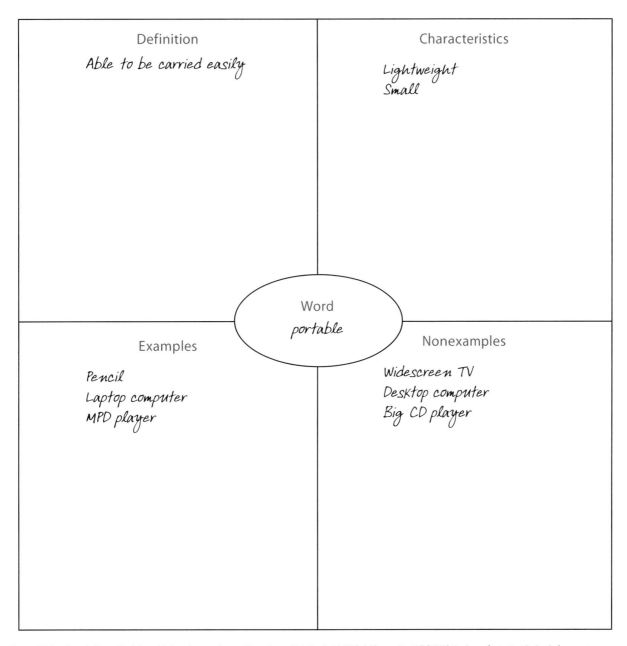

Definition	Characteristics
Able to be carried easily	*Lightweight* *Small*

Word
portable

Examples	Nonexamples
Pencil *Laptop computer* *MPD player*	*Widescreen TV* *Desktop computer* *Big CD player*

Figure 8.26.   Sample Frayer Model used in learning word parts. (From Frayer, D.A., Frederick, W.C., & Klausmeier, H.G. [1969]. *A schema for testing the level of concept mastery [Technical report No. 16].* Madison, WI: University of Wisconsin Research and Development Center for Cognitive Learning; adapted by permission.)

GENERALIZATION

Ask students for examples of situations in which using the word-part strategy would be helpful when they come to unfamiliar words as they are reading. Emphasize the fact that they can use the strategy every time they read.

MONITOR STUDENT LEARNING

Check students' understanding of the concept by rotating among partners, asking questions, and checking their graphic organizers. Ask students to explain how the word parts contribute to the meaning of the words they form.

PERIODIC REVIEW AND MULTIPLE OPPORTUNITIES TO PRACTICE

Teachers should emphasize and model the word-part strategy whenever the opportunity presents itself. Some examples include the following:

- Within a vocabulary lesson: If you are planning a larger vocabulary lesson such as Semantic Mapping or Possible Sentences and one of the target words has a prefix or suffix, then you can emphasize the word parts during the discussion of that specific word.

- Discussion during reading: You may come across a prefixed or suffixed word while preparing a selection to be read with your class. If the students do not need to understand the word to comprehend the selection, then this word does not necessarily need to be pretaught; however, you may use the word to review the word-part strategy within the context of whole-class or small-group discussion.

- Frequent modeling and use of the word-part strategy: Students benefit when teachers frequently model the word-part strategy through think-alouds and give students ample opportunities to practice identifying roots, base words, and affixes.

Think aloud with your students. For example, imagine that you encounter this sentence in your reading: "William was told to transport the money to his contact in Rome." In this case, you would begin by writing the word *transport* on the board.

Teacher: I know that the Latin root *port* means "to carry" and that the prefix *trans-* means "across or from one to another," so *transport* must mean "to carry from one place to another." What was William told to do with the money (pause to allow think time)…Sylvia?

WORD-PART ANALYSIS

Note: This would be taught in a separate lesson.

It is important to mention that the analysis of word parts may not always work as we expect it to work. Students need to be taught to recognize and think about word parts, not just plug them into a formula. One way to help students think about word parts in this way is to use a word-part clue evaluation chart. This type of chart is discussed in the *Vocabulary Handbook* (Diamond & Gutlohn, 2006) and is an excellent tool to help students understand and think about word parts. Initially, find words in a reading text or content-area text that are appropriate to illustrate each column in the chart. Figure 8.27 is an example of such a chart.

The key element of this chart is the discussion of each word with your students. Model the process of analyzing word parts through think-alouds. Consider the following example:

Teacher: The first word is *unhealthy*. First, I see the prefix *un-* and the root word *health* with the suffix *-y*: *healthy*.

Demonstrate covering the prefix with your thumb to reveal the root word.

So, there is a prefix and a root word.

Fill in the second column: Prefix and root word.

Now, I know the prefix *un-* means "not." Does *unhealthy* mean "not healthy"? Yes, it does.

Word-Part Clue Evaluation Chart

Word	No prefix and root word	Prefix and root word	Prefix + root = meaning	Prefix + root ≠ meaning
Unhealthy		Un + healthy	Not healthy	
Interest	In + terest			
Uneasy		Un + easy		Nervous
Return		Re + turn	To turn again; to come back	
Distance	Dis + tance			

Figure 8.27. Sample Word-Part Clue Evaluation Chart. (From Diamond, L., & Gutlohn, L., *Vocabulary Handbook*, 89, 118, 120, Copyright © 2006 by CORE, published by Paul H. Brookes Publishing Co., Inc. Adapted by permission of the publisher.)

Fill in the third column.

> Now I am going to look at the next word, *interest*. I know that *in-* is a prefix. Is *terest* a base word or a root? No, *terest* is not a real word or a root. So, *interest* does not have a prefix and root word.

Fill in the first column.

> Now, let me think about the word *uneasy*. I see the prefix *un-*, which we know means "not." The base word is *easy*. Let me put those together: "not easy." Actually, that is wrong! I know that *uneasy* means "nervous." We could say, "The girl felt uneasy about walking alone when it was dark." In this case, analyzing the word parts did not work! We need to write this word in the last column because the word parts added together do not equal the correct meaning of the word. Using word parts to figure out word meanings often works very well, but it doesn't always work. You have to *think* about the words. This is why it is important to check your guess about the meaning of a word by putting your definition back into the sentence in place of the difficult word to see if it makes sense. If we said, "The girl felt not easy about walking alone when it was dark," that would not make sense!

Fill in the fourth column.

Continue to complete the rest of the table in the same way.

As students get older, they are expected to read more multisyllabic words. This can be overwhelming to a struggling reader. Teaching students to both recognize and analyze word parts is a powerful tool to help them unlock the meaning of the many multisyllabic words they are expected to understand.

| # Word Learning
Using Context Clues

INTRODUCTION

Context clues give students clues, or hints, about what an unfamiliar word might mean. Such clues are found in the text and/or illustrations surrounding the unknown word. The different types of context clues that can be used to infer a word's meaning are listed in Table 8.6, along with examples of how those clues might appear in text. Students benefit from explicit instruction in a strategy for finding and using context clues, such as the one that appears in Figure 8.28 (photocopiable version in the Appendix).

Explain to students that finding and interpreting context clues is not a formula; it is a tool to be tried alongside other tools such as word-part clues. Explain that they can look *inside* a word to find word part clues, and they can look *outside* of a word to find context clues. Some context clues can be misleading, and students must realize that word-learning strategies involve thinking—not just plugging words into a formula. The following lesson is an introductory context clue lesson that teaches the first type of clue—the definition clue. This lesson can be used as a guide to teach the other four types of context clues: synonym, antonym, example, and general clues.

OBJECTIVE

Students will learn to find and interpret context clues to help them infer the meanings of unfamiliar words. Students will be able to recognize and interpret five types of context clues: definition, synonym, antonym, example, and general.

Table 8.6. Types of context clues to be directly taught

Type of context clue	Example*
Definition: The author explains the meaning of the word in the sentence or selection.	When Sara was hiking, she accidentally walked through a patch of **brambles**, *prickly vines and shrubs*, which resulted in many scratches to her legs.
Synonym: The author uses a word similar in meaning.	Josh walked into the living room and accidentally tripped over the **ottoman**. He then mumbled, "I wish people would not leave the *footstool* right in the middle of the room. That's dangerous!"
Antonym: The author uses a word nearly opposite in meaning.	The supermarket manager complained, "Why do we have such a **plethora** of boxes of cereal on the shelves? *In contrast*, we have a real *shortage* of pancake and waffle mix. We've got to do a better job ordering."
Example: The author provides one or more example words or ideas.	There are many members of the **canine** family. *For example, wolves, foxes, coyotes*, and pets such as *collies, beagles*, and *golden retrievers* are all canines.
General: The author provides several word's or statements that give clues to the word's meaning.	It was a **sultry** day. The day was *very hot and humid*. If you moved at all, you would *break out in a sweat*. It was one of those days to *drink water* and *stay in the shade*.

From Baumann, J.F., Font, G., Edwards, E.C., & Boland, E. (2005). Strategies for teaching middle-grade students to use word-part and context clues. In Teaching and learning vocabulary : bringing research to practice by Hiebert, Elfrieda H.; Kamil, Michael L. Copyright 2012 Reproduced with permission of TAYLOR & FRANCIS GROUP LLC – BOOKS in the format Textbook via Copyright Clearance Center.

*Note: In the Example column, words in italics provide context clues for bold words.

Context Clue Strategy

1. Reread the sentence that contains the unknown word. Be on the lookout for signal words or punctuation.

2. Reread the sentences before and after the sentence that contains the unknown word.

3. Based on the clues, try to figure out the meaning of the word.

4. Insert your meaning in the original sentence to see whether it makes sense.

Figure 8.28. Context Clue Strategy. (From Diamond, L., & Gutlohn, L., *Vocabulary Handbook*, 130, Copyright © 2006 by CORE, published by Paul H. Brookes Publishing Co., Inc. Adapted by permission of the publisher.)

MATERIALS

- Figure 8.29: Types of Context Clues chart (photocopiable version in the Appendix)
- Transparency of sample sentences or copy for SMART Board
- Student copies of sentences
- Figure 8.28: Context Clue Strategy chart (photocopiable version in the Appendix)
- Figure 8.30: Guide for Context Clues Practice (photocopiable version in the Appendix)

DAILY REVIEW

Teacher: Yesterday, we looked for word-part clues to help us figure out the meanings of unfamiliar words. What is one type of word part that will give us a clue, or hint, to a word's meaning…Billy? Yes, a prefix may help us determine a word's meaning. Sheila? Yes, if we can find a root word and know what it means, that will help us determine the meaning of the unknown word.

STATE OBJECTIVE OR PURPOSE

Genre: Expository (or narrative)

Teacher: As you read—whether it is your textbook, a newspaper, a magazine, or a story—you will encounter words that are not familiar to you. Because you will not always have someone nearby to help you and I can't teach you every word you need to know, I want to teach you how to figure out unfamiliar words on your own. One way to figure out a word is to look *inside* a word for word parts such as prefixes, suffixes, and roots. Another strategy

Types of Context Clues

Type of context clue	What to look for	Signal words	Sample sentence
Definition	A definition in the sentence	*Is, are, is called, means, or* Signal punctuation: Set off by commas	Brick made of sun-dried clay *is called* **adobe**. The Native Americans used **adobe**, *or* bricks made of sun-dried clay, to build their homes.
Synonym	A word with a similar meaning to the unknown word	*Also, as, like, same, similarly, too*	The Zuni built their homes with brick made of sun-dried clay. The Hopi *also* used **adobe** to build their homes.
Antonym	A word or phrase with the opposite meaning of the unknown word	*But, however, in contrast, on the other hand, though, unlike*	The Hopi lived in single-family houses, *but* the Iroquois lived in **longhouses**.
Example	Several examples in a list	*Such as, for example, for instance, like, including*	The Pueblo people grew many **crops** *such as* corn, beans, and squash.
General	General or inexact clues		After 1700, the Pueblos got sheep from the Spanish, and wool replaced cotton as the most important **textile**.

Figure 8.29. Types of Context Clues. (From Baumann, J.F., Font, G., Edwards, E.C., & Boland, E. [2005]. Strategies for teaching middle-grade students to use word-part and context clues. In Teaching and learning vocabulary : bringing research to practice by Hiebert, Elfrieda H.; Kamil, Michael L. Copyright 2012 Reproduced with permission of TAYLOR & FRANCIS GROUP LLC – BOOKS in the format Textbook via Copyright Clearance Center.)

is to look *outside* of the word at the sentences and illustrations around the unknown word. Today, I am going to teach you how to find clues in the words and phrases that come before and after a particular word. These clues are called *context* clues because they are found in the context, or words and phrases, around the unfamiliar word. Learning to recognize and analyze context clues will help you discover the meaning of words on your own.

MODEL AND TEACH

Grouping: Whole class

> **Teacher:** There are several types of context clues. Over the next few weeks, I am going to teach you five different types of context clues to look for.

Briefly show Figure 8.29, and simply list the different types of clues.

A copy of Figure 8.29 is found in the Appendix. It may be distributed to students as a handout, but you may consider developing sample sentences with content matter that is related to your content area.

> **Teacher:** Today, we are going to concentrate on just one type of context clue—the definition. A definition clue provides the meaning of the word right in the sentence. If you see any of the signal words—*is, are, is called,* or *means*—be on the lookout for a definition. You

Guide for Context Clues Practice

Unfamiliar word	Signal word or punctuation	Type of context clue: Definition, synonym, antonym, example, or general	My definition

Figure 8.30. Guide for Context Clues Practice. (From Baumann, J.F., Font, G., Edwards, E.C., & Boland, E. [2005]. Strategies for teaching middle-grade students to use word-part and context clues. In Teaching and learning vocabulary : bringing research to practice by Hiebert, Elfrieda H.; Kamil, Michael L. Copyright 2012 Reproduced with permission of TAYLOR & FRANCIS GROUP LLC – BOOKS in the format Textbook via Copyright Clearance Center; and Diamond, L., & Gutlohn, L., *Vocabulary Handbook*, 142, Copyright © 2006 by CORE, published by Paul H. Brookes Publishing Co., Inc. Adapted by permission of the publisher.)

can also look for signal punctuation to help to find definition clues. If you see the signal word *or* and a phrase set apart by commas, be on the lookout for a definition. Look at the following sentences:

Project Figure 8.31 containing sample sentences with the overhead or SMART Board (or sentences that use the same formats but align with your content area). Then, cover sentences so that only the first sentence is visible. Think aloud.

Teacher: The first sentence says, "Brick made of sun-dried clay is called adobe." I don't know what adobe is.

Circle the word adobe.

So, I'm going to look at the words and phrases around the word, or context clues, to help me figure out the meaning. First I am going to reread the sentence.

Brick made of sun-dried clay is called **adobe**.

The Navajo lived in **hogans**, or dome-shaped houses that were made of logs and mud.

Figure 8.31.   Sample sentences using definition context clues

Reread the sentence.

I see the signal words *is called*.

Underline "is called."

Okay, what is called *adobe*?

Point to the beginning of the sentence.

Brick made of sun-dried clay is called adobe. So, adobe is brick made of clay that is dried in the sun. This type of context clue is simple. I just have to be on the lookout for the signal words—like a detective searching for clues.

Now I'm going to look at the next sentence.

Read the sentence.

I do not know what *hogans* are.

Circle the word hogans.

First I am going to reread the sentence.

Reread the sentence.

I see the signal word *or*, and I also see a comma.

Underline the word or *and circle the comma.*

I am going to read the phrase after the comma.

Read the phrase.

Hogans must be dome-shaped houses. If I insert my definition into the sentence it would read, "The Navajo lived in dome-shaped houses made of logs and mud." That makes sense.

In both of these sentences, the definition was right in the sentence. This kind of context clue is called a *definition* context clue.

GUIDED PRACTICE

Grouping: Whole class and/or partners

1. Project between four and six more sentences with the overhead or SMART Board. These sentences can be taken directly from your students' science or social studies texts, or you can write sentences using any content that is relevant to your students' curriculum. Figure 8.32 provides more examples of sample sentences using definition context clues.

2. Give students a copy of the sentences in Figure 8.32.

3. Review the context clue strategy provided in Figure 8.28.

4. Lead the students through finding the meaning of the underlined word in the first sentence of Figure 8.32 by looking for definition context clues.

Everyone has different physical characteristics, or <u>traits</u>. Some of us are tall, and others are short. Some of us have brown eyes, and others have green eyes.

<u>Heredity</u> is the passing of traits from parents to their children.
The things that control such traits are called <u>genes</u>.

Gregor Mendel founded <u>genetics</u>, or the study of heredity and genes, in the 19th century.

Figure 8.32.   More sample sentences using definition context clues.

Ask for a volunteer to read the sentence.

Teacher: I don't know what traits are.

Circle the word traits *and ask students to do the same on their papers.*

What is the first thing I need to do when I come to a word that is unfamiliar to me?

Accept student responses.

That's right: I need to reread the sentence. What do I need to look for, like a detective?

Accept student responses.

Yes, I need to look for signal words or punctuation.

Point to Figure 8.29, the types of context clues chart, and ask a student to read the signal words and punctuation for a definition context clue. Ask a volunteer to reread the sentence and ask the class to be on the lookout for signal words and punctuation. After the volunteer has reread the sentence, ask students to turn to their partners and point to any signal words or punctuation they see.

Did anyone see any signal words or punctuation?

Accept student responses. On the overhead, underline the word or *and circle the comma. Ask students to do the same.*

In this case, the unfamiliar word is set apart by the comma and the signal word *or*. Where should I look, then, to find the definition?

Accept student responses.

That's right. The words right before the signal word are *physical characteristics*. So *traits* must mean "physical characteristics." Let's try it in the sentence: "Everyone has different traits." Everyone has different physical characteristics. Does that definition make sense? Yes. What are traits? Yes, traits are physical characteristics. Let's look at the next sentence to see whether we can find some examples of traits.

5. Allow partners 2–3 minutes to find the meaning of the underlined word in the second sentence by looking for definition context clues. Circulate around the room and be available for guidance. After 2–3 minutes, work through the sentence with the class. Follow the same procedure for the last two sentences.

INDEPENDENT PRACTICE

Grouping: Pairs

1. Provide partners with a short passage that you create or take directly from a student textbook. Figure 8.33 provides a sample passage for practice using definition context clues.

2. Tell students that they are going to practice using definition context clues to find the meanings of the underlined words.

3. Give students a sample context clues chart such as the one in Figure 8.34 to guide their work.

4. Circulate around the room and be available for guidance. Figure 8.35 provides a completed version of a sample context clues chart.

GENERALIZATION

Teacher: Think about your other classes. Do you think using context clues might help you with any of your reading outside of this class?

Student: I think I've seen definition context clues in our science book.

Teacher: I'm sure you have. Textbook authors want you to understand what you are reading and will help you by planting clues in the text to help you understand new words. Raise your hand if you can tell me what signal words or punctuation marks you can look for to help you find definition context clues.

> When someone who is not very well known unexpectedly wins a nomination for public office, that person is called a dark horse candidate. James A. Polk, a dark horse candidate, won the Democratic presidential nomination in 1844. Polk was in favor of the annexation, or the adding of a territory to another country, of both Texas and Oregon. Henry Clay, Polk's opponent, was also in favor of annexation.

Figure 8.33. Sample passage for practice using definition context clues.

Unfamiliar word	Signal word or punctuation	Our definition
Dark horse candidate		
Annexation		

Figure 8.34. Sample context clues chart. (From Baumann, J.F., Font, G., Edwards, E.C., & Boland, E. [2005]. Strategies for teaching middle-grade students to use word-part and context clues. In Teaching and learning vocabulary : bringing research to practice by Hiebert, Elfrieda H.; Kamil, Michael L. Copyright 2012 Reproduced with permission of TAYLOR & FRANCIS GROUP LLC – BOOKS in the format Textbook via Copyright Clearance Center; and Diamond, L., & Gutlohn, L., Vocabulary Handbook, 142, Copyright © 2006 by CORE, published by Paul H. Brookes Publishing Co., Inc. Adapted by permission of the publisher.)

Unfamiliar word	Signal word or punctuation	Our definition
Dark horse candidate	Is called	When someone who is not famous wins a political nomination unexpectedly
Annexation	Commas, or	Adding a territory to another country

Figure 8.35. Sample completed context clues chart. (From Baumann, J.F., Font, G., Edwards, E.C., & Boland, E. [2005]. Strategies for teaching middle-grade students to use word-part and context clues. In Teaching and learning vocabulary : bringing research to practice by Hiebert, Elfrieda H.; Kamil, Michael L. Copyright 2012 Reproduced with permission of TAY-LOR & FRANCIS GROUP LLC – BOOKS in the format Textbook via Copyright Clearance Center; and Diamond, L., & Gutlohn, L., Vocabulary Handbook, 142, Copyright © 2006 by CORE, published by Paul H. Brookes Publishing Co., Inc. Adapted by permission of the publisher.)

Student: We can look for the signal words *is called* or for phrases set apart by commas.

Teacher: That's right. Be on the lookout for context clues in your other classes.

MONITOR STUDENT LEARNING

Check Figure 8.34 for appropriate responses, including the following:

- Correct identification of signal words and punctuation
- Correct definitions derived from the context clues

PERIODIC REVIEW AND MULTIPLE OPPORTUNITIES TO PRACTICE

Periodically give students a passage that you either create or take directly from students' textbooks. Underline words that may be unfamiliar to students, and have them work either independently or with partners to find the meaning of the underlined words. Once you have taught other types of context clues, modify the guide so that students must identify and use the different kinds of context clues. Figure 8.30 provides a chart for tracking all of the different types of context clues.

||| # Word Learning
The Outside-In Strategy

INTRODUCTION

Once you have taught students about meaningful word parts and context clues, you can teach them how to combine these two strategies into a strategy, or routine, for figuring out the meanings of unknown words. The Outside-In Strategy (Ebbers & Denton, 2008) is a systematic way of thinking through the process of discovering the meaning of an unknown word during reading. The goal, of course, is for students to use this strategy independently and in a variety of settings. The name of the strategy is deliberately "catchy" to help students remember it and use it when they are not in the reading classroom.

OBJECTIVE

Students will use the Outside-In Strategy of using information from meaningful word parts and context clues to figure out the meanings of unknown words.

MATERIALS

- Figure 8.36: Outside-In Strategy chart (photocopiable version in the Appendix)
- Figure 8.37: Outside-In Strategy Worksheet transparency or copy for SMART Board, and student copies (photocopiable version in the Appendix)

||| ## The Outside-In Strategy

If you read a word that you do not understand:

1. Look OUTSIDE the word for context clues. Reread the sentence and the surrounding sentences.
2. Look INSIDE the word for word-part clues. Can you break the word into parts? (If not, go to Step 3.)
   a. Is there a PREFIX? What does it mean?
   b. Is there a SUFFIX? What does it mean?
   c. Is there a ROOT or BASE WORD? What does it mean?
   d. Put the meanings of the word parts together. What is the meaning of the whole word?
3. GUESS what the word means.
4. INSERT your meaning into the original sentence to see whether it makes sense.
5. If needed, use the DICTIONARY to confirm your meaning.

Figure 8.36. The Outside-In Strategy chart. (From Baumann, J.F., Font, G., Edwards, E.C., & Boland, E. [2005]. Strategies for teaching middle-grade students to use word-part and context clues. In Teaching and learning vocabulary : bringing research to practice by Hiebert, Elfrieda H.; Kamil, Michael L. Copyright 2012 Reproduced with permission of TAYLOR & FRANCIS GROUP LLC – BOOKS in the format Textbook via Copyright Clearance Center; and Diamond, L., & Gutlohn, L., Vocabulary Handbook, 216, Copyright © 2006 by CORE, published by Paul H. Brookes Publishing Co., Inc. Adapted by permission of the publisher.)

The Outside-In Strategy Worksheet

Word: _____

Context sentence: _____
_____

1. **Look OUTSIDE the word for context clues.**

   a. Reread the sentence, looking for signal words and punctuation.

Signal words and punctuation:

   b. Reread the sentences before and after the sentence with the word in it.

Context clues:

2. **Look INSIDE the word for word parts you know. Tell what each word part means.**

Prefix:

Suffix:

Base word or root:

Put the parts together. What does it mean?

3. What do you think the word means? _____
   _____

4. Try your meaning in the sentence in the text. Does it make sense? _____

5. Check the word with a dictionary if you need to. Remember that many words have more than one meaning, so look for the one that goes with the sentence in the book. Were you right? _____

Figure 8.37.   The Outside-In Strategy Worksheet. (From Baumann, J.F., Font, G., Edwards, E.C., & Boland, E. [2005]. Strategies for teaching middle-grade students to use word-part and context clues. In Teaching and learning vocabulary : bringing research to practice by Hiebert, Elfrieda H.; Kamil, Michael L. Copyright 2012 Reproduced with permission of TAYLOR & FRANCIS GROUP LLC – BOOKS in the format Textbook via Copyright Clearance Center; and Diamond, L., & Gutlohn, L., *Vocabulary Handbook*, 216, Copyright © 2006 by CORE, published by Paul H. Brookes Publishing Co., Inc. Adapted by permission of the publisher.)

- Sample text with challenging words for which the meanings may be inferred through the use of context clues and word-part analysis
- Dictionaries
- Science or social studies text

DAILY REVIEW

Teacher: When you are reading on your own and you come to a word for which you do not know the meaning, what is one way you can figure out the meaning of the word?

Accept responses.

Yes, Candace. You can try to break the word into parts. What are some of the parts that may give you clues to a word's meaning?

Accept responses.

Correct, you can look at prefixes, suffixes, and root words. Can anyone remember another way to find out what a word means?

Accept responses.

Yes, we can look at context clues. Where do we find context clues?

Accept responses.

Exactly, in the words and phrases around the unknown word. Raise your hand if you can remember one type of context clue that we have learned.

Quickly review the five types of context clues you have already taught: definition, synonym, antonym, example, and general.

STATE OBJECTIVE OR PURPOSE

Genre: Expository or narrative

Teacher: You have already learned different ways to figure out unknown words by yourself as you are reading. Today, I am going to show you how to use *both* word parts and context clues to figure out the meanings of unknown words as you read. Raise your hand if you can tell me what might happen if you just skip over words that you don't know.

That's right. You will probably misunderstand what you are reading. What does the prefix *mis-* mean, Sylvia? Yes, *mis-* means "wrong." So, Sylvia, if you misunderstand what you are reading, you do what? Yes, you understand it wrong. Would that be confusing? Good, so today I am going to teach you the Outside-In Strategy. This strategy will help you use your knowledge of word parts and context clues to figure out the meanings of unfamiliar words.

MODEL AND TEACH

Grouping: Whole class

1. Present the Outside-In Strategy chart, shown in Figure 8.36, to the class, and read through each step.

Teacher: We are going to use something called the *Outside-In Strategy*. The name of the strategy reminds you what to do when you come to an unfamiliar word. First, look *outside* of the word for context clues. Then, look *inside* of the word for meaningful word parts. "Outside-

In" reminds me of the expression "inside-out." For example, you might say that you turned your socks inside-out. But for unknown words, it works best to start on the outside to look for context clues and *then* look inside the word, so the strategy is called "outside-in." This chart is going to guide your thinking as you learn to apply the strategy to find out what an unknown word means. Eventually, I would like you to be able to go through this thinking process on your own. But for now, this chart is going to be our guide.

2. Choose a brief passage from your text and display it on the overhead or SMART Board. You may need to modify a textbook passage to add examples of context clues and words with prefixes and suffixes for this activity. The following example has been modified from a passage on Texas history. "Sam Houston was the first president of the Texas **republic**. He sent an **ambassador**, an official who represents a country, to the United States. This ambassador's job was to ask that Texas be **annexed**, or added to the country. President Jackson **disapproved**. So, Texas remained an **independent** nation for 10 years."

Teacher: As I read this passage aloud, follow along and read the last word of every sentence together with me.

Follow along with your finger as you read.

Teacher: Sam Houston was the first president of the Texas…

Students: …Republic.

Teacher: He sent an ambassador, an official who represents a country, to the United…

Students: …States.

Continue in this way until you have read the entire passage.

3. Model word one.

Teacher: Okay, the first word with which I am unfamiliar is *republic*. The first step of the Outside-In Strategy tells us to look outside of the word for context clues. I'm going to reread the sentence with the word *republic* in it: "Sam Houston was the first president of the Texas republic." Okay, so a republic has a president. What else do I know that has a president? A country has a president, so maybe a republic is a country. I don't see an example or a definition of a republic; this clue is kind of general.

The second step tells me to look inside the word for word parts I recognize. Well, I see the prefix *re-*. *Re-* means "again." And the root word looks like *public*. So, if this were a prefix and a root word, the whole word would mean "to be public again." I don't think that makes much sense. Maybe this isn't really a prefix and a root word. I'm going to keep that in mind and move on to Step 3.

Step 3 says to guess what the word means. I think the best definition I have so far is that a *republic* is a *country*. So I'm going to insert my meaning into the original sentence and see whether it makes sense. "Sam Houston was the first president of the Texas country… or country of Texas." Well, that would make sense if Texas were a country at the time.

I'm going to double-check by looking in the dictionary. Caleb, will you turn to page 300 of the dictionary and read the definition of *republic* for us?

You can look up the definition before the lesson so that you don't waste any class time waiting on students to locate the word. You can either direct the students to the page or tab the page for them. The most important thing is that students learn to use the dictionary to double-check their own thinking.

Student: The dictionary says that a republic is "a state or country in which people elect representatives to exercise power for them."

Teacher: Okay, so that makes sense. Texas was a republic, a state or country, and they elected Sam Houston as their president. Since he is called a president, I think Texas was a country at that time.

4.   Model word two.

Teacher: The next word I am going to try to figure out is *ambassador*. Look at the chart and raise your hand if you can tell me the first thing I need to do.

Accept responses.

Teacher: That's right. I'm going to look *outside* the word for context clues by rereading the sentence and the surrounding sentences.

Reread the sentence.

Teacher: "He sent an ambassador, an official who represents a country, to the United States." There are no signal words, but there is signal punctuation: two commas surrounding the phrase, "an official who represents a country." So, I think that is the definition.

Next, I will still look *inside* the word to see whether I can break the word into smaller parts. I see the suffix *-or*, which means *someone who does something*, like a *governor* is *someone who governs*. But "someone who ambassads" doesn't make any sense, so I don't think this is a word I can break into parts. I will move on to Step 3.

Step 3 asks me to guess the meaning of *ambassador*. Well, I think it is an official person who represents a country. The definition context clue told me that. So now I am going to insert it and see whether it makes sense. "He sent an official person who represents a country to the United States." Yes, that makes sense. Sam Houston sent someone to represent the country of Texas to the United States.

I can check the dictionary to make sure on this one, but usually if the context clue is a definition clue like this, I can be pretty confident that I have the right definition. Let's look, though. Maria, will you look on page 20 of the dictionary and tell me what *ambassador* means?

Student: An ambassador is "an official of the highest ranking sent by one country as its representative to another country."

Teacher: So was my definition correct, everyone?

Students: Yes.

5.   Model word three.

Teacher: Now I want to figure out the meaning of the word *independent*. What is the first thing I need to do, Juanita?

Accept response.

Teacher: Yes, I need to look outside the word for context clues. Step 1 tells me to reread the sentence and surrounding sentences, looking for clues.

Reread the sentence.

Teacher: "So, Texas remained an independent nation for 10 years." Okay, I don't see any clues or signal words in that sentence. So, I will reread the sentence before.

Reread the sentence.

Teacher: "President Jackson disapproved." That doesn't really give me any clues, but, logically, I wonder what President Jackson disapproved of. If I look at the sentence before, it says that he disapproved of Texas being added to the country. So Texas is not part of the United States; it is by itself. So maybe *independent* means "by yourself." What should I do next, Tamika?

Accept response.

Teacher: Yes, now I need to look *inside* the word and try to break it into parts. I see the prefix *in-*, which means "not." And the root word is *dependent* or *depend*. I know that a child might depend on his Mom or be dependent on his Mom. What might that word mean, Julie?

Accept response.

Teacher: Yes, Julie. *Depend* might mean "to need someone or something." So, if I put those two meanings together, *independent* might mean "to not need someone or something."

Step 3 asks me to guess the meaning of the word. If I put both clues together—the context clues and the word-part clues—I think *independent* means "to be alright alone and not need anyone else."

To follow Step 4, I will insert my meaning into the sentence. "So, Texas remained a nation by itself, not needing anyone else, for 10 years." That sort of makes sense.

I'm going to follow Step 5 and check the dictionary to make sure. Joel, will you turn to page 100 of the dictionary and tell us the definition for *independent*?

Student: The dictionary says that *independent* means "free from any authority or control of something else and able to operate and stand on its own."

Teacher: So, my definition was close, but the dictionary definition makes complete sense. Texas was free from authority from any other nation and able to operate on its own for 10 years. Sometimes, the Outside-In Strategy will give you an idea of the word's meaning, but word parts and context clues may not help you understand *exactly* what a word means.

GUIDED PRACTICE

Grouping: Whole class and/or sitting with partners

1. Introduce the guided practice activity.

Teacher: Today I am going to show you how to use the Outside-In Strategy worksheet to guide you through the process of using the Outside-In Strategy (see Figure 8.37).

Give each student two copies of a blank Outside-In Strategy Worksheet and project a blank worksheet with the overhead or SMART Board.

Teacher: Using the same social studies passage we worked with yesterday, we are going to look for clues to find the meanings of the words *annexed* and *disapproved*. Let's start with the word *annexed*. The first space asks me to write the unknown word. Our unknown word is *annexed*, so I am going to write *annexed* here. Fill in the first blank on the worksheet.

Below that we need to write our context sentence. The context sentence is the sentence that contains the unknown word. What sentence will I need to write here, Steven?

Student: "This ambassador's job was to ask that Texas be annexed, or added to the country."

Teacher: That is correct. I am going to write the context sentence here.

Fill in the second blank.

Now, when I look at the rest of the worksheet, I can see that there are five main boxes and that each one leads me through the steps on the Outside-In Strategy Chart.

2. Continue to guide students as they complete the chart in partners. Focus first on context clues.

Teacher: The first step tells us to look outside the word and to reread the context sentence and surrounding sentences. With your partner, I want you to reread the sentence, looking for context clues. If you find any signal words or punctuation, write them here (*point to the Signal Words box*), and if you see any clues, write them here (*point to the Context Clue box*).

Review signal words and punctuation if necessary.

Allow partners 1–3 minutes to reread and document any context clues or signal words and/or punctuation. Circulate around the room and be available to help.

Return to the overhead and ask for volunteers to share context clues and signal words and/or punctuation. Record answers.

Students should have found the signal word or, preceded by a comma. Also, they should have been able to locate the definition clue "added to the country."

3. Proceed in the same way as you focus on word-part clues.

    Teacher: Step 2 asks us to look inside the word and determine whether we can break the word into parts. Do I see a prefix? No, so I will draw a slash in the worksheet box that asks for a prefix. Do I see a suffix? Yes, *-ed* is a suffix, and I know that means "past tense."

    Record on worksheet.

    Raise your hand if you can tell me the root word. (Accept responses.) Yes, the root word is *annex*. I will write that here, but the word-part clues haven't given us very much information about the meaning of the word. If I put the meanings together, all I know is that *annexed* is the past tense of *annex*.

4. Guide students through Step 3 of the strategy.

    Teacher: Step 3 asks us what we think the word means. With your partner, use the context clues and word-part clues to come up with a definition. Write your answers under Step 3.

    Allow students a few minutes to discuss and write. They should be able to locate and write the definition clue "added to a country."

    Raise your hand if you can give me a definition.

    Accept responses.

    That's right, we found a definition context clue that gives us the definition! So let's try it in our sentence.

5. Guide students as they complete Step 4, trying the word in a sentence to see whether it makes sense.

    Teacher: Please read the sentence with our definition inserted, Marcus.

    Student: "This ambassador's job was to ask that Texas be added to the country."

    Teacher: Does that make sense?

    Students: Yes.

6. Have students verify their answer using a dictionary.

    Teacher: Okay, we feel pretty confident because our context clue was a definition clue, but let's look it up in the dictionary, just to make sure. Gina, would you look on page 22 and read us the definition of *annex*?

    Student: *Annex* means "to take over a territory and incorporate it with another country or state."

    Teacher: *Incorporate* means "add," so does our definition still make sense?

    Students: Yes.

    Teacher: Yes, it does. Nice work.

7. Following the same procedure as above, lead the students through each step of the worksheet, one section at a time. This time, students will find the meaning of a second word (*disapproved*). Make sure that students understand that each worksheet is used to find the definition for just one word.

INDEPENDENT PRACTICE

Grouping: Partners

*   Choose a selection from the students' science or social studies text.
*   Highlight or write between two and four words that may be unknown to your students.

- Working with a partner, have the students read the text and determine the meaning of the unknown words. Ask pairs to follow the Outside-In Strategy Worksheet and complete one worksheet for each word.
- Circulate around the room and be available for guidance.

When students have mastered applying the strategy using the worksheet, provide practice without the worksheet. Encourage students to memorize the strategy, to remember to *look outside the word* first for context clues, then to *look inside the word* for meaningful word parts, then to *guess* what the word means and *check* their guesses by inserting their definition into the sentence and rereading to see whether it makes sense. Teach them to remember a shortened version of the strategy: Look outside, look inside, guess, and check.

GENERALIZATION

Teacher: Raise your hand if you can tell me a way that the Outside-In Strategy can help you in your other classes.

Student: Well, when we come to a word we don't understand, we can remember to look outside the word for context clues and inside the word for word parts. Then we can use the clues we've found to guess what the word means.

Teacher: Right! You don't have to have a form like the one we used as we learned the strategy. You just need to remember to look outside and inside for *both* context clues and word-part clues. Now, if any of you use this strategy to figure out the meaning of a word in another class, let me know. I'd love for you to share your experience with the rest of the class.

MONITOR STUDENT LEARNING

Check worksheets for appropriate responses.

PERIODIC REVIEW AND MULTIPLE OPPORTUNITIES TO PRACTICE

Periodically, have students use the Outside-In Strategy to find the meaning of one to two words in an instructional-level passage (guided practice) or an independent-level passage (independent practice).

Choose a section from the students' science or social studies text, and highlight a few words that the students might not know. Have the students infer the meaning of the unknown word or words by following the Outside-In Strategy. They may need to use the worksheet at first.

Keep the steps of the Outside-In Strategy posted in your room so that students can refer to it when they come to a word they do not know. Always remind students that they can use this strategy in your class, in their other classes, and any time they read. It is most important that students are able to generalize the strategies you teach them.

Chapter 9

Fluency

TERMS TO KNOW

automaticity   Automatic processing; implementing a skill, strategy, or process with little or no conscious attention to it

fluency   The ability to read text quickly, accurately, and with expression

prosody   Interpreting cues such as punctuation, italics, and boldface words with appropriate pauses, stops, intonation, and pitch variation

rate   The speed of reading

WHY TEACHERS SHOULD CONSIDER FLUENCY WITH MIDDLE SCHOOL READERS

Fluency is said to be the bridge between word recognition and comprehension (Vaughn & Linan-Thompson, 2004). Slow and laborious reading is frustrating for secondary students and often leads them to avoid reading altogether (Rasinski et al., 2005).

In addition to instruction in comprehension strategies and practices, teaching students to read fluently may help them better understand what they read (Fuchs, Fuchs, Hosp, & Jenkins, 2001). If students spend most of their effort focused on word recognition or reading one word at a time without phrasing, then reading text for understanding is compromised. Fluent readers at the middle school level display the following characteristics:

- Read 100–160 words correct per minute (WCPM).
- Have automatic word-recognition skills.
- Group words into meaningful phrases.
- Read with expression.
- Make few word identification errors and usually self-correct when they do make errors.
- Understand what they read.

The goal of fluency instruction is to facilitate the ability to read words with little conscious effort. Students who recognize words without conscious effort are free to focus on comprehending text (Chard, Vaughn, & Tyler, 2002). It is important to note that automatic reading does not solely refer to how quickly a student reads the words on the page. A student may be able to read a passage very quickly but may not necessarily decode words accurately or understand what he or she is reading (Rasinski et al., 2005). Similarly, a student may be able to read every word correctly, but if the student is not reading with **automaticity**, he or she will not be able to understand the ideas behind the words (Chard, Vaughn, & Tyler, 2002). To bridge the gap between word recognition and comprehension, improved **rate** or speed of reading must be accompanied by high accuracy, appropriate expression, and attention to the meaning of the text.

CAVEATS ABOUT ORAL READING FLUENCY IN MIDDLE SCHOOL STUDENTS

Many of the guidelines about monitoring students' progress and establishing benchmarks in oral reading fluency for older students with reading difficulties are based on research with younger children in Grades 1–4. Considerably less is known about fluency practices for older students. Consider the following when interpreting fluency rates with older students:

- The most important outcome for students is that they can understand and learn from the text they read. If students have below-average fluency but demonstrate average or above-average comprehension, it may not be appropriate to spend considerable time on improving their rate of reading.

- Students who read above 100–125 WCPM with 90% accuracy in grade-level text may benefit from time spent on enhancing their background knowledge, vocabulary, and/ or comprehension rather than on fluency instruction.

- Consider the individual needs of adolescent learners, their interest in reading, and their motivation to learn as you interpret oral reading fluency scores and develop interventions.

ASSESSING ORAL READING FLUENCY

The most efficient way to measure fluency is to give a Curriculum-Based Measurement Oral Reading Fluency assessment (CBM/ORF). Originally developed in 1985 by Stanley Deno at the University of Minnesota, a CBM/ORF assessment requires little time to administer. During a CBM/ORF measure, a student is asked to read a passage for 1 minute while the teacher marks mistakes. The teacher then determines the WCPM for the student by subtracting the errors from the total number of words read in 1 minute. See "Assessing Reading Fluency" in Chapter 3 for directions for administering a CBM/ORF assessment.

CBM/ORF assessments can be administered on a regular schedule to monitor students' progress toward fluency goals. If a student is not making sufficient progress, he or she may need fluency practice using one of the approaches described in the following sample lessons. Keeping track of progress on a Fluency Chart (see Figure 9.1; a full-page photocopiable version of this form also appears in the Appendix) can be motivating for older students.

INSTRUCTION TO SUPPORT READING FLUENCY

Select Appropriate Text

The first step in planning fluency instruction is to select appropriate text to use for instruction. Most sources suggest that students read instructional-level text, although some

Fluency Chart

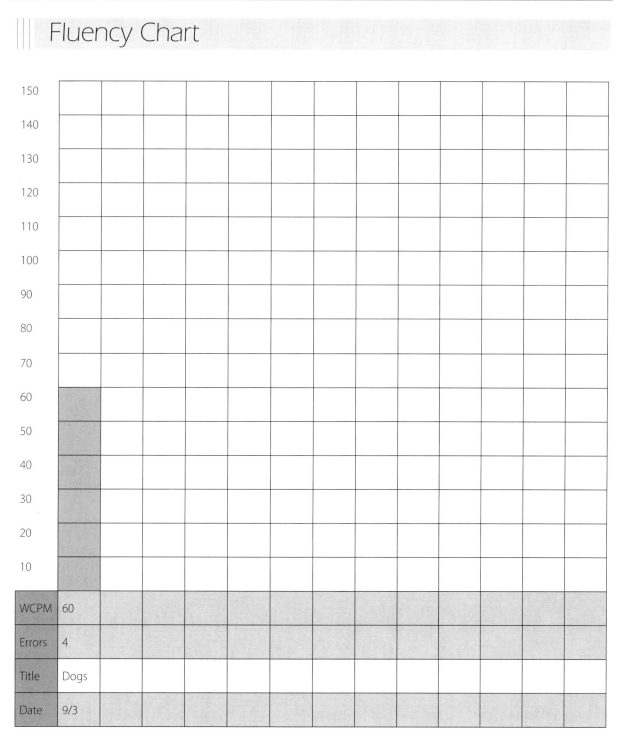

150												
140												
130												
120												
110												
100												
90												
80												
70												
60												
50												
40												
30												
20												
10												
WCPM	60											
Errors	4											
Title	Dogs											
Date	9/3											

Figure 9.1.   Fluency Chart. (*Key:* WCPM, words correct per minute.)

research with younger students suggests that fluency practice can be effective when students read slightly more challenging text (O'Connor, Swanson, & Geraghty, 2010). Refer to the steps suggested in Section I of this book to assess oral reading accuracy and find each student's instructional reading level.

Model Fluent Reading

Students need to hear explicit models of fluent reading. A teacher, parent, tutor, student, audio recording, or computer program can provide this modeling. When you model reading a passage fluently, remember to do the following:

- Read with expression and **prosody**, phrasing and appropriate verbal interpretation of the text.
  - Explain prosody to your students by saying, "I paused here because there is a comma" or, "The question mark tells me to raise my voice a little at the end of this sentence."
- **Demonstrate combining words into meaningful phrases.**
- Demonstrate how to sweep your finger under words and phrases (if needed) instead of pointing to each individual word as you read.

Repeated Reading with Corrective Feedback

The majority of fluency research has focused on elementary students. There is still a great need for further fluency studies with secondary struggling readers, but teachers can provide direct fluency instruction to older readers based on what is known about teaching young readers to be fluent. NICHD (2000) found that guided repeated oral reading practice has "a significant and positive impact on word recognition, fluency, and comprehension across a range of grade levels" (p. 12). When implementing repeated reading to promote fluency, it is important to include the following:

- Explicit modeling of fluent reading
- Teacher or student support with corrective feedback
- Opportunities for students to read text multiple times
- Oral reading practice
- Regular monitoring of student progress

Several repeated reading strategies include all of the above elements. Descriptions of the most promising fluency strategies for secondary struggling readers are provided in the following sections.

| Partner Reading

ASSIGN PARTNERS

In partner reading, students read and reread text with partners. One way to assign partners is to make a list of all students in the class, with the highest-level reader at the top and the lowest-level reader at the bottom. Next, divide the list in half. The highest-level reader will be partnered with the top student on the bottom half of the list. The next student on the top half will be partnered with the next student on the bottom half and so on. See Figure 9.2 for an example. This is only one way to assign partners. For some older readers, rotating pairs frequently has been shown to be an effective way to keep students motivated (Fuchs, Fuchs, & Kazdan, 1999). Knowing your students' personalities and reading levels is the key to having a productive partner reading time.

Consider the following when rotating partner assignments:

- Assign a higher-level reader with a somewhat lower-level reader. The higher-level reader will model fluent reading.

- Consider the personality of your students.

- Choose text that is on the instructional level of the lower-level student.

Student A	95 WCPM
Student B	93 WCPM
Student C	85 WCPM
Student D	70 WCPM
Student E	65 WCPM
Student F	50 WCPM
- - - - - - - - - - - - - -	- - - - - - - -
Student G	48 WCPM
Student H	45 WCPM
Student I	32 WCPM
Student J	30 WCPM
Student K	28 WCPM
Student L	25 WCPM

Figure 9.2. Possible method for assigning reading partners. (*Sources:* Bryant et al., 2000 and Delquadri, Greenwood, Whorton, Carta, & Hall, 1986.) (*Key:* WCPM, words correct per minute.)

TEACH THE PROCEDURE

It is very important to model and teach the partner reading procedure. You can model the procedure with a student or another adult, or you can show a videotape of two students working together. It is essential that students see the procedure in action and are allowed to practice the steps before they are expected to work together independently. When they are proficient, you will be able to focus on working with individual pairs, giving corrective feedback and progress monitoring. Use the steps of effective instruction to teach the partner reading routine. First, model what you want students to do. Then, provide guided and independent practice. If students fail to follow the routine appropriately, rather than reprimand them, simply reteach the procedure—model, provide guided practice, and provide independent practice.

PARTNER READING ROUTINE

The following routine works well for partner reading (Klingner et al., 2001):

1. Partner 1, usually the higher-level reader, reads the first paragraph while Partner 2 follows along.

2. Partner 2, usually the lower-level reader, reads the same paragraph.

3. The pair discusses briefly what they just read by retelling what happened or by identifying the main idea of the paragraph. They can identify the main idea by asking each other "Who or what was the paragraph mainly about?" and, "What was the most important thing about the *who* or the *what*?" See Chapter 7 for a sample lesson plan for teaching this strategy.

4. Repeat steps 1–3 until the passage is complete.

CORRECTION PROCEDURES

The following are guidelines for correcting one's partner during partner reading:

*   If a student reads a word incorrectly, skips a word, or does not know a word, his or her partner will point to the word and say, "What is this word?"

*   If the student reads the word correctly, the partner says, "Yes, that word is _____. What word? Please reread the sentence."

*   If the student does not know the word, the partner says, "That word is _____. What word? Please reread the sentence."

*   The student repeats the word and is asked to reread the sentence.

Your students also will need several opportunities to practice the correction procedure with you and with each other. If you, as a teacher, use this exact procedure for correcting during whole-class instruction, your students will pick up the procedure quickly.

It is essential to teach the partner reading routine and provide guided practice until the procedure becomes a habit. Once the routine is established, students are able to follow the procedure independently. Thus, transition time is reduced, lessons move at a quick pace, and students feel a sense of security by knowing exactly what is expected of them. You may want to provide students with cards to cue them to follow the steps of the partner reading routine. It is particularly helpful to provide cards with the correction procedure on them until this routine has been internalized.

Readers' Theater

Readers' theater involves students in extensive practice and rehearsal of scripted material to be performed for a group (see Worthy & Broaddus, 2002). By the time struggling readers reach middle school and high school, they probably have had several unsuccessful—or even painful—experiences reading in front of their peers. Readers' theater can provide older struggling readers with an opportunity to be successful at reading. This experience may lead to greater student confidence, motivation, and, because of the extensive practice required, improved oral reading fluency (Rinehart, 1999). As with any new activity, you will need to model, or demonstrate, what a readers' theater performance may look like. It would be beneficial to develop a criteria chart with the class to be used for all performances. See Chapter 8 for a more detailed description of the use of criteria charts. Criteria may include but not be limited to the following:

- Readers speak clearly and use an appropriate volume.
- Readers read the text accurately.
- Readers read the text with expression.
- Members of the group cooperate with each other during rehearsal time.
- The group uses their rehearsal time wisely.

PROCEDURE

Select Material to Read

Scripted material can be developed from children's books, poetry, song lyrics, plays, stories, or novels with rich dialogue.

Develop the Script

Assign dialogue to different characters or voices in a story, novel, or poem. Highlight each role so that each student has a copy of the script with his or her role highlighted.

Assign Roles

Readers' theater groups can be as small or as large as needed. It probably will work best to keep groups small at first. When students become confident with the process of rehearsing and performing, you may assign scripts with a larger number of performers.

Practice, Practice, Practice

Allow students ample time to practice and rehearse their script. This repeated practice of familiar text is necessary to improve oral reading fluency to prepare for the "performance" when they read for the class or others. According to Rasinski and colleagues (2005), "When students are asked to perform for others, they have a natural inclination and desire to practice the passage to the point where they can read it accurately, with appropriate rate, and especially with meaningful expression and phrasing" (p. 26). As students are practicing, circulate around the room and be prepared to provide modeling and feedback if students need it to achieve the goals of accurate, fluent reading with appropriate expression and phrasing.

Perform

Students are expected to read the text—not recite their lines from memory. Students may perform for their class, for another class, or for younger students. When students become comfortable with performing, they may want to prepare a piece to perform for parents or for a school assembly.

Discuss

After every performance, discuss with the group and the class the strengths of the performance. Also, give suggestions and have students offer suggestions for improving the performance.

Audio- or Computer-Assisted Reading

Audio-assisted reading requires students to read along orally with a recording of a fluent reader. As a teacher, you may want to record yourself reading fluently or you may choose to purchase one of several fluency programs that provide recorded or computer-generated models of fluent reading. Some of these programs are purposefully recorded several times at different reading rates, with each reading becoming increasingly fluent. Thus, students are more likely to be able to keep up with the initial rate and to read along with the tape at higher levels of fluency with practice. When students are engaged in reading with a recorded model, *it is essential that they actually read along with the tape in a quiet voice rather than simply listening to the tape.* Therefore, the selection cannot be recorded at such a high rate of reading that students will not be able to actually read along with it. Students must be monitored carefully and continually during this activity, especially while they are learning the routines associated with it.

When you introduce this activity, it is important to stress that the object of the game is *not* to simply read fast. Model reading with expression and appropriate phrasing and provide guided practice in this aspect of fluency. It is also important to stress the goal of reading for understanding. It can be a good idea to require that students retell two to four important ideas from the text after they practice with the recording. If they know that they are accountable for the meaning of the text, they will be less likely to turn repeated reading practice into a "speed game."

Before the activity begins, set fluency goals with each student. For example, one student's goal may be to read 100 WCPM with fewer than three mistakes, whereas another student's goal may be to read 70 WCPM with fewer than five mistakes. Each student's goal will depend on the level of difficulty of the passage he or she is reading and his or her current oral reading fluency level. Students should be involved in setting goals and maintaining their own oral reading Fluency Charts. See "Assessing Reading Fluency" in Chapter 3 for a discussion of oral reading rates and Figure 9.1 for a Fluency Chart that can be used to monitor progress (photocopiable version in the Appendix).

Versions of the following procedures are used in several published and unpublished fluency programs. The basic procedures were described by Jay Samuels (1979, 1994).

PROCEDURE

Step 1: First Timed Reading (Before Practice)

Before a student practices reading his or her passage with the recording or computer, the teacher times the student reading the passage independently for 1 minute. This is sometimes called the "cold reading." The teacher then helps the student record the number of words read correctly in 1 minute and reviews any error words. Some computerized fluency programs allow students to time themselves using the computer, identifying words that they hesitate on, stumble on, or find difficult (e.g., by clicking the space bar when they get to a difficult word). These words are recorded by the computer as errors. The computer uses this information to calculate the WCPM. This procedure can be adapted by having the teacher or another adult record the error words as the student reads aloud.

If a computerized program is not available, there are various approaches that can be used for timing students' reading. The teacher may listen to each student individually and time him or her using the procedures described in the "Assessing Reading Fluency" section of Chapter 3; however, this approach can be difficult to implement when several students are ready to read for the teacher at the same time. Some teachers have students time themselves, but care must be taken to ensure that students use timers appropriately. Another approach is to have students work in pairs for the initial timed reading and time everyone in the class simultaneously. One student from each pair will read while the teacher times the reading for 1 minute. Partner 1 reads while Partner 2 listens and tracks the number of words missed by Partner 1; then the partners switch roles, the timer is reset for 1 minute, and Partner 2 reads. The procedure might look like this:

Teacher: Everyone, we will do a timed reading together. You will be working with your partners. Remember, Partner 1 will read first while Partner 2 listens to keep track of misread words and to note where Partner 1 stops when the timer goes off. Partners, get ready…begin.

Start the timer for one minute. One student from each group begins to read orally while his or her partner listens and records errors. Stop the students when the timer goes off.

Teacher: Stop. Partner 2, write down the last word Partner 1 read when the timer went off, along with the number of errors your partner made. Now, switch roles. (*Set the timer again.*) Partner 2, get ready to read while Partner 1 listens. Everyone, ready…begin.

Start the timer. Observe while Partner 2 reads in each group. Stop the students when the timer sounds and have Partner 1 write down the last words Partner 2 read when the timer went off, along with the number of errors made.

Note: If you use one of the available published sources of graded passages designed for oral reading fluency practice, you will notice that numbers aligned with each line of text indicate the total number of words that would be read if a student finished each line when the timer sounded. Partners can be taught to use these numbers to quickly calculate the total number of words read in 1 minute (when the timer went off). Then they can subtract the error words from this total to calculate WCPM. Students may record their scores in a table or on a graph, and these "cold reading" scores can be compared with timed reading scores taken after the students have practiced with the recording.

Step 2: Repeated Oral Reading Practice

While listening to a fluent reader read the text on recording or computer, students *read aloud softly* along with the recording. Students continue to practice with audio support until they are able to read the text independently, usually reading the same passage along with the recording two to three times. Students should be monitored during practice. Encourage them to read accurately and with expression rather than just trying to "read fast."

Step 3: Final Timed Reading

Students signal the teacher when they are confident that they can meet their fluency goals. The teacher times the students reading independently for 1 minute. The teacher then reviews any error words. Since students will complete their reading practice sessions at different times, it sometimes works best to conduct the final reading individually. This also allows the teacher to monitor students' reading to ensure that they are reading with appropriate phrasing and observing punctuation rather than focusing only on reading quickly. The teacher may have students retell two to four important ideas from the text after the timed reading. Some published fluency programs include comprehension questions or brief activities that students complete after the fluency routine.

Another approach is to give students a set amount of time for repeated practice and then conduct a simultaneous second timed reading for the whole class in pairs as described above in Step 1.

Students can compare their scores on the final reading with their cold reading scores and evaluate whether they met their pre-set goals for fluency and accuracy after practicing the passage. Goals may need to be modified based on student progress.

Chapter 10

Word Recognition

TERMS TO KNOW

base word	A word that can stand alone and to which affixes can be added
consonant blend	A combination of consonant letters found before or after a vowel sound in a syllable, in which each consonant represents a unique sound (e.g., *tr-, spr-*)
consonant digraph	A combination of consonant letters that represent one speech sound (e.g., *ph-, ch-*)
decoding	Using sound–symbol relationships to read words
irregular word	A word in which letters or letter combinations do not make their most common, or expected, sounds; a word that does not follow the common conventions of phonics; often taught as sight words
nonsense word (or pseudoword)	A word that is not a real word in English but follows the spelling patterns found in real words; for example, the word *tig* is not a real word, but it follows the consonant-vowel-consonant pattern as in *log*
prefix	A word part that is added to the beginning of a base word or root and modifies its meaning
root	A unit of meaning that cannot stand alone but that can be used to form words with related meanings (e.g., *spect* in *spectacle, inspection, spectator*)
schwa	An indistinct vowel sound found in unstressed English syllables (usually sounds like short *u* or short *i*)
suffix	A word part that is added to the end of a base word or root and modifies its meaning
syllable	A unit of speech organized around a vowel sound

This word recognition method is in common use. For more information and ideas see Archer, A.L., Gleason, M.M., & Vachon, V. (2005a). *REWARDS: Multisyllabic word reading strategies.* Longmont, CO: Sopris West.

INTRODUCTION

The goal of reading is, of course, to make meaning from text, but—as discussed in Chapter 2—students at the secondary level may have difficulties with reading comprehension for a number of reasons. Some students have difficulty with quickly and accurately recognizing the words on the page. For some students, this problem is related to serious difficulties **decoding** even simple words. These students often need long-term, intensive intervention. Other students recognize short words easily but are inaccurate when they try to decode words with more than one or two syllables. These students often benefit from short-term, less intensive instruction in reading multisyllable words.

This chapter focuses on word-recognition instruction, specifically for students who need instruction in reading multisyllable words. These activities are appropriate for students requiring strategic intervention. The chapter concludes with recommendations to guide the selection of instructional materials for interventions with students requiring intensive intervention who have more severe word-reading difficulties.

To design effective word-recognition instruction, it is important to know the following:

- How to teach students to recognize different syllable patterns
- A strategy for reading multisyllable words
- How to plan and implement effective word-recognition instruction
- How to select a scientific research-based word-recognition program for middle school struggling readers

TEACHING STUDENTS TO RECOGNIZE SYLLABLE PATTERNS IN WORDS

When skilled readers encounter unfamiliar multisyllable words, such as technical or scientific terms, they usually look for familiar or pronounceable parts within the words. Then they mentally pronounce each word part to attempt to read the word. You can try this yourself with the words in the following sentence from a medical essay: "Our previous work demonstrated that regulation of apoptotic cell death is a critical factor in controlling lymphomagenesis" (Eischen, 2006).

You probably separated the word *apoptotic* into pronounceable parts such as *a-pop-to-tic*, or you might have divided it as *a-pop-tot-ic*. Either way, you probably were able to make your way through the word with a close approximation of the correct pronunciation. The word *apoptotic* means "pertaining to apoptosis," a kind of programmed cell death in which the body eliminates cells that threaten survival.

For the word *lymphomagenesis*, you may have recognized the **prefix** *lympho-* as a word part you have heard before. You may have associated it with lymph nodes in the body or the cancer lymphoma. You also may have recognized the word *genesis*, meaning "beginning or origin." You may have divided the word into two parts: *lymphoma* and *genesis*, concluding that it has something to do with the beginning of a lymphoma cancer. The word *lymphomagenesis* does, in fact, refer to the development of lymphoma, cancer that affects the body's primary immune system.

Using the strategy of looking for recognizable word parts within these words helped you pronounce the words and gave you clues to the words' meanings. Students with difficulties reading multisyllable words can be taught to use this strategy.

WHAT DO STUDENTS NEED TO KNOW ABOUT SYLLABLES?

To use the strategy of identifying recognizable word parts within long words, students must know the following:

- That these words are composed of pronounceable word parts called *syllables*
- That each **syllable** contains one vowel sound (but that sound may be spelled with a vowel combination as in *maintain*, with the letter *y* as in *slowly or gymnasium*, or even with a contraction in which the vowel letter is "hidden" as in the final syllable of *couldn't*)
- How to recognize syllables composed of common **prefixes**, **suffixes**, and **roots**
- How to divide the word into word parts, read each part, and combine the parts to read the word
- How to be flexible when a word has a part or parts in which letters do not make their expected sounds (often the **schwa** sound for a vowel in an unaccented syllable)

Although students may be taught the "correct" way to divide words into syllables as they are in the dictionary for various other reasons, *it is not necessary that students know the rules for dictionary syllabication in order to read multisyllable words.* What is essential is that when students see a long word they do not know, they quickly look for word parts they recognize, pronounce "chunks" of the word separately, and then put these chunks together to pronounce the entire word. Finding the vowels in the word can help students "chunk" the word into pronounceable parts.

SYLLABLE TYPES

One way to help students recognize pronounceable word parts is to teach them the basic types of syllables that occur often in words and how these syllables typically are pronounced. Six syllable types are taught in several word-recognition programs:

- Closed syllables (*pic-nic*; *ab-sent*)
- Open syllables (*ve-to*; *a-pron*)
- Silent *e* syllables (*de-bate*; *base-ball*)
- Vowel-team syllables (*re-frain*; *car-toon*)
- Vowel-*r* syllables (*en-ter*; *or-phan*)
- Consonant-*le* syllables (*bot-tle*; *bea-gle*)

As you can see from examining this list, the first five syllable types have patterns that are common in short single-syllable words. In describing these patterns, we will use *C* to stand for *consonant* and *V* to stand for *vowel*. Figure 10.1, Vowel Sounds in Syllable Patterns, is a guide to the vowel sounds and spelling patterns found in the various syllable types (photocopiable version in the Appendix). It includes key words to assist students (and teachers!) in remembering the pronunciations of the sound-spellings found in each syllable pattern. You may want to make copies on cardstock for your students or enlarge this page and post it in your classroom.

Closed syllables are made up of the patterns VC (*at*, *in*), CVC (*dig*, *mat*), CCVC (*plot*, *slug*), CVCC (*nest*, *mint*), and other **consonant blend** patterns such as CCVCC (*clamp*). The vowel sound in a closed syllable may be spelled with the letter *y* as in *gym*. Closed

Vowel Sounds In Syllable Patterns

Closed syllables

Sound–spelling pattern	Key word
a	cat
e	let
i	sit
o	hot
u	cup
y	gym

Open syllables

Sound–spelling pattern	Key word
a	paper
e	me
i	hi
o	go, open
u	ruby
___y	my
___y	happy

Silent e syllables

Sound–spelling pattern	Key word
a__e	cake
e__e	these
i__e	like
o__e	note
u__e	cute, tube

Vowel-r syllables

Sound-Spelling Pattern	Key Word
ar	car
er	her
ir	bird
or	for
ur	church

Examples of words with consonant-le syllables

able, article, tackle, riddle, giggle, sparkle, apple, title, sizzle

Examples of words with schwa

about, taken, pencil, other, lesson, beautiful

Vowel team syllables

Sound–spelling pattern	Key word	Sound–spelling pattern	Key word
Patterns that spell long vowel sounds			
Long A		Long O	
ai	rain	oa	boat
ay	day	oe	toe
eigh	eight	ow	show
Long E		Long U	
ea	eat	ue	blue
ee	see	ew	flew
Long I		oo	cool
igh	night		
Patterns that spell other vowel sounds			
al, all	salt, tall	oi	oil
au	haul	oy	boy
aw	saw	ou	out
ea	head	ow	cow
oo	look		

Less common vowel teams

Sound–spelling pattern	Key word	Sound–spelling pattern	Key word
augh	daughter	ei	height
ea	great	ought	fought
ei	vein	ough	dough
ey	they	ough	rough
ey	key	ough	through
ie	chief	ou	soup
ei	either	ui	suit
uy	buy		

Figure 10.1. Vowel Sounds in Syllable Patterns.

syllables also can be spelled using **consonant digraphs**, as in <u>ch</u>in, ma<u>th</u>, and <u>sh</u>op. In each of these words, the vowel makes its short sound. Students can be taught to look for closed syllable patterns and that the vowels in these syllables usually are pronounced with their short sounds. One way to help students remember that these are closed syllables is to show them that these syllables end with a consonant so that the vowel is "closed off" from the rest of the word.

Open syllables are made up of a single vowel (a), the CV pattern (no, hi), or a consonant blend or digraph followed by a vowel (<u>pre-</u>, <u>she</u>). The vowel sound in an open syllable may be spelled with the letter y as in la-<u>dy</u> or fl<u>y</u>. The vowel in an open syllable usually is pronounced with its long sound. Students can be taught to look for open syllable patterns and that the vowels in these syllables will usually be long. One way to help students remember that these are open syllables is to show them that these syllables end with a vowel so that the vowel is "open" to the rest of the word.

Silent e syllables have the VCe pattern found in pine and rope. A silent e syllable may begin with a vowel (<u>ate</u>) or a consonant (<u>huge</u>), and consonants in the pattern may include consonant blends (<u>smile</u>) or consonant digraphs (<u>shake</u>). It can be confusing to identify silent e syllables that occur at the ends of words when certain endings have been added since the final silent e is dropped before adding an ending beginning with a vowel (rep<u>lac</u>ing).

In a vowel-team syllable, the vowel sound is spelled with a letter combination, as in the words r<u>ai</u>n, b<u>oa</u>t, sn<u>ow</u>, b<u>oo</u>t, and pl<u>ay</u>. Usually, the consonants before—and sometimes after—the vowel team form a chunk that can help students read the entire word.

Vowel-r syllables are syllables in which a vowel letter is followed by the letter r. These are sometimes referred to as "r-controlled vowels" because the pronunciation of the vowel is changed when it is followed by the letter r. In vowel-r words or syllables, the vowel and the r that follows it make a single sound. You cannot hear the sound of the vowel separately from the sound of the r. Examples of vowel-r words are p<u>ar</u>k, h<u>er</u>d, s<u>ir</u>, f<u>or</u>, and f<u>ur</u>.

Consonant-le syllables are found in words that end in a consonant followed by the letters le (bot-<u>tle</u>, ca-<u>ble</u>, ma-<u>ple</u>; pud-<u>dle</u>). As with silent e syllables, the final <u>e</u> in consonant-le syllables is dropped before adding some endings, making these patterns difficult for some students to see (e.g., hud<u>dl</u>ing).

Syllables that do not conform to one of these patterns can be included in a category called "other." For example, the suffixes -tion and -sion are not, strictly speaking, vowel-team syllables. A Syllable Types Chart is provided in the Appendix. It may be helpful to make copies of this chart for your students.

A STRATEGY FOR READING MULTISYLLABLE WORDS

As we have described in other sections of this book, a strategy is a multistep plan of action that is implemented to solve a problem or overcome a difficulty. Students who have problems reading multisyllable words benefit from learning and applying a consistent strategy for reading these words. Multisyllable word reading strategies found in different reading programs may vary somewhat, but a basic strategy that many students can learn and apply successfully is described below. This strategy was adapted from one developed by Archer, Gleason, and Vachon (2005a).

1. Find the vowels. Quickly scan the word and locate the vowels *and vowel teams*. Because each syllable will have one vowel sound, the vowels are the keys to locating the syllables in unknown words.

2. Look for word parts you know. Students should be able to recognize common prefixes and suffixes quickly. Identifying these common word parts as well as syllable patterns can make it possible to read unknown multisyllable words quickly and efficiently (see Chapter 8). Students also must look for sound–spelling patterns they recognize, including consonant digraphs, vowel teams, and *r*-controlled vowels. Students must take care not to try to "split up" one of these patterns as they divide the word into syllables (e.g., *raisin* must be divided as *rai-sin*, not *ra-is-in*; *flower* as *flow-er*, not *flo-wer*; *storage* as *stor-age*, not *sto-rage*).

3. Read each word part. Remember that each word part will have one vowel sound.

4. Read the parts quickly. Put the parts together to read the word.

5. Make it sound like a real word. "Flex" the word as needed. Often, letters in multisyllable words do not "follow the rules." For example, vowels in unaccented syllables often make the schwa sound, resembling the sound of short *u* or *i*. Once students put the parts of a multisyllable word together, they may need to "play with" the vowel sounds until the word sounds correct. This step is difficult, if not impossible, if the word is not in the student's spoken vocabulary, but instruction in multisyllable word recognition can help extend this vocabulary.

PLANNING AND IMPLEMENTING WORD-RECOGNITION INSTRUCTION

Middle school students who have difficulty reading multisyllable words benefit from direct, explicit teaching of the syllable types and the multisyllable word reading strategy described above. As described in Chapter 5, this includes the following:

- Setting a purpose for the activity
- Clearly teaching concepts (e.g., syllable types) and modeling skills (e.g., identifying different syllable types in words, using the word-reading strategy)
- Providing guided practice with immediate feedback
- Providing independent practice with close monitoring
- Teaching students how to generalize what they have learned so that they can apply skills in many different contexts

Sample word-recognition lessons are provided to illustrate this process.

Teach the Necessary Subskills

To apply the multisyllable word reading strategy, students must be able to do the following:

- Identify vowel letters and vowel combination patterns.
- Recognize common prefixes and suffixes and common sound–spelling patterns.
- Say the sounds of vowel letters, vowel teams, and *r*-controlled vowels.
- Apply the silent *e* rule in silent *e* syllables.
- Try the schwa sound for vowels in a word part.
- Flex a word by changing the vowel sounds until they arrive at a recognizable word.

It is important to teach these key preskills while (or before) teaching the strategy. Provide daily instruction and review in the sounds of vowels and vowel combinations and in quickly recognizing common prefixes and suffixes. Instruction in the meanings of these word parts can help extend students' vocabularies. (See the sample lesson on the word-part strategy in Chapter 8.)

Teach Syllable Types and the Multisyllable Word Reading Strategy

Students should be taught to recognize and pronounce each syllable type. Introduce the syllable types one at a time and provide practice on newly taught syllable types combined with previously learned syllable types. Vowel sounds often are confusing to struggling readers, so it is very important to review the vowel sounds that occur in each syllable type. Instruction and review in vowel sound–spelling patterns can be done in brief 3-to-5-minute segments every day as an introduction to word-reading instruction or at the beginning of each reading class as a warm-up activity. For example, when introducing closed syllables, review the sounds of the short vowels (e.g., /a/ as in *bat*, /e/ as in *egg*) and when introducing vowel-*r* syllables, review the sounds of the r-controlled vowels (e.g., /ar/ as in *car*, /er/ as in *her*, /ir/ as in *girl*, /or/ as in *for*, and /ur/ as in *fur*). More time will need to be taken to review the many vowel combinations found in vowel-team syllables (e.g., *ai* in *rain*, *oi* in *oil*, *ay* in *play*); we recommend that you introduce words with only a few vowel teams at a time.

If students have problems remembering the various vowel combinations, teaching them to use a key-word strategy can be helpful. Provide a key word for each combination that students know well and can easily recognize *and* spell (e.g., *eat* for *ea*, *her* for *er*, *girl* or *bird* for *ir*, *boy* for *oy*; *cow* and *slow* for the two sounds of *ow*; *look* and *boot* for the two sounds of *oo*). Then, if a student forgets a sound–spelling pattern when trying to read a word, prompt the student by saying something such as, "Do you know another word like that?" rather than just giving him or her the sound or telling the word. Figure 10.1, Vowel Sounds in Syllable Patterns (photocopiable version in the Appendix), contains sample key words for each vowel team and sound-spelling pattern. Notice that there is one table with the most common vowel team patterns and a second table with less common patterns. Most students will not need to learn the less common patterns, but they are provided in case they are needed.

The following is a possible sequence for teaching syllable types:

1. Introduce closed syllables. Review short vowel sounds. Practice reading closed syllables. Practice reading words made up of only closed syllables.

2. Introduce open syllables. Review long vowel sounds. Practice reading open syllables. Practice reading open syllables mixed in with closed syllables. Practice reading words made up of open and closed syllables.

3. Introduce silent *e* syllables. Review the silent *e* rule. Practice reading silent *e* syllables. Practice reading silent *e* syllables mixed in with open and closed syllables. Practice reading words made up of open syllables, closed syllables, and silent *e* syllables.

4. Continue this pattern of introducing the new syllable type and reviewing the corresponding vowel sounds, practicing the new syllable type, practicing it mixed in with previously learned syllable types, and practicing reading words with all the syllable types learned so far.

Teachers of older struggling readers have found that they can teach and review very basic word-reading skills such as reading CVC patterns (found in simple words such as *log*, *pig*, and *mat*) by having students practice reading CVC *syllables* in two-syllable words. In this way, older struggling readers can review the basics of decoding without reading "first-grade words." Rather than practicing reading *rat* or *mop*, students practice closed-syllable words with the CVC pattern, such as *cus-pid*, *dis-miss*, and *con-trast*. Similarly, teachers can review the silent *e* rule by having students read words such as *statement* and *translate*.

Multisyllable Word Reading Strategy

As described previously, students must be taught basic preskills to be able to apply the multisyllable word reading strategy; however, it is not necessary that students master all of these preskills before they begin to apply the strategy to read words. For example, students can learn to apply the strategy while they are also learning and reviewing the different syllable types.

Just as in any strategy instruction, the multisyllable word reading strategy should be clearly modeled for students, and students must have many opportunities to practice each part of the strategy. It may be helpful to teach one or two components of the strategy at a time. For example, one lesson may focus on finding and circling vowels and vowel teams in words, whereas other lessons may teach students to recognize and underline common prefixes. Lists of common prefixes, suffixes, and Greek and Latin roots are included in the Appendix. (See Chapter 8 on vocabulary instruction for information about teaching students to recognize and use these word parts to determine word meanings.) Another lesson or group of lessons will focus on teaching students the schwa sound and how to flex words until they sound correct. Just as the introduction and practice opportunities for the syllable types are cumulative, lessons on the components of the word-reading strategy also build on each other.

The following is a sample sequence for teaching the multisyllable word reading strategy:

1. Set a purpose for learning the strategy. Model the entire strategy with several words while "thinking aloud" to demonstrate thought processes that are involved in applying the strategy.

2. Teach students that words are made up of pronounceable parts called *syllables* and that each syllable contains one vowel sound. Teach students to identify vowels and vowel patterns in words. Have students practice circling vowel letters and vowel combinations in words.

3. Teach students that they will be able to read multisyllable words more quickly and accurately if they can recognize word parts and patterns within the words. Have students practice finding and underlining common prefixes, suffixes, inflectional endings (e.g., *-ing* or *-ed*), along with sound–spelling patterns they recognize (e.g., *-ight* or *-eat*) and any syllable types they have learned so far.

4. Model quickly locating the vowels and recognizable word parts in two-syllable words, reading the words in "chunks," and then reading the chunks quickly to say the whole word. Have students practice in pairs. Start with two-syllable words that do not require "flexing" (words such as *picnic* in which the vowels make their expected sounds) and then progress to three-syllable words.

5. Teach students that sometimes they have to flex, or play with, the vowel sounds in a word until it sounds like a real word. Tell students that vowels in multisyllable words often have a "lazy" sound call a *schwa* and that the schwa sounds like the short *u* or short *i* (make the short *u* and short *i* sounds to demonstrate). Model trying the schwa

sound with a word like *dis-tant*. First read the word with the short vowel sounds that would be expected in closed syllables, pronouncing the *a* as in *hat*. Then flex the word and pronounce the *a* with a schwa sound, producing the word as it is normally said. Have students practice flexing syllables in closed-syllable words such as *happen*, *pencil*, *falcon*, *constant*, *system*, *ransom*, and *indulgent*.

6. Model and provide practice applying the entire multisyllable word reading strategy.

7. Prompt (remind) students to apply the strategy whenever they come to an unknown multisyllable word (or when they misread a multisyllable word) when they are reading text.

Note that this sequence should not be introduced too quickly. Be sure that students have had many opportunities to practice each step before introducing the next step. Monitor the students closely during practice and model again if necessary. Provide scaffolding and feedback as they apply the strategy in text.

In the next sections, we include sample word-recognition lessons designed to teach students to recognize and read common syllable types and to use the strategy to read multisyllable words. As you design your own lessons, you can find lists of words with particular patterns (e.g., silent *e* words, words with *ar*, words with *ea*) on the Internet or in books such as the *Reading Teacher's Book of Lists* (Fry & Kress, 2006).

|| # Word Recognition
The Multisyllable Word Reading Strategy

OBJECTIVE

Students will learn and apply the multisyllable word reading strategy to read unfamiliar multisyllable words. **Note:** Teach this lesson as soon as students have learned to recognize the closed syllable pattern and review this strategy as needed as they learn more syllable patterns.

PREREQUISITE SKILLS

Prior to this lesson, the students already should have had an initial lesson on identifying and pronouncing one-syllable words with the closed **syllable** pattern. They should also have learned the **prefix** un-, the suffix -ly, and the inflectional endings -ing and -ed.

MATERIALS

- Figure 10.2: Multisyllable Word Reading Strategy poster (photocopiable version in the Appendix in the section for Chapter 7)
- Overhead projector or SMART Board
- Transparency or copy of Figure 10.1: Vowel Sounds in Syllable Patterns (photocopiable version in the Apendix)
- Prepared word lists for students (see Preparation, below)

PREPARATION

Prepare a list of between six and eight multisyllable words that contain only closed syllables and prefixes, suffixes, and endings that students have learned. These words should be made up of only closed syllables in which the vowels are pronounced with their short sounds. Do not include words that have syllables in which vowels make the **schwa** sound (e.g., the a in distant). Sample words with closed syllables and common affixes include abstract, conflict, unintended, dismissed, splendid, selfishly, disgusting, unexpected, inspecting, and investing.

DAILY REVIEW

> **Teacher:** You have learned about closed syllables. A closed syllable ends in at least one consonant, and the vowel is short. Remember that the vowel is "closed off" by the consonant at the end of the word. Let's quickly review the sounds the vowels make in closed syllables.
>
> *Place a transparency of Figure 10.1, Vowel Sounds in Syllable Patterns, on the overhead and use it to review the short vowel sounds found in closed syllable words and their key words. As you point to each vowel letter, ask students for the sound and key word. Review and reteach any that are not firm. Then have students read a short list of one-syllable words that follow the closed syllable pattern. Try to select words that are not overly simple, even though they have only one syllable. For example, select words with consonant blends and di-*

graphs (e.g., stamp, grant, slept, blimp, clasp, check, snug, track, strand*). If students make errors point to the vowel in the word and ask for its sound. Then have students reread the word. If necessary, tell students the word. Then, have the students read the word after you. Continue with the other words, but be sure to return to the problem word later and have the students read it without your help. Finally, have individual students take turns reading one or two words each.*

STATE OBJECTIVE AND/OR PURPOSE

Teacher: Today, you will learn a strategy, or plan, to read words with more than one syllable. You will be able to use this strategy in any class to help you read words with more than one syllable.

MODEL AND TEACH

Genre: Expository or narrative

Grouping: Whole class or small group

Display a poster with the steps for the multisyllable strategy written on it. This strategy can be found in Figure 10.2. (photocopiable version in the Appendix). This poster will be kept in the room for student reference as they learn the strategy.

Teacher: I'm going to show you how I would use the strategy if I were trying to read a word I didn't know. You might already be able to read the word that I'm going to write, but if you can, don't say it out loud. I want to show you what you could do if you were trying to read a long word that you *didn't* know.

Write fantastic *on an overhead transparency. Think aloud as you model each step of the strategy for the students.*

Multisyllable Word Reading Strategy

1. Find the vowels.

2. Look for word parts you know.

3. Read each word part.

4. Read the parts quickly.

5. Make it sound like a real word.

Figure 10.2. Multisyllable Word Reading Strategy. (From Archer, A.L., Gleason, M.M., & Vachon, V. [2005a]. *REWARDS: Multisyllabic word reading strategies.* Longmont, CO: Sopris West; adapted by permission.)

The first step in the strategy is to find the vowels. I know that every syllable must have a vowel sound, so finding the vowels will help me find the syllables in the word.

Point to the word fantastic *on the overhead.*

In this word I see an *a*, another *a*, and an *i*. I'm going to circle the vowels in the word.

Circle the vowels in the word fantastic.

Step 2 of the strategy is to look for word parts you know. Hmmm. I see something that looks like *fan* at the beginning. That isn't one of the prefixes we have worked on, but it is a word part I know. I'm going to underline it.

Underline fan *in* fantastic.

I also see two more closed syllables in the word. I'm going to underline the closed syllables.

Underline tas *and* tic *in* fantastic.

Step 3 is to read each word part. Okay, because these are closed syllables, I think the vowels will have their short sounds. *Fan-tas-tic.*

Step 4 is to read the parts quickly. *Fantastic.* That makes sense! The word is *fantastic.*

Step 5 says to make it sound like a real word. The word I read sounds right. *Fantastic.* I don't think I have to change it. It sounds like a real word.

Be sure to emphasize the accented syllable: *fantastic*. At first, it may be helpful to demonstrate how placing the emphasis on the wrong syllable will make it into a **nonsense word:** *fantastic, fantastic*. Changing the emphasis to the correct syllable can be part of Step 5: Make it sound like a real word.

For English language learners, teach this strategy: Whenever you hear a new multisyllable word, pay attention to which syllable has the emphasis. You can write the word and put a dot under or underline the stressed syllable. The next time you hear or read the word, this mark will remind you of the correct pronunciation.

GUIDED PRACTICE

Grouping: Whole group or small group

Teacher: Now, let's do one together.

Write the word unimpressed *on the overhead transparency.*

Teacher: What is the first step of our strategy? Michael?

Student: Find the vowels.

Teacher: Michael, what are all the vowel letters?

Student: *A, e, i, o, u,* and sometimes *y.*

Teacher: Good. Please come up and circle all of the vowel letters you see in this word.

Michael circles u, i, e, *and* e.

Thank you, Michael. What's the next step in the strategy? Terri?

Student: Look for word parts you know.

Teacher: Terri, do you see any word parts you know?

Student: It has *un-* at the beginning.

Teacher: Excellent, Terri. You found the prefix *un-* in the word. What does that mean? Javier? Yes, *un-* means "not." Terri, come up and underline the prefix *un-* in the word. Great, thank you. What other word parts do you see in the word—Simon?

Student: I see *-ed* at the end. That means it's in the past.

Teacher: Excellent, Simon. Please come up and underline *-ed*. Now, do you see any syllable types you know? Remember, the vowels can help you find the syllables since each syllable has one vowel sound in it. Tamika, what do you see?

Student: I think there are two closed syllables: *im* and *press*.

Teacher: Wow, Tamika! You are really using what you know about syllables! Please come underline those two word parts. The next steps in the strategy are to read the parts and then read them quickly. Everyone, read the first part.

Point to un-.

Teacher: Yes, *un-*. Read the part.

Point to im.

Read the part.

Point to press.

Now read those parts together.

Students: *Unimpress.*

Teacher: Good. Now add the ending to show that it happened in the past.

Students: *Unimpressed.*

Teacher: Terrific. Does it sound like a real word? Maia?

Student: I think so. I've heard the word *impress*, like you wear a really cool shirt to try to impress your friends.

Teacher: That's a great example, Maia. You're right. The base word is *impress*. If you impress someone, you make them think that something is very important or special. So what would *impressed* mean? Tamika?

Student: Well, I think the *-ed* ending means I did it in the past.

Teacher: Yes, it can mean that. We could say, "I impressed all my friends when I wore my new shirt." There is another meaning for this word. I could say, "I was impressed when I saw Maia's cool new shirt." That means I saw the shirt and thought it was very special. Now what would it mean if I said, "I was *un*impressed when I heard the boy tell a joke." Anyone?

Student: If *un-* means "not," I guess you did not think it was very special. You didn't like the joke very much.

Teacher: Exactly! If you are unimpressed by something, you don't think it is very special. Simon, can you finish this sentence? "I was unimpressed when…."

Student: I was unimpressed when…I saw last night's basketball game.

Teacher: Why were you unimpressed when you saw the game?

Student: We lost. We played bad.

Teacher: Okay. That makes sense. Everyone, please read the five steps of the strategy together.
Point to the poster as the class reads. Repeat, if necessary.

INDEPENDENT PRACTICE

Grouping: Partners

Teacher: You did a very good job of using the strategy to read this long word. Now, I'm going to give you a chance to read some words with your partner. Listen carefully to my directions. When you get together with your partner, I will give you a list of words. First,

Partner 1 will use the strategy to read a word. Partner 2 will check Partner 1's work and remind Partner 1 how to use the strategy, if needed. If both partners are not sure about how to use the strategy to read the word, raise your hands and I will come to help you figure it out. When you have finished a word, switch jobs, and Partner 2 uses the strategy to read the next word, while Partner 1 helps. I will be coming around and checking your work, so be ready to read your words to me when I come to your group.

What will you do first when you join your partners? Javier?

Student: Partner 1 will read the first word.

Teacher: Yes. Remember that you will use the five steps in our strategy to read the word. What will Partner 2 do? Simon?

Student: Help Partner 1, if needed.

Teacher: What if you both get stuck on the word? Tamika?

Student: Raise our hands and you'll come.

Teacher: Yes. And what will you do when you have figured out a word? Michael?

Student: Switch so the other partner can read the next word.

Teacher: Excellent. Please move over next to your partners.

Give each pair a list of between six and eight multisyllable words that are made of closed syllables and pre-fixes, suffixes, and endings that they have learned. See the section on Preparation for this lesson.

Important! Do not include irregular words or those that have syllables in which the vowels do not make their short sounds, such as words with the schwa sound. At this point students should not have to do Step 5 of the strategy. They should not have to "play with" the vowel sounds in the word to make it sound like a real word. Once students have mastered the strategy, teach a lesson on reading words with the schwa sound, in which you model how to make it sound like a real word. Have students work in partner groups to read the words, following the directions above.

GENERALIZATION

Teacher: How might you use the multisyllable word reading strategy to help you outside of this class?

Student: It could help when we try to read hard words.

Teacher: Yes. When you are reading in your science, social studies, English, or math classes, I want you to remember to try the strategy. It won't work for all the hard words you see, but try it anyway. You may be able to figure out most of the words this way. I'm going to ask you tomorrow how you used the strategy in your other classes. Do you think you might be able to use the strategy at home?

Student: Maybe when I'm reading my new comic book. Sometimes they have some long words in them.

Teacher: Good idea, Simon. Anytime you read, at home or at school, and you come to long words that you don't know, try the strategy. I can't wait to find out how it works for you.

MONITOR STUDENT LEARNING

Check students' work carefully as they work with their partners to read words. Plan several lessons to review the strategy and have students apply it in more challenging words, especially as you teach more syllable types.

Provide opportunities for students to partner-read selected passages with several examples of multisyllable words that contain the syllable types the students have learned. Remind students to try the strategy to read words that have more than one syllable. Have partners remind each other to use the strategy to help them read unfamiliar words. Monitor their reading closely and provide feedback.

PERIODIC AND MULTIPLE OPPORTUNITIES TO PRACTICE

Review the strategy often, and teach more lessons on using the strategy as needed. It may require several lessons and opportunities to practice before students begin to use the multisyllable word reading strategy independently. Share this strategy with your students' content-area teachers so that students can follow the same procedure in other classes and generalize the strategy. Ask the content-area teachers to remind students to try the multisyllable word reading strategy when they come to a long word they don't know.

Word Recognition
The Silent *e* Syllable Type

OBJECTIVE

Students will recognize and read silent *e* syllables, distinguish silent *e* syllables from previously taught syllable types, and read multisyllable words that include silent *e* syllables and previously taught syllable types.

MATERIALS

- Overhead projector or SMART Board
- Syllable Types Chart (photocopiable version in the Appendix)
- Transparency or copy of Figure 10.1: Vowel Sounds in Syllable Patterns (photocopiable version in the Appendix)
- Student text
- Pocket chart
- Index cards

PREPARATION

Choose a passage from the student text and select at least 10 examples of words that contain silent *e* syllables, beginning with one-syllable words. Write each word on an index card. The examples used in this sample lesson are taken from an excerpt from *The Joy Luck Club,* by Amy Tan.

DAILY REVIEW

Use the Syllable Types Chart to quickly review the two types of syllables you have already taught: closed and open syllables (photocopiable version in the Appendix). If needed, use Figure 10.1, Vowel Sounds in Syllable Patterns, to quickly review the vowel sounds found in these two syllable patterns.

Teacher: We have been learning about different syllable types so that we can quickly recognize and pronounce the parts of a word. Raise your hand if you can tell me what a syllable is. Devon? Yes, a syllable is a word part containing one vowel sound. When you are reading and you come to a word that you don't know, you can look for syllable patterns to help you read the word.

Write the words closed *and* open *on index cards and place them in the top row of the pocket chart to create column headings.*

We have learned about closed and open syllables. A closed syllable ends in at least one consonant and the vowel is short. Remember that the vowel is "closed off" by the consonant at the end of the word. Let's think of some examples of words that contain a closed syllable.

Record student responses on index cards and underline the closed syllables in each word. Place the cards in the closed-syllable column. Sort the words into groups by the number of syllables. This should be quick. If students cannot readily generate closed-syllable words, provide examples.

Good work. These words belong in the closed-syllable column: *such, fresh,* and *with.* You also thought of some words that have more than one syllable and that contain closed syllables: *picnic, absent,* and *rabbit.*

Now let's review open syllables. An open syllable ends in one vowel, and the vowel is usually long. Remember that the vowel is at the end of the syllable, so the vowel is "open" to the rest of the word. What is an example of a word that contains an open syllable?

Record student responses on index cards and underline the open-syllable patterns. Place the cards in the open-syllable column of the pocket chart. Sort the words into groups by the number of syllables. If students cannot readily generate open-syllable words, provide examples.

Good work again. I'll place these examples in the open-syllable column: *we, she, so, see,* and *go.* These are all one-syllable words. You also thought of a two-syllable word with an open syllable. The first syllable of the word *paper* is an open syllable: /pā/.

Continue to add student responses to the open-syllable column and underline the open syllable. Prompt students or provide examples if they have problems generating the words on their own.

I'll write these examples in the "open syllable" column and underline the open syllable in each word: <u>ba</u>by, <u>i</u>tem, <u>pro</u>tect, <u>ba</u>con, <u>hu</u>man, and <u>tro</u>phy.

STATE OBJECTIVE AND/OR PURPOSE

Teacher: Today, we are going to learn a new syllable type to help us quickly recognize and pronounce the parts of words; we will learn the silent *e* syllable pattern. Silent *e* syllables normally end in one vowel, one consonant, and a final *e*. The finale *e* is silent and the vowel is long.

Silent *e* syllables follow the same pattern as one-syllable silent *e* words like *cake* and *like.* The *e* at the end tells us that the vowel in the word will have its long sound.

Sometimes, silent *e* syllables or words may have an ending like *-s* or *-d,* or even *-er* or *-est,* that follows the final *e*. These are still silent *e* syllables. Examples are the words *liked, bikes, nicer,* and *safest.*

Write these words on the board or on note cards and show students the silent e *pattern and the ending.*

Sometimes the silent *e* has been dropped before adding an ending that begins with a vowel, as in *joking* (*joke + ing*). These are a bit harder to find, but they are still silent *e* syllables.

Write joking *on the board and demonstrate the fact that it is formed by adding* ing *to a silent* e *word.*

Silent *e* syllables may begin with a vowel, as in the word *ape,* or a consonant, as in the word *tape.* Let's review the long sounds that vowels make.

Review long vowel sounds.

MODEL AND TEACH

Genre: Expository or narrative

Grouping: Whole class or small group

Create a new column in the pocket chart labeled Silent e.

Teacher: Let's begin by reading a set of one-syllable words that contain the silent *e* syllable pattern. I'll read the word first and then you repeat it. Listen for the long vowel sounds in each word.

Display the index cards one at a time, reading the word aloud and having students repeat it after you. After reading each word, place it in the pocket chart. Examples include home, owe, nine, hopes, scale, blame, crazed, poke, quote, whine, *and* use.

Now, let's take a closer look at the silent *e* pattern.

Use the overhead projector, a white board on an easel, or a chart tablet to provide explicit instruction. Write the first word from the list.

Find the first vowel. It is always followed by a consonant and then an *e*. The first vowel is long, and the *e* is silent. I will circle the first vowel and draw a line through the silent *e*. Remember: Silent *e* syllables may begin with a vowel or a consonant. Which words on our list begin with a vowel?

Solicit student input.

That's right; *owe* and *use* begin with vowels.

Write the examples on the overhead, white board, or chart tablet.

I will circle the first vowel in each of these words and draw a line through the silent *e* at the end. That reminds me that the first vowel is long and the silent *e* doesn't have a sound. Which words on our list begin with a consonant?

Solicit student input.

That's right—*home, nine, hopes, scale, blame, crazed, poke, quote,* and *whine* begin with consonants or consonant blends.

Write the examples, thinking aloud and soliciting student input.

Again, I will circle the first vowel in each of these words and draw a line through the silent *e* at the end. What sound does the first vowel make? That's right, the first vowel is long. Why did I draw a line through the *e*? You're right again; because it doesn't have a sound. I notice that the word *crazed* ends with the letter *d* because it is in the past tense. This is still a silent *e* word because it is made from the word *craze* with an ending added to it. We won't cross out the e in crazed because it is part of the *ed* ending.

Introduce two-syllable words that contain syllables that follow the silent e pattern.

All the examples on our list are one-syllable words, but the silent *e* pattern also occurs in words with two or more syllables. Let's look at an example of a two-syllable word that contains the silent *e* pattern.

Write the word cupcake.

There are two syllables in the word *cupcake*. The first syllable is *cup*. I know that *cup* follows the closed syllable pattern because the vowel is closed in by the consonant, so the vowel is short.

The second syllable is *cake*. *Cake* follows the silent *e* syllable pattern, so the first vowel is long and the *e* is silent. I'll circle the first vowel in *cake* and draw a line through the silent *e*. Read it with me: "cake." Now read the whole word: "cupcake." Remember, in words that contain more than one syllable, like *cupcake*, the syllables may follow different syllable patterns.

Now, let's read some two-syllable words from the selection you will read in our textbook that contain syllables that follow the silent *e* pattern. I'll ask a student to find the silent *e* syllable in each word. Then I'll ask you to read each syllable in the word. Finally, you will put the syllables together and read the whole word.

One at a time, show students the note cards containing two-syllable words taken from the text selection. Call on a student to identify and read the silent e *syllable in each word. Underline the silent* e *syllable on the index card. If the student has difficulty, read the silent* e *syllable for the group and have the whole group read it after you. Then, point to each syllable in the word and ask the class to read it. Finally, have the students read the entire word. If the word is likely to be unfamiliar to the students, provide a brief definition of the word and/or an example. Examples of two-syllable silent* e *words include* nick<u>name</u>, cas<u>cade</u>, em<u>braced</u>, un<u>grate</u>ful, *and* <u>taste</u>ful.

Jonathan, read the silent *e* syllable in the first word. Yes, the silent *e* syllable is *name*.

Point to the silent e *syllable.*

Everyone, read the first syllable. Now, read the silent *e* syllable. Read the whole word. Yes, *nickname*. A nickname is a special name we use for our close friends or members of our families. Sometimes it is a shorter way of saying the person's real name. My sister's name is Katherine, but we call her Kate. Kate is her nickname.

Repeat with the other words. If students have problems with a word like embraced, *point out that the silent* e *syllable has the* ed *ending to show that the action happened in the past.*

Have the students practice reading all of the silent e *words on the index cards without you. Include both the one-syllable and two-syllable words on the list. Point to each word, skipping randomly from word to word, and have students read them chorally, answering together as you point to the word. Listen carefully to their responses. If any students misread a word, stop right away and read the word to the students, then have them repeat it with you, and finally have them read it as a group without you. Students should have mostly correct responses. If there are many errors, either 1) slow down a little to give students more think time, 2) point to the silent* e *syllable first and have students read that one and then read the whole word, or 3) reteach how to recognize and read open, closed, and/or silent* e *syllables.*

Once students have practiced reading the words on the cards as a group, call on each student to read one or two words, skipping randomly between the words and including both one-syllable and two-syllable words. If a student makes an error, model how to read the word, have the whole group read it together, and then have the individual student read the word again. Then ask the student who made the error to read a different word alone.

Teacher: Jessica, read this word.

The word on the index card is cascade, *but Jessica says "casted."*

The silent *e* syllable in this word is *cade*, and the word is *cascade*. Everyone, read the silent *e* syllable. Yes, *cade*. Now read the whole word. Yes, *cascade*. Jessica, read the silent *e* syllable. Now read the whole word. Yes, *cascade*. Jessica, now read the silent *e* syllable in this word.

Point to grate *in* ungrateful. *If Jessica struggles, cover the prefix and suffix in the word to isolate* grate *and ask her to provide the sound of the long* a *in the syllable and then read the syllable.*

Yes, the silent *e* syllable is *grate*. Now, Jessica, read the first syllable. Read the next syllable. Read the last syllable. Read the whole word. Yes, the word is *ungrateful*. Everyone, read the word.

Refer to the list of words in the pocket chart.

Now we have learned three syllable patterns: closed, open, and silent *e*. Remember, when you are reading and you come to a word that you don't know, you can look for these three syllable patterns in the word to help you read it. We can sort words by their syllable patterns to review what we have learned.

GUIDED PRACTICE

Prepare additional index cards with words that follow the closed, open, or silent *e* pattern to provide practice with new words.

Grouping: Whole group or small group

> *Remove all the index cards from the pocket chart. Model the sorting procedure.*

Teacher: I will read the first three words and sort them according to syllable types. If the word contains more than one syllable, the syllable to sort by is underlined. After I finish, you will have a turn to sort words on your own. Many of these words are from the selection that we began reading this week—*The Joy Luck Club*, by Amy Tan.

> *Show students the first word. Begin with a silent* e *word, such as* fame.

I know that this is a silent *e* word because the first vowel is followed by a consonant and an *e*. The word is *fame*. It goes in the "Silent *e*" column of our pocket chart.

> *Place the index card in the correct column. Continue modeling how to sort words, choosing one example of a closed syllable and one example of an open syllable. Think aloud about the syllable pattern as you place each word in the correct column of the pocket chart.*

The next word is *tests*. The first vowel in *tests* is *e*. It is a closed syllable because the vowel is closed by the consonants that follow it.

The next word is *piano*. Remember that if the word has more than one syllable, I have underlined the syllable I want you to sort by. The first vowel in the syllable that is underlined is *o*. It is open because it is not followed by a consonant.

> *Provide opportunities for student practice. Distribute the remaining word cards and call on students one at a time to sort the words into groups using the pocket chart categories. Require students to explain their thinking and justify their choices. Provide corrective feedback as needed.*

Janelle, your word is *nickname*. It has two syllables, and the second syllable is underlined. What spelling pattern does *name* follow?

Student: It is a silent *e* word because the first vowel, *a*, is followed by a consonant, and then an *e* comes at the end.

INDEPENDENT PRACTICE

Grouping: Partners

1. Provide partners with a set of word cards to sort into open-, closed-, and silent *e* syllable patterns. Select words from your textbook so that students will encounter the words again in their reading.

2. Tell students that they are going to practice reading words and sorting them by syllable patterns to practice what they have learned. Give each student a handout such as the one in Figure 10.3 with the sorting categories at the top, but with enough rows for students to sort at least 30 words into groups. Include the list of the word-sort words at the bottom of the handout.

3. Have students work with partners to sort their set of word cards according to the three syllable types.

4. Once they have finished the word sort, ask the students to write the words on their own copies of the sorting sheet using the list at the bottom of the page, remembering to underline the syllable in each word by which the word was sorted.

Closed syllable	Open syllable	Silent *e* syllable

Word list: home, ice, owe, we, nine, hopes, scale, ape, cas<u>cade</u>, blame, <u>silent</u>, spoke, crazed, use, poke, quote, shape, whine, cute, un<u>grate</u>ful, theme, em<u>braced</u>, five, nick<u>name</u>, she, so, see, <u>Lin</u>do, take, <u>Chi</u>nese, pia<u>no</u>, <u>tro</u>phy

Figure 10.3. Sample guide for word sort by syllable type. (From *JOHNSTON, FRANCINE; INVERNIZZI, MARCIA; BEAR, DONALD R., WORDS THEIR WAY: WORD SORTS FOR SYLLABLES AND AFFIXES SPELLERS, 1st Edition,* © *2005. Reprinted by permission of Pearson Education, Inc., Upper Saddle River, NJ. Vocabulary selected from Tan, 1989.)*

GENERALIZATION

Teacher: How can you use this to help yourself outside of this class?

Student: Whenever we're reading and we don't know a word, we can look for the syllable types that we know to help us read it.

Teacher: Yes. When you are reading in your science class today, I want you to remember to try looking for open, closed, and silent *e* syllables in difficult words. I'm going to give each of you an index card to use as a bookmark when you are reading in science. If you come to difficult words, make a quick note of some of the words on this bookmark and bring it back to our class tomorrow. We'll look at the words and see whether we can find syllable patterns we know to help us read the words.

MONITOR STUDENT LEARNING

Check students' work on their copies of the sorting sheet. Provide opportunities for students to partner-read (see Chapter 9) selected passages that contain multiple examples of words that contain the three syllable patterns that have been introduced. Have partners remind each other to use the strategy of looking for syllable types to help them read unfamiliar words. Monitor their reading closely and provide feedback.

PERIODIC AND/OR MULTIPLE OPPORTUNITIES TO PRACTICE

Share this strategy of looking for syllable patterns with your students' content-area teachers so that students can be encouraged to follow the same procedure in other classes and generalize the strategy. Tell the content-area teachers about the index cards that students will use as bookmarks and on which students will record challenging words as they read content-area text.

SELECTING AN EFFECTIVE READING INTERVENTION PROGRAM

Most students who have serious difficulties with word recognition, particularly those who need intensive intervention, will benefit from a more systematic approach to word-reading instruction than the one described above. Systematic instruction is based on a carefully designed scope and sequence, in which less difficult skills are introduced before more difficult skills and many opportunities for practice are integrated into the lesson design, including cumulative practice over time. This level of systematic instruction is best provided by implementing a high-quality reading intervention program, usually consisting of published materials. This section will provide guidelines for selecting such a program for middle school students.

The following guidelines are based on characteristics of instruction that are found in effective, evidence-based interventions for struggling readers. Figure 10.4 is designed to be used by groups of educators as they evaluate reading-intervention programs (a photocopiable version of this form also appears in the Appendix). This is from a document that was developed to assist the Curriculum and Instruction Team at the Florida Center for Reading Research (FCRR) at Florida State University as they reviewed reading programs for Grades 4–12 to determine alignment with current reading research. It is important to note that this document is designed to evaluate a *comprehensive* reading program, so it covers all of the five components of reading identified by NICHD: phonemic awareness (sound analysis), phonics (word identification and decoding), fluency, vocabulary, and comprehension. In some cases, however, educators may need a program that emphasizes one of these components more than the others, or even exclusively. In that case, they may use only portions of this document.

STUDENTS WHO DO NOT RESPOND ADEQUATELY TO INTERVENTION

Some middle school students with severe reading difficulties and disabilities do not make adequate progress in word recognition, even when they are provided with small-group intervention using research-validated, high-quality programs. These students may need the kind of long-term, highly intensive intervention that can best be provided in special education. Students who are provided with quality small-group intervention in general education but who do not make adequate progress after two semesters may need to be referred for evaluation for a learning disability. Students with severe reading disabilities who are already served in special education must be provided with highly intensive interventions (very small groups for extended periods of time) delivered by well-qualified teachers using programs that have evidence of effectiveness with students with severe and persistent reading difficulties. Some of these students may need different kinds of intervention approaches than have been described in this manual.

Guidelines for Reviewing a Reading Program

USING THE GUIDELINES

When reviewing a reading program thoroughly, it is not sufficient to examine only a sample of lessons. In order to determine whether a program is aligned with current reading research, it is essential to review all the teacher and student materials. This document was developed to help navigate a reviewer through the lengthy but important process of reviewing a reading program. It was designed to be utilized in conjunction with the resources listed below. When using this document, place a check mark in either the yes or no column after each question. If the answer is not clear or not evident, write "not evident" in the comments column and leave the yes/no columns blank. It is very important to use the comments column to detail specific examples, note questions, etc. When a question is marked "no" or "not evident" it is a concern that the program may not be fully aligned with current reading research. That is, if a reading program is aligned with current reading research, then "yes" will be marked on most or all of the questions with evidence to support this assertion written in the comments column. No program is perfect, and sometimes teachers will need to make adaptations to their instruction such as providing additional cumulative practice opportunities.

The following resources on the Florida Center for Reading Research Web site (http://www.fcrr.org) will assist educators who use this tool to guide their review of a reading program:

- Glossary of Reading Terms (boldface words in the Guidelines are found in the Glossary).
- Continuum of Phonological Awareness Skills.
- Continuum of Word Types.
- FCRR Reports (reviews of reading programs already posted).
- References and Resources for Review of Reading Programs.

OVERALL INSTRUCTIONAL DESIGN OF THE READING PROGRAM

Characteristic	Yes	No	Comments (e.g., specific examples, strengths, concerns, questions)
Is there a clear "road map" or "blueprint" for teachers to get an overall picture of the program (e.g., scope and sequence)?			
Are goals and objectives clearly stated?			
Is instruction consistently explicit (including direct explanations and models, clear examples, guided practice, and independent practice)?			
Is instruction consistently systematic (progressing from easier to more challenging skills, with confusing elements separated, teaching necessary preskills prior to introducing complex strategies)?			
Are there consistent, "teacher-friendly" instructional routines that include direct instruction, modeling, guided practice, student practice and application with feedback, and generalization?			
Are there aligned student materials?			
Are there ample guided practice opportunities, including multiple opportunities for explicit teaching and teacher feedback?			
Are teachers encouraged to give immediate corrective feedback and/or instructional scaffolding?			

(continued)

Figure 10.4. Guidelines for Reviewing a Reading Program. (From the Florida Center for Reading Research, http://www.fcrr.org.)

OVERALL INSTRUCTIONAL DESIGN OF THE READING PROGRAM *(continued)*

Characteristic	Yes	No	Comments (e.g., specific examples, strengths, concerns, questions)
Is scaffolding a prominent part of the lessons?			
Are there specific instructions for scaffolding?			
Are all of the activities (e.g., centers) reading-related (i.e., word building, fluency practice), and are they designed to provide independent practice in objectives that have already been taught and practiced with teacher support?			
Is differentiated instruction prominent?			
Is instruction individualized based on assessment?			
Is instruction provided to small groups of students with similar needs?			
Are there guidelines for flexible grouping based on assessment results, with movement from group to group based on student progress?			

TEXT READING

Characteristic	Yes	No	Comments (e.g., specific examples, strengths, concerns, questions)
Do the instructional routines of the program include daily text reading?			
Does the program include a variety of high-quality text for students to read?			
Is text available at a variety of reading levels so that each student can read on his or her independent and instructional levels?			
Does the level of difficulty of the text increase as students' skills are strengthened?			
Are sufficient quantities of both narrative and informational text included?			
Does the program include text in which students can successfully apply word identification skills and strategies?			
Does the program include text appropriate for fluency practice?			
Does the program include text to support vocabulary instruction?			
Does the program include text that is suitable for instruction and application of various comprehension strategies?			

Figure 10.4. *(continued)*

INSTRUCTION IN DECODING, WORD IDENTIFICATION, AND SPELLING

Characteristic	Yes	No	Comments (e.g., specific examples, strengths, concerns, questions)
Is there a component of the program devoted to instruction in word identification, decoding, and spelling?			
Overall, does instruction progress from easier word reading skills and activities to more difficult ones?			
Is instruction and practice in word reading, decoding, and spelling provided for about 10 to 20 minutes daily?			
Does the program include explicit, systematic instruction in common sound-spelling patterns (e.g., vowel teams, letter combinations)?			
Does the program include placement tests and/or mastery tests that can be used to individualize instruction so that students are taught the specific sound-spelling patterns they do not know?			
Does the program provide opportunities to practice reading decodable words in isolation as well as in text?			
Does the program include explicit, systematic instruction to support the automatic recognition of high-frequency words, particularly those that are not decodable (e.g., was, of)?			
Does the program teach students to use structural analysis strategies to read multi-syllable words?			
Does the program include explicit instruction In the recognition of syllable types?			
Are there ample opportunities to read multisyllabic words daily?			
Does the program include instruction in using meaningful word parts, such as prefixes, suffixes, and basic roots, to pronounce unknown words and infer word meanings?			
Are word parts that occur with high frequency (such as un, re, and in) introduced over those that occur in only a few words?			
Are decoding and word identification skills and strategies applied while reading connected text that contains many examples of the sound-spelling patterns and word types that have been taught?			
Does the program include instruction and practice activities focused on spelling the same word types that students are taught to decode (e.g., word sorts, word-building activities, analogical reasoning activities)?			
Are students required to apply their word knowledge as they write sentences and more extended writing assignments?			

Figure 10.4.   *(continued)*

FLUENCY INSTRUCTION

Characteristic	Yes	No	Comments (e.g., specific examples, strengths, concerns, questions)
Is fluency assessed regularly?			
Does the program include instruction and activities designed to promote reading fluency?			
Does fluency-based instruction focus on developing accuracy, rate, and prosody?			
Are ample practice materials provided at appropriate reading levels (independent and/or instructional)?			
Does fluency instruction include regular oral reading practice with feedback from a teacher or other more-able reader, including repeated reading of the same text and continuous wide reading for exposure to many different texts?			
Does fluency instruction include modeling and guided practice in fluent, phrased reading with expression, with feedback?			
Do fluency-building routines include goal setting and self-monitoring to promote reading accuracy and rate, including regular timed readings?			

VOCABULARY INSTRUCTION

Characteristic	Yes	No	Comments (e.g., specific examples, strengths, concerns, questions)
Is vocabulary instruction incorporated into the program?			
Are a limited number of words selected for robust, explicit vocabulary instruction?			
Are only important (words students must know to understand a concept or text), useful (words that may be encountered many times), and challenging (e.g., multiple meanings) words taught?			
Is instruction provided to promote the knowledge and use of academic vocabulary, words that students encounter often in academic texts, tests, and other school contexts?			
Does the instructional routine for vocabulary include: introducing the word, presenting a student-friendly explanation, illustrating the word with examples (and non-examples), and checking the students' understanding?			

Figure 10.4. *(continued)*

VOCABULARY INSTRUCTION   *(continued)*

Characteristic	Yes	No	Comments (e.g., specific examples, strengths, concerns, questions)
Is vocabulary instruction provided in the context of read-aloud texts, student-read texts, and content area texts?			
Are vocabulary words reviewed cumulatively?			
Are multiple exposures to vocabulary words provided in different contexts?			
Are there activities for distinguishing and interpreting words with multiple meanings?			
Does the program include the study of word origins, derivations, synonyms, antonyms, and idioms to determine and clarify the meanings of words and phrases?			
Are word-learning strategies taught, and are ample opportunities provided to practice and apply these strategies?			
Is systematic and explicit instruction in morphemic analysis provided to support the understanding of word meanings through knowledge of roots, prefixes, and suffixes?			
Is there explicit instruction in the use and limitations of analyzing context clues to determine word meanings?			
Does the program include the use of grade-appropriate dictionaries as well as student-friendly explanations of word meanings?			
Is vocabulary taught both directly and indirectly?			
Is word awareness supported through strategies such as having students keep vocabulary logs and through practice activities that are engaging, provide multiple exposures to words, encourage deep processing, and connect word meanings to prior knowledge?			
Are opportunities provided to engage in oral vocabulary activities?			
Is high-level terminology used to bring richness of language to the classroom?			
Are there ample activities provided to practice writing vocabulary words in sentences and extended text?			
Is exposure to diverse vocabulary provided through listening and reading both narrative and informational text?			

Figure 10.4.   *(continued)*

COMPREHENSION INSTRUCTION

Characteristic	Yes	No	Comments (e.g., specific examples, strengths, concerns, questions)
Is comprehension monitoring taught?			
Is explicit instruction in reading comprehension strategies provided?			
Are students taught how to determine which strategies to use in different situations (metacognition)?			
Is strategy instruction cumulative over the course of the year?			
Are sufficient opportunities to practice and apply strategies provided?			
Are there ample opportunities to read, discuss, and respond to narrative and informational text?			
Is prior knowledge activated before reading?			
Are there ample opportunities to engage in discussions relating to the meaning of text?			
Does the teacher model making inferences to explain and integrate ideas across a text? Are students taught to connect ideas across a single text and to make inferences by using information from the text along with their background knowledge?			
Is explicit instruction in recognizing different text structures included?			
Are graphic organizers used, including story maps and diagrams of various informational text structures?			
Are there frequent opportunities to discuss elements of narrative text and compare the use of these elements in different narratives?			
Are students taught to generate different kinds of questions and answer their own questions during reading to improve engagement with and processing of text?			
Are opportunities provided to interpret information from charts, graphs, tables, and diagrams and connect it to information in text?			
Is a strategy for finding main ideas explicitly taught (e.g., using pictures, then individual sentences, then paragraphs, etc.)?			
Are ample opportunities provided to employ main idea strategies using increasingly complex texts, including text in which the main ideas are not explicitly stated?			
Are summarization strategies taught? Do students routinely produce written or oral summaries of texts they have read?			
Is there an element of the program that requires students to follow specific oral directions in order to perform or complete activities to promote listening comprehension?			
Are there ample opportunities to listen to text read aloud and to discuss and respond to these texts?			

Figure 10.4. *(continued)*

MOTIVATION AND ENGAGEMENT

Characteristic	Yes	No	Comments (e.g., specific examples, strengths, concerns, questions)
Does the program foster intrinsic motivation in students (e.g., student selection of books, various genres of book titles, multicultural/international book titles, opportunities to learn about topics of significant interest to individual students)?			
Is there a component of the program that fosters extrinsic motivation in students (e.g., external recognition, rewards, or incentives)?			
Are there ample opportunities for students to engage in group activities to promote active student involvement and motivation?			
Are there opportunities for students to set individual goals (usually along with the teacher) and receive feedback on progress toward their goals?			

ASSESSMENT

Characteristic	Yes	No	Comments (e.g., specific examples, strengths, concerns, questions)
Is high-quality assessment included in the program?			
Are the assessment instruments reliable and valid?			
Do the assessments measure progress or mastery of objectives in word identification, fluency, vocabulary, and comprehension?			
Does the program include diagnostic assessments to provide specific information about individual students' instructional needs (such as which sound-spelling patterns or vocabulary words they do not know)?			
Does assessment aid teachers in making individualized instruction decisions?			
Does the program provide teacher guidance in how to use assessment results effectively?			

Figure 10.4.   *(continued)*

PROFESSIONAL DEVELOPMENT FOR THE READING INTERVENTIONIST

Characteristic	Yes	No	Comments (e.g., specific examples, strengths, concerns, questions)
Is professional development available from the publisher or another source to prepare teachers to implement the program with high fidelity?			
Are strategies included for providing in-class coaching or some form of ongoing support as teachers learn to implement the program?			
Are teachers taught how to administer and interpret assessments that accompany the program?			
Is professional development for the program customized to meet the varying needs of the participants (e.g., first-year teachers, coaches, principals)?			
Does the professional development help the teacher understand the rationale for the instructional approach and strategies utilized in the program (e.g., articles, references, and reliable Web sites) as well as how to implement them?			
Does the program provide materials (e.g., principal checklists, a video/CD with modeled lessons, printed teaching charts, graphs, transparencies) to supplement the professional development and facilitate high-fidelity implementation?			

Figure 10.4. *(continued)*

CONCLUSION

Comprehension problems often result from difficulties in quickly and accurately reading words. Students who cannot accurately read the words on the page often have problems with higher-level skills requiring inference and interpretation of text.

Some middle school struggling readers benefit from instruction in word identification. Students who can read simple words quickly and accurately but are inaccurate readers of multisyllable words may need instruction in recognizing common syllable patterns as well as common prefixes and suffixes along with a strategy for reading multisyllable words. Students with more serious word-reading problems may need a highly systematic and explicit intervention program. Decisions about the need for word identification instruction should be based on diagnostic assessments and continuous progress monitoring (see Chapter 3).

It is important to use instructional approaches and published programs supported by evidence from scientific research, especially when instructing struggling readers at the secondary level. These students do not have the luxury of time to experiment with reading programs or instructional approaches that do not have solid evidence of effectiveness from high-quality research. If this kind of evidence is not available, it is necessary to evaluate the components of programs to find out whether they have characteristics that have been identified as essential for the progress of middle school students with severe reading problems. Figure 10.1, which can also be found in the Appendix, can be used to evaluate programs.

References

Anders, P.L. & Bos, C.S. (1986). Semantic feature analysis: An interactive strategy for vocabulary development and text comprehension. *Journal of Reading*, 29, 610–616.

Anderson, J.R. (1980). *Cognitive psychology and its implications.* San Francisco, CA: W.H. Freeman and Co.

Anderson, R.C., & Nagy, W.E. (1992). The vocabulary conundrum. *American Educator, 16,* 14–18, 44–47.

Archer, A.L., Gleason, M.M., & Vachon, V. (2005a). *REWARDS: Multisyllabic word reading strategies.* Longmont, CO: Sopris West.

Archer, A.L., Gleason, M.M., & Vachon, V. (2005b). *REWARDS Plus: Reading strategies applied to social studies passages.* Longmont, CO: Sopris West.

Armbruster, B.B., Lehr, F., & Osborn, J. (2003). *Put reading first: The research building blocks for teaching children to read* (2nd ed.). Washington, DC: National Institute for Literacy.

Baumann, J.F., Font, G., Edwards, E.C., & Boland, E. (2005). Strategies for teaching middle-grade students to use word-part and context clues. In E.H. Hiebert & M.L. Kamil (Eds.), *Teaching and learning vocabulary: Bringing research to practice.* Mahwah, NJ: Lawrence Erlbaum Associates.

Baumann, J.F., & Kame'enui, E.J. (1991). Research on vocabulary instruction: Ode to Voltaire. In J. Flood, J.M. Jenson, D. Lapp, & J.R. Squire (Eds.), *Handbook of research on teaching the language arts* (pp. 602–632). New York, NY: Macmillan.

Baumann, J.F., & Kame'enui, E.J. (2003). *Vocabulary instruction: Research to practice.* New York, NY: Guilford Press.

Bear, D., Invernizzi, M., Templeton, S.R., & Johnston, F. (2003). *Words their way: Word sorts for syllables and affixes spellers.* Upper Saddle River, NJ: Pearson.

Beck, I.L., & McKeown, M.G. (2001). Text talk: Capturing the benefits of read-aloud experiences for young children. *The Reading Teacher,* 55, 10–20.

Beck, I.L., McKeown, M.G., & Kucan, L. (2002). *Bringing words to life: Robust vocabulary instruction.* New York, NY: Guilford.

Betts, E.A. (1946). *Foundations of reading instruction, with emphasis on differentiated guidance.* New York, NY: American Book Company.

Biancarosa, G., & Snow, C.E. (2004). *Reading next: A vision for action and research in middle and high school literacy: A report to Carnegie Corp. of New York.* Washington, DC: Alliance for Excellent Education.

Blachowicz, C.L.Z., & Fisher, P. (2000). Vocabulary instruction. In R. Barr, M.L. Kamil, P.B. Mosenthal, & P.D. Pearson (Eds.), *Handbook of reading research* (Vol. III, pp. 503–523). New York, NY: Longman.

Bos, C.S., & Anders, P.L. (1992). A theory-driven interactive instructional model for text comprehension and content learning. In B.Y.L. Wong (Ed.), *Contemporary intervention research in learning disabilities: An international perspective* (pp. 81–95). New York, NY: Springer-Verlag.

Burns, M.S., Griffin, P., & Snow, C.E. (Eds.). (1999). *Starting out right: A guide to promoting children's reading success.* Washington, DC: National Academy.

Bryant, D.P. (2003). Promoting effective instruction for struggling secondary students: Introduction to the special issue. *Learning Disability Quarterly, 26,* 70–72.

Bryant, D.P., Vaughn, S., Linen-Thompson, S., Ugel, N., Hamff, A., & Hougen, M. (2000). Reading outcomes for students with and without reading disabilities in general education middle-school content area classes. *Learning Disability Quarterly, 23,* 238–252.

Carroll, J.B. (1963). A model of school learning. *Teachers College Record,* 64, 723–733.

Chard, D.J., Vaughn, S., & Tyler, B. (2002). A synthesis of research on effective intervention for building reading fluency with elementary students with learning disabilities. *Journal of Learning Disabilities, 35,* 386–406.

Chomsky, C. (1978). When you still can't read in third grade: After decoding, what? In S.J. Samuels (Ed.), *What research has to say about reading instruction.* Newark, DE: International Reading Association.

Cunningham, P.M., & Allington, R.L. (1999). *Classrooms that work: They can all read and write.* New York, NY: Longman.

Daly, E.J., & Martens, B.K. (1994). A comparison of three interventions for increasing oral reading performance: Application of the instructional hierarchy. *Journal of Applied Behavior Analysis, 27,* 459–469.

Delquadri, J., Greenwood, C.R., Whorton, D., Carta, J.J., & Hall, R.V. (1986). Classwide peer tutoring. *Exceptional Children, 52,* 535–542.

Denton, C.A., Barth, A., Fletcher, J.M., Wexler, J., Vaughn, S., Cirino, P.T., Romain, M., & Francis, D.J. (2011). The relations among oral and silent reading fluency and comprehension in middle school: Implications for identification and instruction of students with reading difficulties. *Scientific Studies of Reading, 15,* 109–135.

Diamond, L., & Gutlohn, L. (2006). *Vocabulary handbook.* Baltimore, MD: Paul H. Brookes Publishing Co.

Dickson, S.V., Simmons, D.C., & Kame'enui, E.J. (1998). Text organization: Research bases (pp. 239–277). In D.C. Simmons & E.J. Kame'enui (Eds.), *What reading research tells us about children with diverse learning needs: Bases and basics.* Mahwah, NJ: Lawrence Erlbaum Associates.

Ebbers, S. (2011). *Vocabulary through morphemes: Suffixes, prefixes, and roots for intermediate and secondary grades* (2nd ed.). Longmont, CO: Cambium Learning/Sopris West.

Ebbers, S.E. (2012, February 19). Invaders of the English language. *Vocabulogic Edublog.* Retrieved May 30, 2012, from http://vocablog-plc.blogspot.com/2012/02/invaders-of-english-language.html

Echevarria, J., Vogt, M.E., & Short, D.J. (2004). *Making content comprehensible for English language learners: The SIOP model* (2nd ed.). Boston, MA: Pearson.

Eischen, C.M. (2006). *Apoptic cell death in controlling lymphomagenesis.* Proposal submitted to the National Institute for Health.

Elbaum, B., Vaughn, S., Hughes, M.T., & Moody, S.W. (1999). Grouping practices and reading outcomes for students with disabilities. *Exceptional Children, 65*(3), 399–415.

Elbaum, B., Vaughn, S., Hughes, M.T., & Moody, S.W. (2000). How effective are one-to-one tutoring programs in reading for elementary students at risk for reading failure? A meta-analysis of the intervention research. *Journal of Educational Psychology, 92*(4), 605–619.

Espin, C.A., & Foegen, A. (1996). Validity of three general outcome measures for predicting secondary students' performance on content-area tasks. *Exceptional Children, 62,* 497–514.

Feldman, K., & Kinsella, K. (2005). *Narrowing the language gap: The case for explicit vocabulary instruction.* New York, NY: Scholastic.

Frayer, D.A., Frederick, W.C., & Klausmeier, H.G. (1969). *A schema for testing the level of concept mastery (Technical report No. 16).* Madison, WI: University of Wisconsin Research Development Center for Cognitive Learning.

Fry, E.B., & Kress, J.E. (2006). *The reading teacher's book of lists.* San Francisco, CA: Jossey-Bass.

Fuchs, L.S., Fuchs, D., Hosp, M.K., & Jenkins, J.R. (2001). Oral reading fluency as an indicator of reading competence: A theoretical, empirical, and historical analysis. *Scientific Studies of Reading, 5,* 239–256.

Fuchs, L.S., Fuchs, D., & Kazdan, S. (1999). Effects of peer-assisted learning strategies on high school students with serious reading problems. *Remedial and Special Education, 20,* 309–318.

Fuchs, D., Fuchs, L.S., Thompson, A., Svenson, E., Yen, L., Al Otaiba, S., & ... Saenz, L. (2001). Peer-assisted learning strategies in reading: Extensions for kindergarten, first grade, and high school. *Remedial and Special Education, 22*(1), 15–21.

Gambrell, L.B., & Bales, R.J. (1986). Mental imagery and the comprehension-monitoring performance of fourth- and fifth-grade poor readers. *Reading Research Quarterly, 21,* 454–464.

Garcia, G.E. (2003). The reading comprehension development and instruction of English-language learners. In A.P. Sweet & C.E. Snow (Eds.), *Rethinking reading comprehension* (pp. 30–50). New York, NY: Guilford.

Graves, M.F., Juel, C., & Graves, B.B. (1998). *Teaching reading in the 21st century.* Needham Heights, MA: Allyn and Bacon.

Greenwood, C.R., Delquadri, J.C., & Hall, R.V. (1989). Longitudinal effects of classwide peer tutoring. *Journal of Educational Psychology, 81,* 371–383.

Grognet, A., Jameson, J., Franco, L., & Derrcki-Mescua, M. (2000). *Enhancing English language learning in elementary classrooms.* McHenry, IL: Center for Applied Linguistics and Delta Systems.

Guthrie, J.T., Schafer, W.D., Von Secker, C., & Alban, T. (2000). Contributions of integrated reading instruction and text resources to achievement and engagement in a statewide school improvement program. *Journal of Educational Research, 93,* 211–226.

Hammil, D.D., Wiederholt, J.L., & Allen, E.A. (2006). *Test of Silent Contextual Reading Fluency.* Austin, TX: PRO-ED.

Heimlich, J.E., & Pittelman, S.D. (1986). *Semantic mapping: Classroom applications.* Newark, DE: International Reading Association.

Johnson, D., Pittelman, S., & Heimlich, J. (1986). Semantic mapping. *The Reading Teacher, 29,* 778–783.

Jones, B.F., Pierce, J., & Hunter, B. (1988). Teaching students to construct graphic representations. *Educational Leadership, 46*(4), 20–25.

Kame'enui, E.J., & Carnine, D.W. (1998). *Effective teaching strategies that accommodate diverse learners.* Upper Saddle River, NJ: Prentice-Hall.

Kim, A.H., Vaughn, S., Wanzek, J., & Wei, S. (2004). Graphic organizers and their effects on the reading comprehension of students with LD: A synthesis of research. *Journal of Learning Disabilities, 37*(2), 105–118.

Klingner, J.K., & Vaughn, S. (1996). Reciprocal teaching of reading comprehension strategies for students with learning disabilities who use English as a second language. *Elementary School Journal, 96*(3), 275–293.

Klingner, J.K., Vaughn, S., Dimino, J., Schumm, J.S., & Bryant, D. (2001). *Collaborative strategic reading: Strategies for improving comprehension.* Longmont, CO: Sopris West.

Klingner, J.K., Vaughn, S., & Schumm, J.S. (1998). Collaborative strategic reading during social studies in heterogeneous fourth-grade classrooms. *Elementary School Journal, 99,* 3–22.

LaPray, M., & Ross, R. (1969). The graded word list: Quick gauge of reading ability. *Journal of Reading, 12*(4), 305–307.

Lehr, F., Osborn, J., & Hiebert, E.H. (2004). *A focus on vocabulary.* Honolulu, HI: Pacific Resources for Education and Learning.

Lowry, L. (1989). *Number the stars.* New York, NY: Bantam Doubleday Dell Books for Young Readers.

Lyon, G.R., & Moats, L.C. (1997). Critical conceptual and methodological considerations in reading intervention research. *Journal of Learning Disabilities, 30*(6), 578–588.

Mastropieri, M.A., & Scruggs, T.E. (2002). *Effective instruction for special education.* Austin, TX: ProEd.

Mather, N., Hammill, D.D. Allen, E.A., & Roberts, R. (2004). *Test of Silent Word Reading Fluency.* Austin, TX: PRO-ED.

McCray, A.D., Vaughn, S., & Neal, L.I. (2001). Not all students learn to read by third grade: Middle school students speak out about their reading disabilities. *Journal of Special Education, 35*(1), 17–30.

McNeil, J.D. (1992). *Reading comprehension: New directions for classroom practice* (3rd ed.). New York, NY: Harper Collins.

Moats, L.C. (2001). When older students can't read. *Educational Leadership, 58*(6), 36–40.

Moore, D.W., & Moore, S.A. (1986). Possible sentences. In E.K. Dishner, T.W. Bean, J.E. Readence, & D.W. Moore (Eds.), *Reading in the content areas* (pp. 174–178). Dubuque, IA: Kendall-Hunt.

Muniz-Swicegood, M. (1994). The effects of metacognitive reading strategy training on the reading performance and fluent reading analysis strategies of third-grade bilingual students. *Bilingual Research Journal, 18,* 83–97.

National Center for Education Statistics. (2011). *The nation's report card: Reading 2011* (NCES 2012–457). Washington, DC: U.S. Department of Education, Institute of Education Sciences.

National Institute of Child Health and Human Development. (2000). *Report of the National Reading Panel. Teaching children to read: An evidence-based assessment of the scientific research literature on reading and its implications for reading instruction* (NIH Publication No. 00-4769). Washington, DC: U.S. Government Printing Office

O'Connor, R.E., Swanson, H.L., & Geraghty, C. (2010). Improvement in reading rate under independent and difficult text levels: Influences on word and comprehension skills. *Journal of Educational Psychology, 102*(1), 1–19.

Oxford Advanced Learner's Dictionary (7th ed.). (2007). Retrieved January 15, 2007, from http://www.oup.com/elt/catalogue/teachersites/oald7/?cc=global

Palinscar, A.S., & Brown, A.L. (1989). Classroom dialogues to promote self-regulated comprehension. In J. Brophy (Ed.), *Advances in research on teaching* (pp. 35–71). New York, NY: JAI.

Pressley, M., Wood, W., Woloshyn, V.E., Martin, V., King, A., & Menke, D. (1992). Encouraging mindful use of prior knowledge: Attempting to construct explanatory answers facilitates learning. *Educational Psychologist, 27*(1), 91–109.

Raphael, T.E. (1986). Teaching question answer relationships, revisited. *Reading Teacher, 39*(6), 516–522.

Raphael, T.E., & Au, K.H. (2005). QAR: Enhancing comprehension and test taking across grades and content areas. *Reading Teacher, 59*(3), 206–221.

Raphael, T.E., & Pearson, P.D. (1985). Increasing students' awareness of sources of information for answering questions. *American Educational Research Journal, 22,* 217–235.

Rasinski, T.V. (2004). *Assessing reading fluency.* Honolulu, HI: Pacific Resources for Education and Learning.

Rasinksi, T.V., Padak, N.D., McKeon, C.A., Wilfong, L.G., Friedaur, J.A., & Heim, P. (2005). Is reading fluency a key for successful high school reading? *Journal of Adolescent and Adult Literacy, 49,* 22–27.

Reed, D. (2004). Unpublished supplemental material produced for SEDL.

Reed, J.H., Schallert, D.L, Beth, A.D., & Woodruff, A.L. (2004). Motivated reader, engaged writer: The role of motivation in the literate acts of adolescents. In T.L. Jetton & J.A. Dole (Eds.), *Adolescent literacy research and practice* (pp. 251–282). New York, NY: Guilford.

Reyes, E.I., & Bos, C.C. (1998). Interactive semantic mapping and charting: Enhancing content area learning for language minority students. In R. Gersten & R. Jiminez (Eds.), *Innovative practices for language minority students.* Pacific Grove, CA: Brooks/Cole.

Rinehart, S.D. (1999). "Don't think for a minute that I'm getting up there": Opportunities for reader's theater in a tutorial for children with reading problems. *Journal of Reading Psychology, 20,* 71–89.

Rivera, M.O., Moughamian, A.C., Lesaux, N.K., & Francis, D.J. (2008). *Language and reading interventions for English language learners and English language learners with disabilities.* Portsmouth, NH: RMC Research Corporation, Center on Instruction.

Rosenshine, B., Meister, C., & Chapman, S. (1996). Teaching students to generate questions: A review of the intervention studies. *Review of Educational Research, 66*(2), 181–221.

Rumelhart, D.E. (1980). Schemata: The building blocks of cognition. In R.J. Spiro, B.C. Bruce, & W.F. Brewer (Eds.), *Theoretical issues in reading comprehension* (pp. 33–58). Mahwah, NJ: Lawrence Erlbaum Associates.

Sachar, L. (1998). *Holes.* New York, NY: Scholastic.

Saenz, L.M., & Fuchs, L.S. (2002). Examining the reading difficulty of secondary students with learning disabilities: Expository versus narrative text. *Remedial & Special Education, 23*(1), 31–41.

Samuels, S.J. (1979). The method of repeated readings. *The Reading Teacher, 32,* 403–408.

Samuels, S.J. (1994). Toward a theory of automatic information processing in reading, revisited. In R.B. Ruddell, M.R. Ruddell, & H. Singer (Eds.), *Theoretical models and processes of reading* (4th ed., pp. 816–861). Newark, DE: International Reading Association.

Scanlon, D.J., Duran, G.Z., Reyes, E.I., & Gallego, M.A. (1992). Interactive semantic mapping: An interactive approach to enhancing LD students' content area comprehension. *Learning Disabilities and Research Practice, 7,* 142–146.

Schifini, A. (1994). Language, literacy, and content instruction: Strategies for teachers. In K. Spangenberg-Urbschat & R. Pritchard (Eds.), *Kids come in all languages: Reading instruction of ESL students* (pp. 158–179). Newark, DE: International Reading Association.

Schwartz, N.H., Ellsworth, L.S., Graham, L., & Knight, B. (1998). Accessing prior knowledge to remember text: A comparison of advance organizers and maps. *Contemporary Educational Psychology, 23,* 65–89.

Science Explorer: Grade 7. (2002). Upper Saddle River, NJ: Prentice-Hall.

Shin, J., Deno, S.L., & Espin, C. (2000). Technical adequacy of the maze tasks for curriculum-based measurement of reading growth. *Journal of Special Education, 34,* 164–172.

Simmons, D., Rupley, W., & Vaughn, S. (2006). Materials developed by the Teacher Quality Research Project through funding from the U.S. Department of Education's Institute of Education Sciences, grant contract number R305M050121A (*Enhancing the quality of expository text instruction and comprehension through content and case-situated professional development*).

Snow, C.E., Burns, S., & Griffin, P. (Eds.). (1998). *Preventing reading difficulties in young children.* Washington, DC: National Academy.

Sperry, A. (1984). The ghost of the lagoon. In C.G. Waugh & M.H. Greenberg (Eds.), *The Newbery Award Reader: A collection of short fiction by writers who have won the John Newbery Medal* (pp. 261–270). Orlando, FL: Harcourt Brace Jovanovich.

Stahl, S.A. (1999). *Vocabulary development.* Newton Upper Falls, MA: Brookline Books.

Stahl, S.A. (2003). How words are learned incrementally over multiple exposures. *American Educator, 27*(1), 18–19, 44.

Stahl, S.A., & Fairbanks, M.M. (1986). The effects of vocabulary instruction: A model-based meta-analysis. *Review of Educational Research, 56*(1), 72–110.

Stahl, S.A., & Kapinus, B.A. (1991). Possible sentences: Predicting word meanings to teach content area vocabulary. *The Reading Teacher, 45,* 36–43.

Stahl, S.A., & Kapinus, B.A. (2001). *Word power: What every educator needs to know about teaching vocabulary.* Washington, DC: National Education Association.

Stahl, S.A., & Vancil, S.J. (1986). Discussion is what makes semantic maps work in vocabulary instruction. *Reading Teacher, 40*(1), 62–67.

Stanovich, K.E. (1986). Matthew effects in reading: Some consequences of individual differences in the acquisition of literacy. *Reading Research Quarterly, 31,* 360–397.

Sternberg, R.J. (1987). Most vocabulary is learned from context. In M.G. McKeown & M.E. Curtin (Eds.), *The nature of vocabulary acquisitions* (pp. 89–106). Mahwah, NJ: Lawrence Erlbaum Associates.

Swan, E.A., (2004). Motivating adolescent readers through concept-oriented reading instruction. In T.L. Jetton & J.A. Dole (Eds.), *Adolescent literacy research and practice.* New York, NY: Guilford.

Swanson, H.L., & Deshler, D. (2003). Instructing adolescents with learning disabilities: Converting a meta-analysis to practice. *Journal of Learning, 36,* 124–135.

Taboada, A., & Guthrie, J.T. (2006). Contributions of student questioning and prior knowledge to construction of knowledge from reading information text. *Journal of Literacy Research, 38*(1), 1–35.

Tan, A. (1989). *The joy luck club.* New York, NY: Putnam.

Texas Reading Initiative. (2000). *Promoting vocabulary development: Components of effective vocabulary instruction.* Austin, TX: Texas Education Agency.

Therrien, W.J., Wickstrom, K., & Jones, K. (2006). Effect of a combined repeated reading and question generation intervention on reading achievement. *Learning Disabilities Research & Practice, 21*(2), 89–97.

University of Texas Center for Reading and Language Arts. (2003a). *Meeting the needs of struggling readers: A resource for secondary English language arts teachers.* Austin, TX: Author.

University of Texas Center for Reading and Language Arts. (2003b). *Special education reading project (SERP) secondary institute—Effective instruction for secondary struggling readers: Research-based practices.* Austin, TX: Author.

Vaughn Gross Center for Reading and Language Arts at the University of Texas at Austin. (2005). *Introduction to the 3-tier reading model: Reducing reading difficulties for kindergarten through third grade students* (4th ed.). Austin, TX: Author.

Vaughn, S., & Bos, C.S. (2012). *Strategies for teaching students with learning and behavior problems* (8th ed.). Boston, MA: Pearson.

Vaughn, S., & Klingner, J.K. (1999). Teaching reading comprehension through collaborative strategic reading. *Intervention in School and Clinic, 43*, 284–292.

Vaughn, S., Klingner, J.K., & Schumm, J.S. (1996). *Collaborative strategic reading.* Miami, FL: School-Based Research, University of Miami.

Vaughn, S., & Linan-Thompson, S. (2004). *Research-based methods of reading instruction.* Alexandria, VA: Association for Supervision and Curriculum Development.

Vaughn, S., Linan-Thompson, S., Louzekanani, K., Bryant, D.P., Dickinson, S., & Blozis, S.A. (2003). Reading instruction grouping for students with reading difficulties. *Remedial and Special Education, 24*(5), 301–315.

Wagner, R.K., Torgesen, J.K., Rashotte, C.A., Hecht, S.A., Barker, T.A., Burgess, S.R., et al. (1997). Changing relations between phonological processing abilities and word-level reading as children develop from beginning to skilled readers: A 5-year longitudinal study. *Developmental Psychology, 33*(3), 468–79.

Wagner, R.K., Torgesen, J.K., Rashotte, C.A., & Pearson, N. (2010). *The Test of Silent Reading Efficiency and Comprehension.* Austin, TX: PRO-ED.

Wexler, J., Wanzek, J. & Vaughn, S. (2009). Preventing and remediating reading difficulties for elementary and secondary students. In G.D. Sideridis and T.A. Citro (Eds.), *Strategies in reading for struggling learners.* Lanham, MD: Rowman & Littlefield.

White, T.G., Sowell, J., & Yanagihara, A. (1989). Teaching elementary students to use word-part clues. *The Reading Teacher, 42*, 302–307.

Wiley, H.I., & Deno, S.L. (2005). Oral reading and maze measures as predictors of success for English learners on a state standards assessment. *Remedial and Special Education, 26*, 207–214.

Williamson, G.L. (2006, April). *Student readiness for postsecondary endeavors.* Paper presented at the Annual Meeting of the American Educational Research Association, San Francisco, CA.

Wood, K.D., & Harmon, J.M. (2001). *Strategies for integrating reading and writing in middle and high school classrooms.* Westerville, OH: National Middle School Association.

Worthy, J., & Broaddus, K. (2002). Fluency beyond the primary grades: From group performance to silent independent reading. *Reading Teacher, 55*, 334–343.

Yates, E. (1950). *Amos Fortune, free man.* New York, NY: Aladdin Books.

Appendix

CONTENTS

Planning Checklist for
Implementing Schoolwide Reading Intervention

STEP 1. SELF-EVALUATION: REVIEW CURRENT READING PRACTICES WITHIN THE SCHOOL TO DETERMINE NEEDS AND PRIORITIES

☐ Does the school have a unified vision and plan for ensuring that all students are able to read and learn from academic text and are motivated to read? Are administrators and teachers committed to implementing the plan?

☐ Is there a safe and positive school environment that is conducive to learning?

☐ Do teachers and administrators have high academic standards for their students based on grade-level expectations?

☐ Do teachers provide effective instruction supported by strong instructional leadership from the principal or another person or persons in the school?

☐ Is academic achievement given priority in scheduling, budgeting, and allocation of personnel?

☐ Do content-area teachers consistently teach and encourage students to implement evidence-based vocabulary and comprehension strategies? Is the same limited set of strategies used across all classes?

☐ Are benchmark reading assessments administered three times per year to identify students who need supplemental reading classes or intervention?

☐ Do reading teachers or tutors implement research-supported programs and teaching approaches to provide strategic intervention to students who perform somewhat below grade level and have problems comprehending academic text?

☐ Do reading teachers or other teachers implement research-supported, explicit, systematic reading programs to provide intensive intervention to students with more severe reading difficulties?

☐ Is the progress of students in strategic and intensive intervention monitored regularly to determine whether they are responding adequately to intervention?

STEP 2. DEVELOP A PLAN FOR COLLECTING, MANAGING, AND USING BENCHMARK AND PROGRESS-MONITORING DATA

☐ Who will administer benchmark assessments?

☐ Who will organize the results and analyze them to determine which students need strategic or intensive intervention?

☐ Reading teachers or interventionists should administer progress-monitoring assessments but may need some assistance. If so, who will assist them?

☐ Who will compile progress-monitoring data and display them as easily interpreted graphs or in other accessible formats?

☐ It is recommended that groups of reading teachers, other teachers, and, ideally, administrators meet regularly to examine the progress-monitoring data so that they can identify students who are not making adequate progress and collaborate to make plans for accelerating the progress of these students. Who will organize these meetings?

Adapted with permission from the Vaughn Gross Center for Reading and Language Arts at the University of Texas at Austin. (2005).
Introduction to the 3-Tier reading model: Reducing reading difficulties for kindergarten through third grade students (4th ed.). Austin, TX: Author.

In *Effective Instruction for Middle School Students with Reading Difficulties: The Reading Teacher's Sourcebook*
by Carolyn A. Denton, Sharon Vaughn, Jade Wexler, Deanna Bryan, and Deborah Reed (2012).
Published by Paul H. Brookes Publishing Co., Inc. 1-800-638-3775; www.brookespublishing.com

STEP 3. DEVELOP A SCHOOLWIDE PLAN FOR IMPLEMENTING CONTENT-AREA STRATEGIES AND ROUTINES

☐ If there is a need for professional development in a system of positive behavioral supports to ensure a safe and positive school environment, then who will provide this professional development and who will ensure that the system is implemented?

☐ Is there a plan for providing quality professional development to content-area teachers to prepare them to incorporate evidence-based vocabulary and comprehension strategies and to use collaborative grouping to increase active student involvement? Does this plan include ongoing support in the form of regular study group sessions and/or coaching?

☐ Are content-area teachers committed to implementing research-based strategies and routines across classes to ensure that students learn key vocabulary and are able to read and understand academic text in each discipline?

☐ Are content-area and reading teachers given adequate time to plan and collaborate to overcome obstacles to integrating these strategies and routines into their instruction?

☐ Is a system established for problem solving and decision making related to this component of school-wide intervention?

STEP 4. DEVELOP A PLAN FOR IMPLEMENTING STRATEGIC INTERVENTION

☐ Who will provide strategic intervention?

☐ Will strategic intervention take place in reading classes or in tutoring sessions?

☐ How will class sizes of 12–18 students be ensured?

☐ When will strategic intervention be provided?

☐ Where will strategic intervention be implemented?

☐ Is a system in place for monitoring the progress of strategic intervention students between one and two times per month and using the results to guide instructional decisions?

☐ Are criteria established for entry and exit from strategic intervention?

☐ How will assessment data be used to group and regroup students, to plan targeted instruction, and to make adaptations to ensure students meet grade-level benchmarks and/or objectives?

☐ Is a system established for problem solving and decision making related to strategic intervention?

☐ Is time provided for collaboration among reading intervention teachers?

☐ Who will ensure that reading interventionists receive quality professional development emphasizing scientific research-based programs and practices in teaching students with reading difficulties? Who will provide them with ongoing support?

Adapted with permission from the Vaughn Gross Center for Reading and Language Arts at the University of Texas at Austin. (2005). *Introduction to the 3-Tier reading model: Reducing reading difficulties for kindergarten through third grade students* (4th ed.). Austin, TX: Author.

(page 2 of 3)

In *Effective Instruction for Middle School Students with Reading Difficulties: The Reading Teacher's Sourcebook* by Carolyn A. Denton, Sharon Vaughn, Jade Wexler, Deanna Bryan, and Deborah Reed (2012). Published by Paul H. Brookes Publishing Co., Inc. 1-800-638-3775; www.brookespublishing.com

239

STEP 5. DEVELOP A PLAN FOR IMPLEMENTING INTENSIVE INTERVENTION

☐   Who will provide intensive intervention (e.g., reading teacher, special education teacher, other well-qualified teacher)?

☐   When and how often will intensive intervention be provided?

☐   Where will intensive intervention be implemented?

☐   What scientific research-based, explicit, systematic program(s) will be used to provide intensive intervention?

☐   Has the relationship of intensive intervention with Section 504 and special education services been clarified?

☐   Is a system in place for monitoring the progress of intensive intervention students between two and four times per month and using the results to guide instructional decisions?

☐   Are criteria established for entry and exit from intensive intervention?

☐   How will assessment data be used to plan targeted instruction and to make adaptations to ensure students meet grade-level benchmarks and/or objectives?

☐   Is a system established for problem solving and decision making related to intensive intervention?

☐   Is time provided for collaboration among intervention teachers?

☐   Who will ensure that intensive intervention teachers receive quality professional development emphasizing scientific research-based programs and practices in teaching students with reading difficulties? Who will provide them with ongoing support?

Adapted with permission from the Vaughn Gross Center for Reading and Language Arts at the University of Texas at Austin. (2005). *Introduction to the 3-Tier reading model: Reducing reading difficulties for kindergarten through third grade students* (4th ed.). Austin, TX: Author.

(page 3 of 3)

Accuracy Guidelines

INDEPENDENT LEVEL

No more than 1 in 20 words is difficult.   95%–100% accuracy

INSTRUCTIONAL LEVEL

No more than 1 in 10 words is difficult.   90%–94% accuracy

FRUSTRATION LEVEL

Difficulty with more than 1 in 10 words.   ≤ 90% accuracy

Source: Betts, 1946.

(page 1 of 1)

Sample Instructional Sequence for Reading Instruction (Based on a 45-minute class)

EVERY DAY FOR THE FIRST 4–6 WEEKS OF INTERVENTION

COMPONENTS	TIME RANGE (IN MINS.)
Fluency (partner reading)	7–10
Vocabulary instruction (prefixes, suffixes, base words, and roots)	8–10
Multisyllable word reading instruction and practice	18–24
Spelling dictation	4–6

SAMPLE WEEKLY SCHEDULE FOR REMAINDER OF INTERVENTION

COMPONENTS	TIME RANGE (IN MINS.)
MONDAY	
Fluency (if needed) or other text reading (partner reading)	7–10
Multisyllable word reading practice or vocabulary word part review	6–8
Vocabulary instruction	15–25
Spelling dictation	6–8
TUESDAY	
Fluency (if needed) or other text reading (partner reading)	7–10
Vocabulary review and practice	5–7
Comprehension strategy instruction (modeling and guided practice)	10–15
Passage reading, applying comprehension strategy	15–20
WEDNESDAY	
Fluency (if needed) or other text reading (partner reading)	7–10
Vocabulary review and practice	5–7
Comprehension strategy instruction, continued	8–10
Passage reading, applying comprehension strategy	20–25
THURSDAY	
Fluency (if needed) or other text reading (partner reading)	7–10
Multisyllable word reading practice or vocabulary word part review	6–8
Vocabulary review and practice	8–10
Comprehension strategy instruction, continued; passage reading, applying comprehension strategy	25–35
FRIDAY	
Fluency (if needed) or other text reading (partner reading)	7–10
Comprehension review	6–8
Expository writing (Write a summary of the passage or write an essay using the same text structure as the passage, guided by a graphic organizer.)	25–35

(page 1 of 1)

Guide to Adapting Instruction

ADAPTATION CATEGORY	DEFINITION	EXAMPLES
Instructional Content	Skills and concepts that are the focus of teaching and learning	Determining main ideas Reading words with closed syllable patterns Summarization
Instructional Activity	The actual lessons used to teach and reinforce skills and concepts	Semantic mapping Main idea strategy lesson Teaching the multisyllable word reading strategy
Delivery of Instruction	The procedures and routines used to teach instructional activities	Grouping—whole class, small group, or partners Modeling and thinking aloud Connecting to background knowledge Multiple opportunities for practice
Instructional Materials	Supplemental aids that are used to teach and reinforce skills and concepts	Narrative or expository text Manipulatives Charts Flashcards Recorded text

Adapted with permission from The University of Texas Center for Reading and Language Arts. (2003b). *Special education reading project (SERP) secondary institute—Effective instruction for secondary struggling readers. Research-based practices.* Austin, TX. Author.

(page 1 of 1)

In *Effective Instruction for Middle School Students with Reading Difficulties: The Reading Teacher's Sourcebook*
by Carolyn A. Denton, Sharon Vaughn, Jade Wexler, Deanna Bryan, and Deborah Reed (2012).
Published by Paul H. Brookes Publishing Co., Inc. 1-800-638-3775; www.brookespublishing.com

243

Characteristics of Effective Readers

COMPREHENSION

- Establish a purpose for reading.
- Activate background knowledge.
- Monitor reading for understanding.
- Construct mental images while reading.
- Identify main idea and supporting details.
- Summarize text.
- Generate and answer questions.
- Recognize text structure.
- Distinguish fact and opinion.

VOCABULARY

- Use background knowledge to understand word meaning.
- Are aware of multiple-meaning words.
- Are aware of word origins.
- Understand word parts.
- Generalize word meanings across content areas.
- Use strategies to understand new word meaning.
- Are motivated to learn new words.

FLUENCY

- Read 100–150 words per minute.
- Have automatic word recognition skills.
- Self-correct.
- Group words into meaningful chunks.
- Read with expression.
- Chunk words into meaningful phrases.
- Demonstrate prosody: the ability to interpret reading cues such as punctuation with appropriate pauses, stops and intonation.
- Understand that reading practice leads to fluent reading.

WORD RECOGNITION

- Apply knowledge of letter-sound correspondence in order to recognize words.
- Use structural analysis to recognize words.
- Use knowledge of word parts to identify words.

Adapted with permission from The University of Texas Center for Reading and Language Arts. (2003b). *Special education reading project (SERP) secondary institute—Effective instruction for secondary struggling readers: Research-based practices.* Austin, TX: Author.

(page 1 of 1)

In *Effective Instruction for Middle School Students with Reading Difficulties: The Reading Teacher's Sourcebook*
by Carolyn A. Denton, Sharon Vaughn, Jade Wexler, Deanna Bryan, and Deborah Reed (2012).
Published by Paul H. Brookes Publishing Co., Inc. 1-800-638-3775; www.brookespublishing.com

Previewing Planning Sheet

1. ## Preteach proper nouns or critical concept nouns.

   Introduce, read, and define. Students write brief definitions in learning log.

   Who:

   Where:

   What:

2. ## Preview text.

   Introduce the big idea of the text selection.

   What is the most important idea that you want all students to understand and remember from this reading?

   Important key concepts, subheadings, bolded print, etc.

   Connections to prior learning:

Adapted with permission from materials developed by the Teacher Quality Research Project through funding from the U.S. Department of Education's Institute of Education Sciences, grant contract number R305M050121A (*Enhancing the quality of expository text instruction and comprehension through content and case-situated professional development*; Simmons, D., Vaughn, S., & Edmonds, M., 2006). *(page 1 of 1)*

In *Effective Instruction for Middle School Students with Reading Difficulties: The Reading Teacher's Sourcebook*
by Carolyn A. Denton, Sharon Vaughn, Jade Wexler, Deanna Bryan, and Deborah Reed (2012).
Published by Paul H. Brookes Publishing Co., Inc. 1-800-638-3775; www.brookespublishing.com

245

Multisyllable Word Reading Strategy

1. Find the vowels.

2. Look for word parts you know.

3. Read each word part.

4. Read the parts quickly.

5. Make it sound like a real word.

From Archer, A.L., Gleason, M.M., & Vachon, V. (2005a). *REWARDS: Multisyllabic word reading strategies.* Longmont, CO: Sopris West; adapted by permission.

(page 1 of 1)

In *Effective Instruction for Middle School Students with Reading Difficulties: The Reading Teacher's Sourcebook*
by Carolyn A. Denton, Sharon Vaughn, Jade Wexler, Deanna Bryan, and Deborah Reed (2012).
Published by Paul H. Brookes Publishing Co., Inc. 1-800-638-3775; www.brookespublishing.com

Preview and Questioning Learning Log

Name: _____ Partner's name: _____ Date: _____

Chapter or selection name: _____

Unfamiliar Proper Nouns or Big-Idea Words	
1.	☐ Person ☐ Place ☐ Thing/event
2.	☐ Person ☐ Place ☐ Thing/event
3.	☐ Person ☐ Place ☐ Thing/event
4.	☐ Person ☐ Place ☐ Thing/event

What is the topic (or "big idea") of the selection?

What do I already know about the topic?

Make a prediction: What will I learn about the topic?

Generate three questions about the important ideas (use *who, what, when, where, why,* and *how*).

Level ___ 1.	
Answer:	*Provide the evidence! How do you know that?*

Level ___ 2.	
Answer:	*Provide the evidence! How do you know that?*

Level ___ 3.	
Answer:	*Provide the evidence! How do you know that?*

Adapted with permission from materials developed by the Teacher Quality Research Project through funding from the U.S. Department of Education's Institute of Education Sciences, grant contract number R305M050121A (*Enhancing the quality of expository text instruction and comprehension through content and case-situated professional development;* Simmons, D., Vaughn, S., & Edmonds, M., 2006).

(page 1 of 1)

Planning Sheet

LEVEL 1 QUESTIONS

1. **Preteach proper nouns or critical concept nouns.**

    Introduce, read, and define. Students write brief definition in learning log.

    Who:

    Where:

    What:

2. **Preview text.**

    Introduce the big idea of the text selection.

    What is the most important idea that you want all students to understand and remember from this reading?

    Important key concepts, subheadings, bolded print, etc.

    Connections to prior learning:

3. **Model Level 1 questions.**

    Questions to use as examples:

Adapted with permission from materials developed by the Teacher Quality Research Project through funding from the U.S. Department of Education's Institute of Education Sciences, grant contract number R305M050121A (*Enhancing the quality of expository text instruction and comprehension through content and case-situated professional development*; Simmons, D., Vaughn, S., & Edmonds, M., 2006).

(page 1 of 1)

In *Effective Instruction for Middle School Students with Reading Difficulties: The Reading Teacher's Sourcebook*
by Carolyn A. Denton, Sharon Vaughn, Jade Wexler, Deanna Bryan, and Deborah Reed (2012).
Published by Paul H. Brookes Publishing Co., Inc. 1-800-638-3775; www.brookespublishing.com

Level 1: Right-There Questions

☐ Questions can be answered in one word or one sentence.

☐ Answers can be found word-for-word in the text.

⋏ Who?　⋏ Where?

⋏ What?　⋏ Why?

⋏ When?　⋏ How?

Effective Instruction for Middle School Students with Reading Difficulties, Denton et al., Brookes Publishing Co. (2012).

Level 1: Right-There Questions

☐ Questions can be answered in one word or one sentence.

☐ Answers can be found word-for-word in the text.

⋏ Who?　⋏ Where?

⋏ What?　⋏ Why?

⋏ When?　⋏ How?

Effective Instruction for Middle School Students with Reading Difficulties, Denton et al., Brookes Publishing Co. (2012).

Level 1: Right-There Questions

☐ Questions can be answered in one word or one sentence.

☐ Answers can be found word-for-word in the text.

⋏ Who?　⋏ Where?

⋏ What?　⋏ Why?

⋏ When?　⋏ How?

Effective Instruction for Middle School Students with Reading Difficulties, Denton et al., Brookes Publishing Co. (2012).

Level 1: Right-There Questions

☐ Questions can be answered in one word or one sentence.

☐ Answers can be found word-for-word in the text.

⋏ Who?　⋏ Where?

⋏ What?　⋏ Why?

⋏ When?　⋏ How?

Effective Instruction for Middle School Students with Reading Difficulties, Denton et al., Brookes Publishing Co. (2012).

*Photocopy on red card stock.

Adapted with permission from materials developed by the Teacher Quality Research Project through funding from the U.S. Department of Education's Institute of Education Sciences, grant contract number R305M050121A (*Enhancing the quality of expository text instruction and comprehension through content and case-situated professional development*; Simmons, D., Vaughn, S., & Edmonds, M., 2006).

(page 1 of 1)

In *Effective Instruction for Middle School Students with Reading Difficulties: The Reading Teacher's Sourcebook*
by Carolyn A. Denton, Sharon Vaughn, Jade Wexler, Deanna Bryan, and Deborah Reed (2012).
Published by Paul H. Brookes Publishing Co., Inc. 1-800-638-3775; www.brookespublishing.com

249

Right-There Question Cards (Back)*

Level 1: Examples

- ☐ What is the primary responsibility of the judicial branch of the federal government?

- ☐ Who was David Crockett?

- ☐ When did Texas become a state?

Effective Instruction for Middle School Students with Reading Difficulties, Denton et al., Brookes Publishing Co. (2012).

Level 1: Examples

- ☐ What is the primary responsibility of the judicial branch of the federal government?

- ☐ Who was David Crockett?

- ☐ When did Texas become a state?

Effective Instruction for Middle School Students with Reading Difficulties, Denton et al., Brookes Publishing Co. (2012).

Level 1: Examples

- ☐ What is the primary responsibility of the judicial branch of the federal government?

- ☐ Who was David Crockett?

- ☐ When did Texas become a state?

Effective Instruction for Middle School Students with Reading Difficulties, Denton et al., Brookes Publishing Co. (2012).

Level 1: Examples

- ☐ What is the primary responsibility of the judicial branch of the federal government?

- ☐ Who was David Crockett?

- ☐ When did Texas become a state?

Effective Instruction for Middle School Students with Reading Difficulties, Denton et al., Brookes Publishing Co. (2012).

*Photocopy on red card stock.

Adapted with permission from materials developed by the Teacher Quality Research Project through funding from the U.S. Department of Education's Institute of Education Sciences, grant contract number R305M050121A (*Enhancing the quality of expository text instruction and comprehension through content and case-situated professional development*; Simmons, D., Vaughn, S., & Edmonds, M., 2006).

(page 1 of 1)

Putting-It-Together Question Cards (Front)*

Level 2: Putting It Together

- ☐ Questions can be answered by looking in the text.
- ☐ Answers require one or more sentences.
- ☐ To answer the questions, you have to look in more than one place and put information together.

  - ⋀ Who?
  - ⋀ What?
  - ⋀ When?
  - ⋀ Where?
  - ⋀ Why?
  - ⋀ How?

Effective Instruction for Middle School Students with Reading Difficulties, Denton et al., Brookes Publishing Co. (2012).

Level 2: Putting It Together

- ☐ Questions can be answered by looking in the text.
- ☐ Answers require one or more sentences.
- ☐ To answer the questions, you have to look in more than one place and put information together.

  - ⋀ Who?
  - ⋀ What?
  - ⋀ When?
  - ⋀ Where?
  - ⋀ Why?
  - ⋀ How?

Effective Instruction for Middle School Students with Reading Difficulties, Denton et al., Brookes Publishing Co. (2012).

Level 2: Putting It Together

- ☐ Questions can be answered by looking in the text.
- ☐ Answers require one or more sentences.
- ☐ To answer the questions, you have to look in more than one place and put information together.

  - ⋀ Who?
  - ⋀ What?
  - ⋀ When?
  - ⋀ Where?
  - ⋀ Why?
  - ⋀ How?

Effective Instruction for Middle School Students with Reading Difficulties, Denton et al., Brookes Publishing Co. (2012).

Level 2: Putting It Together

- ☐ Questions can be answered by looking in the text.
- ☐ Answers require one or more sentences.
- ☐ To answer the questions, you have to look in more than one place and put information together.

  - ⋀ Who?
  - ⋀ What?
  - ⋀ When?
  - ⋀ Where?
  - ⋀ Why?
  - ⋀ How?

Effective Instruction for Middle School Students with Reading Difficulties, Denton et al., Brookes Publishing Co. (2012).

*Photocopy on white card stock.

Adapted with permission from materials developed by the Teacher Quality Research Project through funding from the U.S. Department of Education's Institute of Education Sciences, grant contract number R305M050121A (*Enhancing the quality of expository text instruction and comprehension through content and case-situated professional development*: Simmons, D., Vaughn, S., & Edmonds, M., 2006).

(page 1 of 1)

In *Effective Instruction for Middle School Students with Reading Difficulties: The Reading Teacher's Sourcebook* by Carolyn A. Denton, Sharon Vaughn, Jade Wexler, Deanna Bryan, and Deborah Reed (2012). Published by Paul H. Brookes Publishing Co., Inc. 1-800-638-3775; www.brookespublishing.com

251

Level 2: Examples

- ☐ How did ranchers get their cattle to the markets?

- ☐ What were the factors that contributed to Western expansion?

- ☐ Why was it harder for enslaved people to have a family life than it was for plantation owners?

Effective Instruction for Middle School Students with Reading Difficulties, Denton et al., Brookes Publishing Co. (2012).

Level 2: Examples

- ☐ How did ranchers get their cattle to the markets?

- ☐ What were the factors that contributed to Western expansion?

- ☐ Why was it harder for enslaved people to have a family life than it was for plantation owners?

Effective Instruction for Middle School Students with Reading Difficulties, Denton et al., Brookes Publishing Co. (2012).

Level 2: Examples

- ☐ How did ranchers get their cattle to the markets?

- ☐ What were the factors that contributed to Western expansion?

- ☐ Why was it harder for enslaved people to have a family life than it was for plantation owners?

Effective Instruction for Middle School Students with Reading Difficulties, Denton et al., Brookes Publishing Co. (2012).

Level 2: Examples

- ☐ How did ranchers get their cattle to the markets?

- ☐ What were the factors that contributed to Western expansion?

- ☐ Why was it harder for enslaved people to have a family life than it was for plantation owners?

Effective Instruction for Middle School Students with Reading Difficulties, Denton et al., Brookes Publishing Co. (2012).

*Photocopy on white card stock.

Adapted with permission from materials developed by the Teacher Quality Research Project through funding from the U.S. Department of Education's Institute of Education Sciences, grant contract number R305M050121A (*Enhancing the quality of expository text instruction and comprehension through content and case-situated professional development;* Simmons, D., Vaughn, S., & Edmonds, M., 2006).

(page 1 of 1)

In *Effective Instruction for Middle School Students with Reading Difficulties: The Reading Teacher's Sourcebook*
by Carolyn A. Denton, Sharon Vaughn, Jade Wexler, Deanna Bryan, and Deborah Reed (2012).
Published by Paul H. Brookes Publishing Co., Inc. 1-800-638-3775; www.brookespublishing.com

Level 3: Making Connections

☐ Questions cannot be answered by using text alone.

☐ Answers require you to think about what you just read, what you already know, and how it fits together.

➤ How is _____ like (similar to) _____?

➤ How is _____ different from _____?

➤ How is _____ related to _____?

Effective Instruction for Middle School Students with Reading Difficulties, Denton et al., Brookes Publishing Co. (2012).

Level 3: Making Connections

☐ Questions cannot be answered by using text alone.

☐ Answers require you to think about what you just read, what you already know, and how it fits together.

➤ How is _____ like (similar to) _____?

➤ How is _____ different from _____?

➤ How is _____ related to _____?

Effective Instruction for Middle School Students with Reading Difficulties, Denton et al., Brookes Publishing Co. (2012).

Level 3: Making Connections

☐ Questions cannot be answered by using text alone.

☐ Answers require you to think about what you just read, what you already know, and how it fits together.

➤ How is _____ like (similar to) _____?

➤ How is _____ different from _____?

➤ How is _____ related to _____?

Effective Instruction for Middle School Students with Reading Difficulties, Denton et al., Brookes Publishing Co. (2012).

Level 3: Making Connections

☐ Questions cannot be answered by using text alone.

☐ Answers require you to think about what you just read, what you already know, and how it fits together.

➤ How is _____ like (similar to) _____?

➤ How is _____ different from _____?

➤ How is _____ related to _____?

Effective Instruction for Middle School Students with Reading Difficulties, Denton et al., Brookes Publishing Co. (2012).

*Photocopy on blue card stock.

Adapted with permission from materials developed by the Teacher Quality Research Project through funding from the U.S. Department of Education's Institute of Education Sciences, grant contract number R305M050121A (*Enhancing the quality of expository text instruction and comprehension through content and case-situated professional development*; Simmons, D., Vaughn, S., & Edmonds, M., 2006).

(page 1 of 1)

In *Effective Instruction for Middle School Students with Reading Difficulties: The Reading Teacher's Sourcebook*
by Carolyn A. Denton, Sharon Vaughn, Jade Wexler, Deanna Bryan, and Deborah Reed (2012).
Published by Paul H. Brookes Publishing Co., Inc. 1-800-638-3775; www.brookespublishing.com

253

Level 3: Social Studies Examples

☐ Why is Lincoln's Gettysburg address important in U.S. history?

☐ How is the Magna Carta similar to the U.S. Declaration of Independence?

☐ How is the Civil War different from the Mexican-American War?

Effective Instruction for Middle School Students with Reading Difficulties, Denton et al., Brookes Publishing Co. (2012).

Level 3: Social Studies Examples

☐ Why is Lincoln's Gettysburg address important in U.S. history?

☐ How is the Magna Carta similar to the U.S. Declaration of Independence?

☐ How is the Civil War different from the Mexican-American War?

Effective Instruction for Middle School Students with Reading Difficulties, Denton et al., Brookes Publishing Co. (2012).

Level 3: Social Studies Examples

☐ Why is Lincoln's Gettysburg address important in U.S. history?

☐ How is the Magna Carta similar to the U.S. Declaration of Independence?

☐ How is the Civil War different from the Mexican-American War?

Effective Instruction for Middle School Students with Reading Difficulties, Denton et al., Brookes Publishing Co. (2012).

Level 3: Social Studies Examples

☐ Why is Lincoln's Gettysburg address important in U.S. history?

☐ How is the Magna Carta similar to the U.S. Declaration of Independence?

☐ How is the Civil War different from the Mexican-American War?

Effective Instruction for Middle School Students with Reading Difficulties, Denton et al., Brookes Publishing Co. (2012).

*Photocopy on blue card stock.

Adapted with permission from materials developed by the Teacher Quality Research Project through funding from the U.S. Department of Education's Institute of Education Sciences, grant contract number R305M050121A (*Enhancing the quality of expository text instruction and comprehension through content and case-situated professional development;* Simmons, D., Vaughn, S., & Edmonds, M., 2006).

(page 1 of 1)

In *Effective Instruction for Middle School Students With Reading Difficulties: The Reading Teacher's Sourcebook* by Carolyn A. Denton, Sharon Vaughn, Jade Wexler, Deanna Bryan, and Deborah Reed (2012). Published by Paul H. Brookes Publishing Co., Inc. 1-800-638-3775; www.brookespublishing.com

Planning Sheet

LEVEL 2 QUESTIONS

1. **Preteach proper nouns or critical concept nouns.**

   Introduce, read, and define. Students write brief definition in learning log.

   Who:

   Where:

   What:

2. **Preview text.**

   Introduce the big idea of the text selection.

   What is the most important idea that you want all students to understand and remember from this reading?

   Important key concepts, subheadings, bolded print, and so forth:

   Connections to prior learning:

3. **Model Level 2 questions.**

   Questions to use as examples:

Adapted with permission from materials developed by the Teacher Quality Research Project through funding from the U.S. Department of Education's Institute of Education Sciences, grant contract number R305M050121A (*Enhancing the quality of expository text instruction and comprehension through content and case-situated professional development*; Simmons, D., Vaughn, S., & Edmonds, M., 2006).

(page 1 of 1)

In *Effective Instruction for Middle School Students with Reading Difficulties: The Reading Teacher's Sourcebook*
by Carolyn A. Denton, Sharon Vaughn, Jade Wexler, Deanna Bryan, and Deborah Reed (2012).
Published by Paul H. Brookes Publishing Co., Inc. 1-800-638-3775; www.brookespublishing.com

255

LEVEL 3 QUESTIONS

1. **Preteach proper nouns or critical concept nouns.**

    Introduce, read, and define. Students write brief definition in learning log.

    Who:

    Where:

    What:

2. **Preview text.**

    Introduce the big idea of the text selection.

    What is the most important idea that you want all students to understand and remember from this reading?

    Important key concepts, subheadings, bolded print, and so forth:

    Connections to prior learning:

3. **Model Level 3 questions.**

    Questions to use as examples:

Adapted with permission from materials developed by the Teacher Quality Research Project through funding from the U.S. Department of Education's Institute of Education Sciences, grant contract number R305M050121A (*Enhancing the quality of expository text instruction and comprehension through content and case-situated professional development*; Simmons, D., Vaughn, S., & Edmonds, M., 2006).

(page 1 of 1)

Mental Imagery Log

Title:	
Paragraph 1	Paragraph 5
Paragraph 2	Paragraph 6
Paragraph 3	Paragraph 7
Paragraph 4	Paragraph 8

Adapted with permission from The University of Texas Center for Reading and Language Arts. (2003a). *Meeting the needs of struggling readers: A resource for secondary English language arts teachers.* Austin, TX: Author; based on McNeil, J.D. (1992). *Reading comprehension: New directions for classroom practices (3rd ed.).* New York: Harper Collins; Wood, K.D., & Harmon, J.M. (2001). *Strategies for integrating reading and writing in middle and high school classrooms.* Westerville, OH: National Middle School Association; and Gambrell, L.B., & Bales, R.J. (1986). Mental imagery and the comprehension-monitoring of fourth- and fifth-grade poor readers. *Reading Research Quarterly, 21,* 454–464.

Main Idea Form

Name(s): _____ Date: _____

Title or topic of the selection _____

Paragraph	Who or what is the paragraph about?	Most important information about the *who* or *what*	Key details

From Klingner, J.K., Vaughn, S., Dimino, J., Schumm, J.S., & Bryant, D. (2001). *Collaborative strategic reading: Strategies for improving comprehension.* Longmont, CO: Sopris West; adapted by permission.

In *Effective Instruction for Middle School Students with Reading Difficulties: The Reading Teacher's Sourcebook* by Carolyn A. Denton, Sharon Vaughn, Jade Wexler, Deanna Bryan, and Deborah Reed (2012). Published by Paul H. Brookes Publishing Co., Inc. 1-800-638-3775; www.brookespublishing.com

Main Idea Log

Title of passage: _____

Identify three or four important ideas from the passage:

1. _____

2. _____

3. _____

4. _____

Write the main idea of the entire passage (10 words or less):

_____

_____

Generate three questions about the important ideas:
(Who? What? When? Where? Why? How?)

1. _____

2. _____

3. _____

Create one question about the passage that might be on a test:

_____

_____

Reprinted with permission from The University of Texas Center for Reading and Language Arts. (2003b). *Special education reading project (SERP) secondary institute—Effective instruction for secondary struggling readers: Research-based practices.* Austin, TX: Author.

(page 1 of 1)

In *Effective Instruction for Middle School Students with Reading Difficulties: The Reading Teacher's Sourcebook*
by Carolyn A. Denton, Sharon Vaughn, Jade Wexler, Deanna Bryan, and Deborah Reed (2012).
Published by Paul H. Brookes Publishing Co., Inc. 1-800-638-3775; www.brookespublishing.com

259

Elements of Narrative Text

Examples	Fiction	Historical fiction	Science fiction	Plays
	Autobiographies	Biographies	Fantasies	Mysteries
	Legends	Folktales	Myths	
Purpose	To entertain or inform			
Characteristics	Follow a familiar story structure: Beginning: Introduction of setting, characters, and conflict Middle: Progression of plot, which includes rising action, climax, and falling action End: Resolution or solution to the problem			
Narrative Terms (student-friendly definitions)	Exposition	Introduction of setting, characters, background information, and conflict		
	Setting	Time and place		
	Characters	People, animals, or other entities in the text		
	Conflict	Problem		
	Internal conflict	A character's struggle within him- or herself		
	External conflict	A character's struggle with another character		
	Rising action	Events leading up to the climax; trying to solve the problem		
	Climax	Emotional high point of the story; conflict is addressed		
	Falling action	Consequences or events caused by the climax		
	Resolution	Final outcome		

Adapted with permission from The University of Texas Center for Reading and Language Arts. (2003b). *Special education reading project (SERP) secondary institute—Effective instruction for secondary struggling readers: Research-based practices.* Austin, TX: Author.

In *Effective Instruction for Middle School Students with Reading Difficulties: The Reading Teacher's Sourcebook* by Carolyn A. Denton, Sharon Vaughn, Jade Wexler, Deanna Bryan, and Deborah Reed (2012). Published by Paul H. Brookes Publishing Co., Inc. 1-800-638-3775; www.brookespublishing.com

Elements of Expository Text

Examples	Newspapers Textbooks Magazine articles Brochures Catalogs	
Purpose	To inform	
Characteristics	Titles Headings Subheadings Boldface words Charts Tables Diagrams Graphics	
Organization	One expository passage may be organized using several different text structures.	
Types of organization	Cause–effect	How or why an event happened; what resulted from an event
	Chronology or sequence	The order of events or steps in a process
	Compare and contrast	How two or more things are alike and different
	Description	How something looks, moves, works, and so forth; how things with various characteristics fit into categories; a definition or characterization
	Problem–solution	What's wrong and how to fix it
	Position–reason	Why a point or idea should be supported or what's wrong with an idea

Adapted with permission from The University of Texas Center for Reading and Language Arts. (2003b). *Special education reading project (SERP) secondary institute—Effective instruction for secondary readers. Research-based practices.* Austin, TX. Author.

In *Effective Instruction for Middle School Students with Reading Difficulties: The Reading Teacher's Sourcebook*
by Carolyn A. Denton, Sharon Vaughn, Jade Wexler, Deanna Bryan, and Deborah Reed (2012).
Published by Paul H. Brookes Publishing Co., Inc. 1-800-638-3775; www.brookespublishing.com

Signal Words

Cause–effect

How or why an event happened; what resulted from an event

Accordingly	For this reason	Next
As a result of	Hence	Resulting from
Because	How	Since
Begins with	If...then	So that
Consequently	In order to	Therefore
Due to	Is caused by	Thus
Effects of	It follows	When...then
Finally	Leads/led to	Whether

Chronological order or temporal sequencing

The order of events or steps in a process

After	Following	On (date)
Afterward	Formerly	Preceding
Around	Immediately	Previously
As soon as	In front of	Second
At last	In the middle	Shortly
Before	Initially	Soon
Between	Last	Then
During	Later	Third
Eventually	Meanwhile	To begin with
Ever since	Next	Until
Finally	Not long after	When
First	Now	While

Compare and contrast

How two or more things are alike and different

Although	Even though	Nevertheless
And	However	On the contrary
As opposed to	In common	On the other hand
As well as	In comparison	Opposite
Better	In contrast	Otherwise
Both	In the same way	Same
But	Instead of	Similar to
Compared with	Just as/like	Similarly
Despite	Less	Still
Different from	Likewise	Whereas
Either	More than	Yet

Unpublished supplemental material created by Deborah Reed in 2004 and produced for SEDL. Reprinted with permission.

(page 1 of 2)

In *Effective Instruction for Middle School Students with Reading Difficulties: The Reading Teacher's Sourcebook*
by Carolyn A. Denton, Sharon Vaughn, Jade Wexler, Deanna Bryan, and Deborah Reed (2012).
Published by Paul H. Brookes Publishing Co., Inc. 1-800-638-3775; www.brookespublishing.com

Description

How something looks, moves, works, and so forth; a definition or characterization

Above	Down	Near
Across	For example	On top of
Along	For instance	Onto
Appears to be	Furthermore	Outside
As in	Generally	Over
Behind	Identify	Refers to
Below	In addition	Such as
Beside	In back of	To illustrate
Between	In front of	To the right/left
Consists of	Including	Typically
Describe	Looks like	Under

Problem-solution

What's wrong and how to fix it

Answer	Problem	The problem facing
Challenge	Puzzle	The task was
Clarification	Question	Theory
Difficulty	Reply	This had to be accomplished
Dilemma	Resolution	To fix the problem
How to resolve the issue	Response	To overcome this
Lies	Riddle	Trouble
Obstacles	Solution	Unknown
One solution was	Solved by	What to do
Overcomes	The challenge was	What was discovered
Predicament		

Position-reason

Why a point or idea should be supported; what's wrong with an idea

Accordingly	It is contended	Therefore
As illustrated by	It is evident that	Thesis
Because	It will be argued that	This contradicts the fact that
Consequently	Must take into account	This must be counterbalanced by
For instance	Since	This view is supported by
For this reason	The claim is limited due to	Turn more attention to
In conclusion	The implication is	What is critical
In order for	The position is	What is more central is
It can be established	The strengths of	

Unpublished supplemental material created by Deborah Reed in 2004 and produced for SEDL. Reprinted with permission.

(page 2 of 2)

In *Effective Instruction for Middle School Students with Reading Difficulties: The Reading Teacher's Sourcebook*
by Carolyn A. Denton, Sharon Vaughn, Jade Wexler, Deanna Bryan, and Deborah Reed (2012).
Published by Paul H. Brookes Publishing Co., Inc. 1-800-638-3775; www.brookespublishing.com

263

Identifying Text Structure

If the author wants you to know…	The text structure will be…
How or why an event happened; what resulted from an event	Cause–effect
The order of events or steps in a process	Chronological order or sequencing
How two or more things are alike and different	Compare and contrast
How something looks, moves, works, and so forth; a definition or characterization	Description
What's wrong and how to fix it	Problem–solution
Why a point or idea should be supported; what's wrong with an idea	Position–reason

Unpublished supplemental material created by Deborah Reed in 2004 and produced for SEDL. Reprinted with permission.

In *Effective Instruction for Middle School Students with Reading Difficulties: The Reading Teacher's Sourcebook*
by Carolyn A. Denton, Sharon Vaughn, Jade Wexler, Deanna Bryan, and Deborah Reed (2012).
Published by Paul H. Brookes Publishing Co., Inc. 1-800-638-3775; www.brookespublishing.com

Story Map

Climax:

Rising action:

Falling action:

Conflict:

Resolution:

Exposition:

In *Effective Instruction for Middle School Students with Reading Difficulties: The Reading Teacher's Sourcebook* by Carolyn A. Denton, Sharon Vaughn, Jade Wexler, Deanna Bryan, and Deborah Reed (2012). Published by Paul H. Brookes Publishing Co., Inc. 1-800-638-3775; www.brookespublishing.com

Main Idea Web

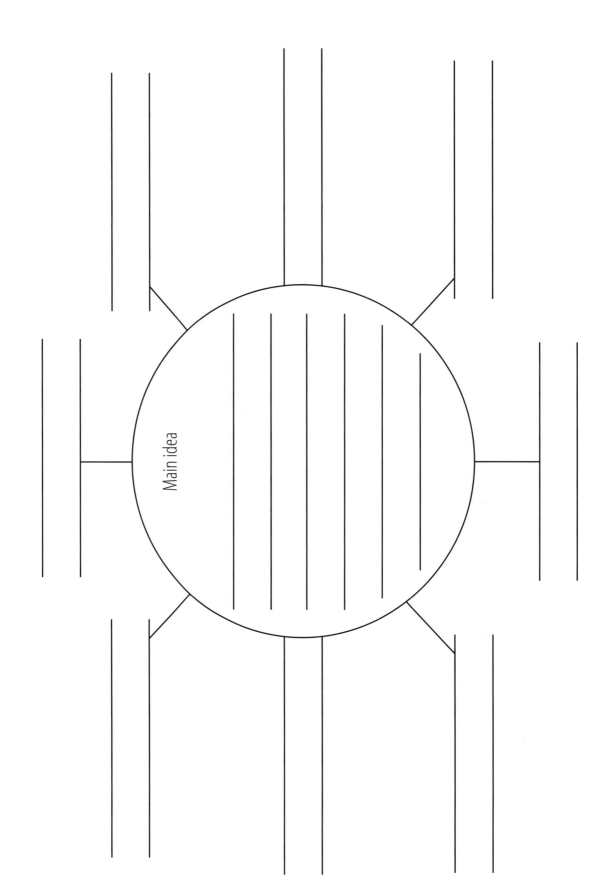

Main idea

Effective Instruction for Middle School Students with Reading Difficulties: The Reading Teacher's Sourcebook
by Carolyn A. Denton, Sharon Vaughn, Jade Wexler, Deanna Bryan, and Deborah Reed. Copyright © 2012 University of Texas System/Texas Education Agency.
All rights reserved. Published by Paul H. Brookes Publishing Co., Inc. 1-800-638-3775; www.brookespublishing.com.

Cause-Effect Chart (Basic)

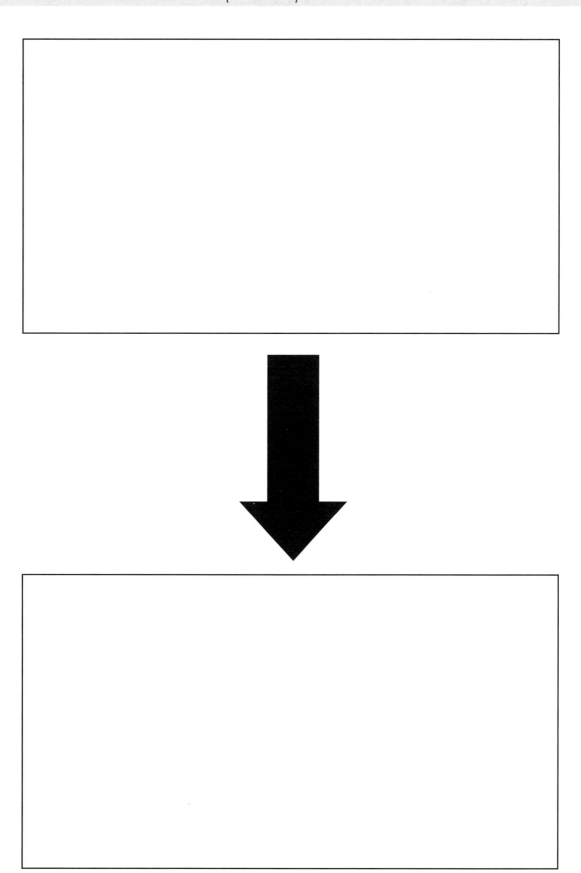

Cause–Effect Herringbone

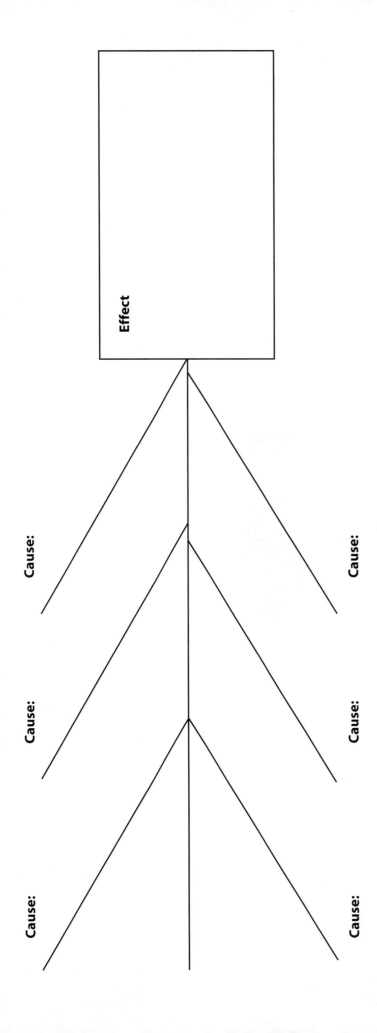

Effect

Cause:

Cause:

Cause:

Cause:

Cause:

Cause:

From "Teaching Students to Construct Graphic Representations," by Beau Fly Jones, Jean Pierce & Barbara Hunter, 1988, *Educational Leadership 46*(4), pp. 20–25. © 1988 by ASCD. Reprinted with permission. Learn more about ASCD at www.ascd.org.

In *Effective Instruction for Middle School Students with Reading Difficulties: The Reading Teacher's Sourcebook* by Carolyn A. Denton, Sharon Vaughn, Jade Wexler, Deanna Bryan, and Deborah Reed (2012). Published by Paul H. Brookes Publishing Co., Inc. 1-800-638-3775; www.brookespublishing.com

(page 1 of 1)

Cause–Effect Semantic Map

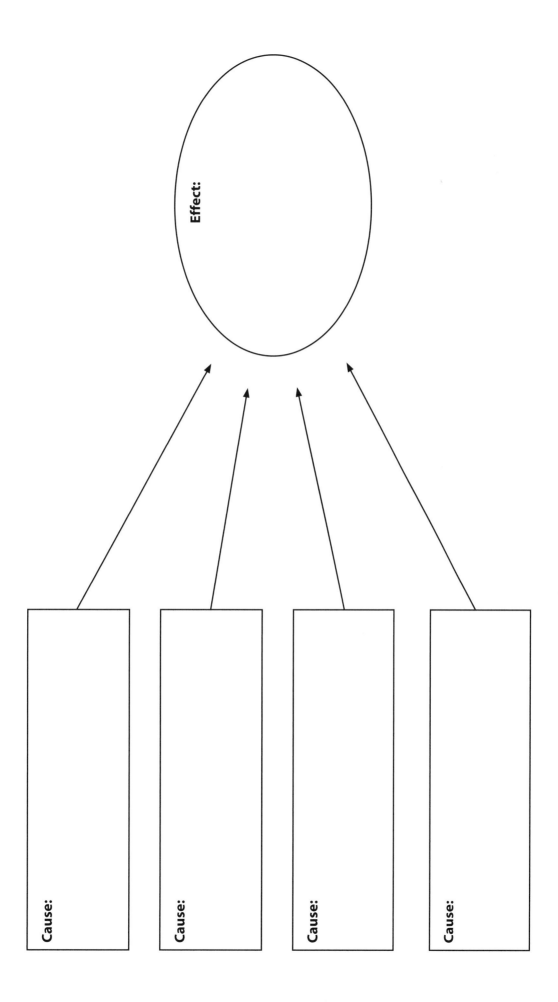

Effect:

Cause:

Cause:

Cause:

Cause:

Effective Instruction for Middle School Students with Reading Difficulties: The Reading Teacher's Sourcebook
by Carolyn A. Denton, Sharon Vaughn, Jade Wexler, Deanna Bryan, and Deborah Reed. Copyright © 2012 University of Texas System/Texas Education Agency.
All rights reserved. Published by Paul H. Brookes Publishing Co., Inc. 1-800-638-3775; www.brookespublishing.com

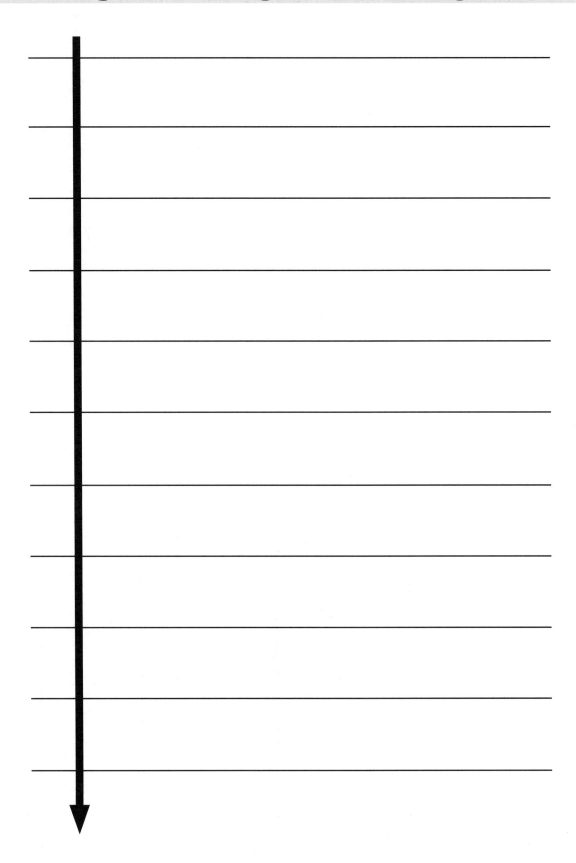

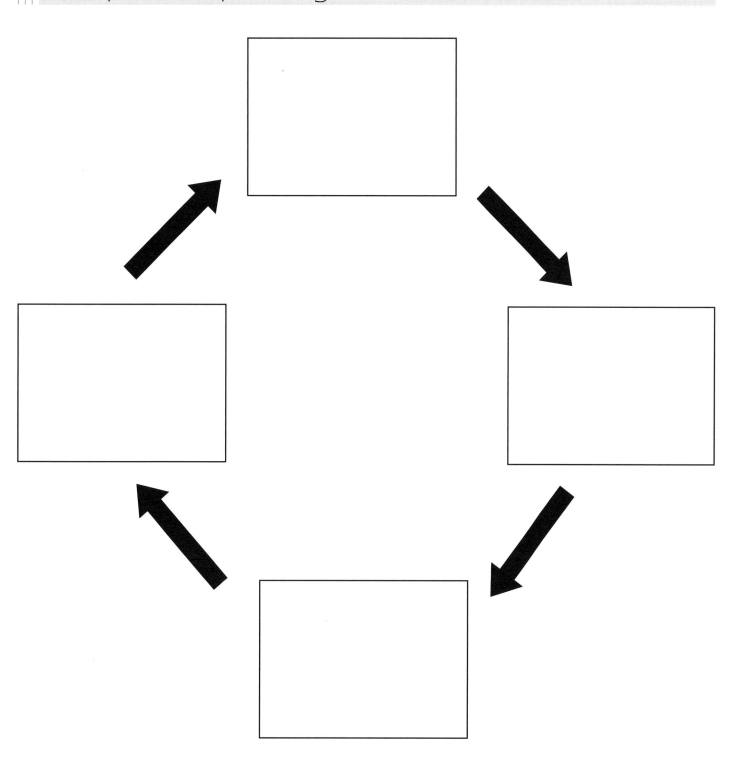

Compare and Contrast Graphic Organizer

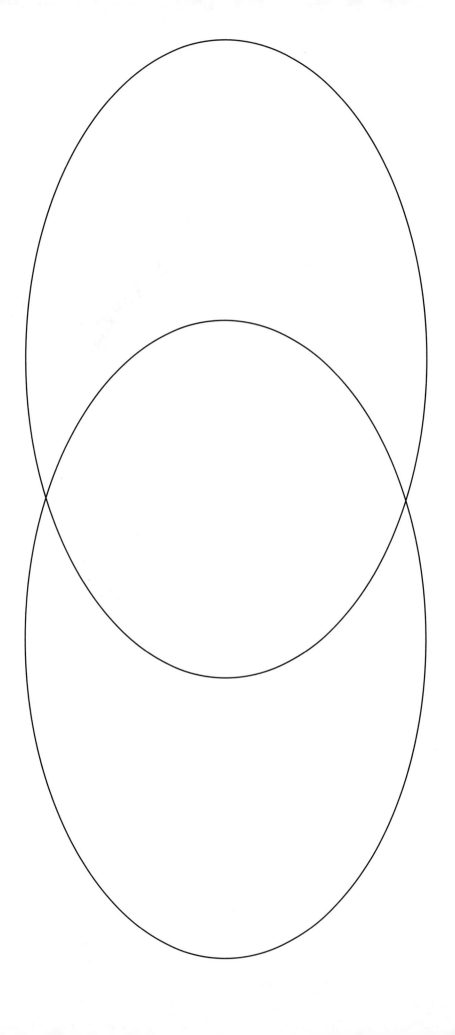

Description (Web)

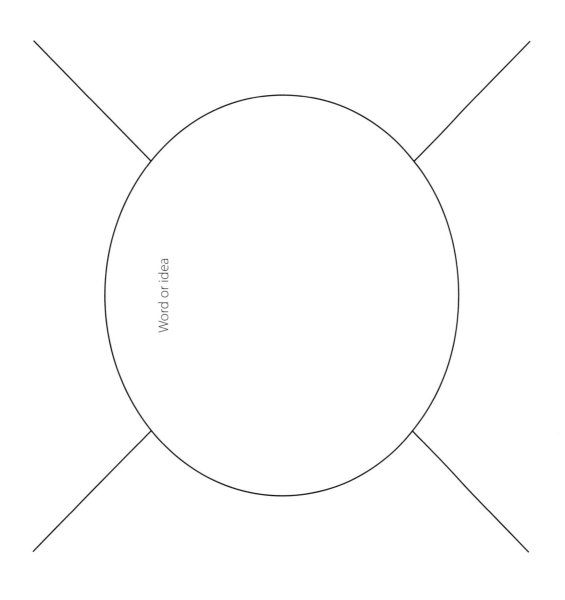

Word or idea

Effective Instruction for Middle School Students with Reading Difficulties: The Reading Teacher's Sourcebook
by Carolyn A. Denton, Sharon Vaughn, Jade Wexler, Deanna Bryan, and Deborah Reed. Copyright © 2012 University of Texas System/Texas Education Agency.
All rights reserved. Published by Paul H. Brookes Publishing Co., Inc. 1-800-638-3775; www.brookespublishing.com

Description (Chart)

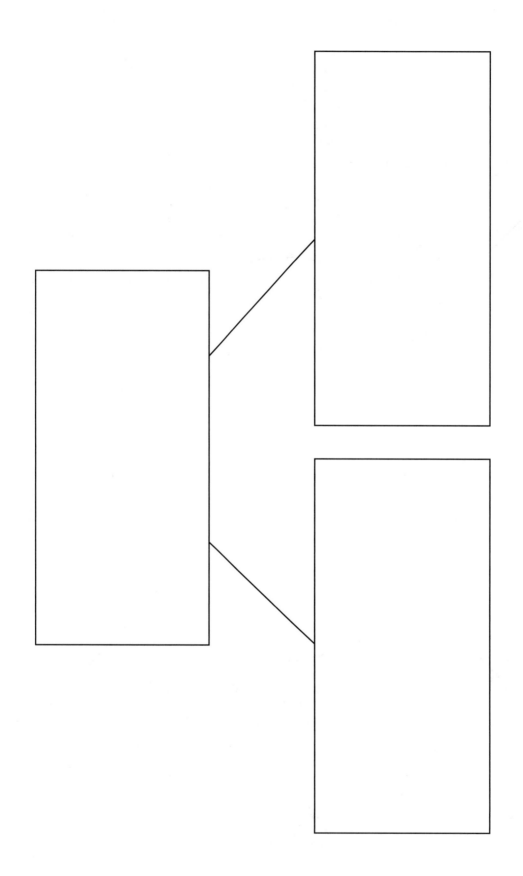

Effective Instruction for Middle School Students with Reading Difficulties: The Reading Teacher's Sourcebook
by Carolyn A. Denton, Sharon Vaughn, Jade Wexler, Deanna Bryan, and Deborah Reed. Copyright © 2012 University of Texas System/Texas Education Agency.
All rights reserved. Published by Paul H. Brookes Publishing Co., Inc. 1-800-638-3775; www.brookespublishing.com

Problem–Solution Graphic Organizer

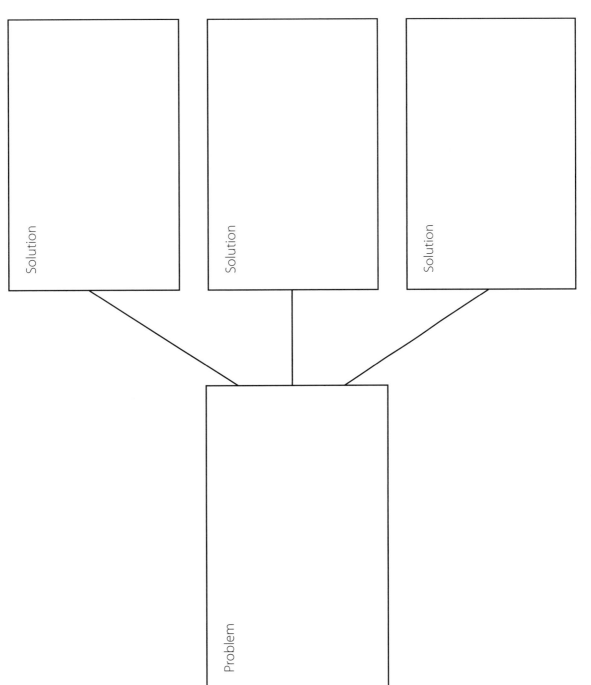

Problem

Solution

Solution

Solution

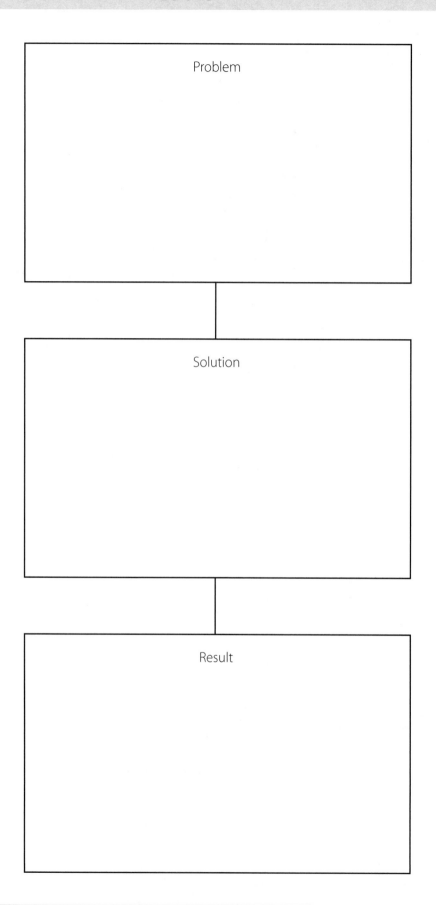

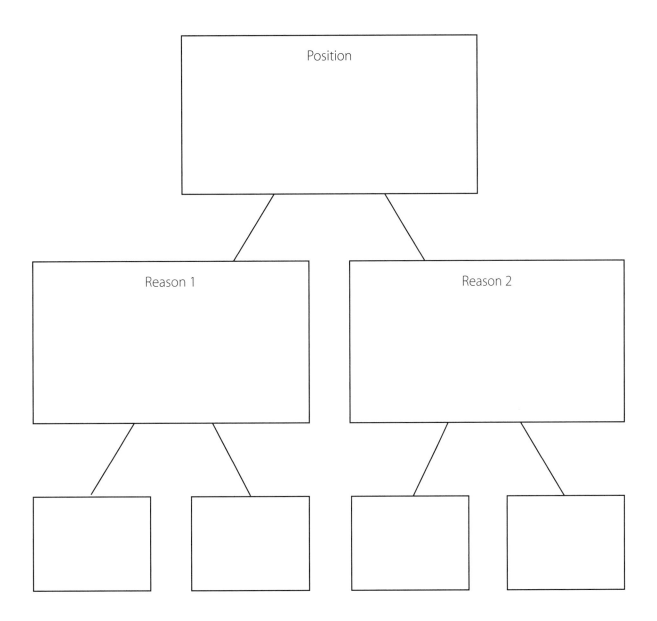

How to Write a Summary

Summary: A shortened version of something that includes only the most important ideas

Step 1:	**List** the main ideas for each paragraph in the passage.
Step 2:	**Underline** the main idea statements that include the most important ideas from the passage.
Step 3:	**Combine** any ideas that could go into one sentence.
Step 4:	**Number** the ideas in a logical order.
Step 5:	**Write** your summary in one paragraph.
Step 6:	**Edit** your summary.

From Archer, A.L., Gleason, M.M., & Vachon, V. (2005b). *REWARDS Plus: Reading strategies applied to social studies passages*. Longmont, CO: Sopris West; adapted by permission.

In *Effective Instruction for Middle School Students with Reading Difficulties: The Reading Teacher's Sourcebook* by Carolyn A. Denton, Sharon Vaughn, Jade Wexler, Deanna Bryan, and Deborah Reed (2012). Published by Paul H. Brookes Publishing Co., Inc. 1-800-638-3775; www.brookespublishing.com

Semantic Feature Analysis Grid

Concept:							
Features							
Examples							

Frayer Model

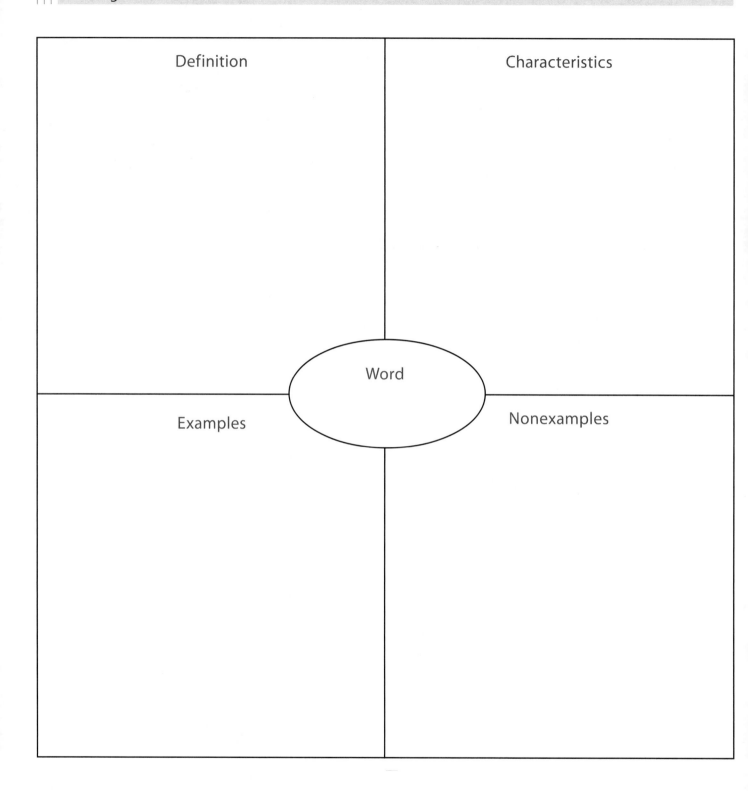

Definition	Characteristics

Word

Examples	Nonexamples

From Frayer, D.A., Frederick, W.C., & Klausmeier, H.G. (1969). *A schema for testing the level of concept mastery (Technical report No. 16)*. Madison, WI: University of Wisconsin Research and Development Center for Cognitive Learning; adapted by permission.

(page 1 of 1)

In *Effective Instruction for Middle School Students with Reading Difficulties: The Reading Teacher's Sourcebook*
by Carolyn A. Denton, Sharon Vaughn, Jade Wexler, Deanna Bryan, and Deborah Reed (2012).
Published by Paul H. Brookes Publishing Co., Inc. 1-800-638-3775; www.brookespublishing.com

Common Prefixes

Recommended order	Prefixes and meanings	Example words	Notes[a]
1. Common prefixes that mean *not* or *the opposite of*	un-; non-; im-, in-, il-, ir-; dis- (not; the opposite of); de- (not; a reversal or removal)	unhappy, nonfiction, impossible, inactive, illegal, irregular, dishonest, decaffeinated	About half of all prefixed words contain just these prefixes.
2. Common prefixes that are related to time	re- (again); pre- (before); fore- (before)	repay, preview, forethought	Lists 1–2 cover about 70% of all prefixed words.
3. Common prefixes that are related to position	in-, im (in; into); ex- (out); sub- (under); inter- (between); trans- (across); mid- (middle); tele- (far away)	input, imprison, export, subway, interstate, transatlantic, midnight, television	Lists 1–3 cover about 82% of all prefixed words.
4. Common prefixes that are related to quantity or quality	over- (too much); under- (too little); super- (above or better than normal); semi- (half)	overcooked, underpay, supermodel, semicircle	Lists 1–4 cover about 88% of all prefixed words.
5. Other common prefixes	en-, em- (cause to; in); mis- (wrongly); anti- (against)	enable, embed, misunderstand, antiwar	Lists 1–5 cover about 96% of all prefixed words.

[a]Estimates of word coverage from White, Sowell, & Yanagihara (1989).

(page 1 of 1)

Common Suffixes

Recommended order	Suffixes	Example words	Notes[a]
1. Inflectional endings	-s, -es (plural of a noun); -ed (past tense of a verb); -ing (progressive tense of a verb)	frogs, boxes, sailed, jumping	About 65% of all suffixed words contain just these inflectional endings.
2. Noun suffixes	-er, -or (one who...); -tion, -sion, -ition; -ity, -ty; -ment; -ness (an abstract noun)	runner, actor, education, confession, activity, loyalty, payment, kindness	Lists 1–2 cover about 76% of all suffixed words.
3. Adjective (and one adverb) suffixes	-ly (usually an adverb, but can be an adjective); -able, ible (able to); -al, ial; -y; -ic	lovely (adjective)/ quickly (adverb); fixable, convertible, medical, racial, sleepy, poetic	Lists 1–3 cover about 88% of all suffixed words.
4. More adjective suffixes	-ous, -ious; -er (more than); -est (the most); -ive, -ative, -tive; -ful (full of) , -less (without)	dangerous, glorious, taller, strongest, active, talkative, beautiful, careless	Lists 1–4 cover about 93% of all suffixed words.

[a] Estimates of word coverage from White, Sowell, & Yanagihara (1989).

(page 1 of 1)

Common Latin and Greek Roots

Root	Origin	Meaning	Examples
aud	Latin	Hear	Auditorium, audition, audience, audible, audiovisual
astro	Greek	Stars or heavens	Astronaut, astronomy, asterisk, asteroid, astrology
bio	Greek	Life	Biology, biography, biochemistry, biome, biomass
cept	Latin	Take	Intercept, accept, reception
dict	Latin	Speak or tell	Dictation, dictate, predict, contradict, dictator
duct or duce	Latin	Lead	Conduct, induct, conductor, productive, seductive, deductive, inductive, produce, deduce
geo	Greek	Earth	Geography, geology, geometry, geophysics
graph	Greek	Write or draw	Autograph, biography, photograph, polygraph, graphic, graphite
ject	Latin	Throw	Eject, reject, projectile, inject
meter	Greek	Measure	Thermometer, barometer, centimeter, diameter
min	Latin	Little or small	Miniature, minimum, minimal
mit or mis	Latin	Send	Mission, transmit, missile, dismiss, submit
ped or pod	Latin	Foot or feet	Pedal, pedestal, pedestrian, tripod, podiatrist, hexapod
phon	Greek	Sound	Telephone, symphony, microphone, phonics, phoneme
port	Latin	Carry	Transport, portable, import, export, porter
rupt	Latin	Break	Disrupt, erupt, rupture, interrupt, bankrupt
scrib or script	Latin	Write	Scribble, scribe, inscribe, describe, prescribe, manuscript, prescription, script, transcript, scripture
spect	Latin	See or look	Inspect, suspect, respect, spectacle, spectator
struct	Latin	Build or form	Construct, destruct, instruct, structure
tele	Greek	From afar	Telephone, telegraph, teleport
tract	Latin	Pull	Traction, tractor, attract, subtract, extract
vers or vert	Latin	Turn or change	Reverse, inverse, convert, convertible, divert, vertigo

Sources: Diamond and Gutlohn (2006); Ebbers (2011); Stahl and Kapinus (2001).

The Origins of English

This story explains why our English language is so complicated. It explains that English is a mixture of Greek and Latin and French and German, with borrowed words from many other languages.

Greek is a very old language, but it is found in modern English—the language we speak today. Greek words go way back, to about 3,000 years ago. We like to use old Greek roots to name new terms in medicine or science: *dinosaur, technology,* and *esophagus.* Even some simple words stem from old Greek: *anchor, school, phone.* About 10 percent of our English words are Greek. Some of the letters of our alphabet are Greek. Even the word alphabet is a Greek word!

Long ago, the Romans spoke a language called Latin. Latin is another ancient language. Today Rome is only a city in Italy, but 2,000 years ago the Roman Empire covered most of Europe. Many of the languages spoken in Europe today were originally Latin-based, including Spanish, French, Portuguese, and Italian. The Romans ruled a big chunk of the world.

The Romans even invaded the Celtic (pronounced /kel-tic/) people in England; only back then England was called Britton. Romans lived in Britton for about 500 years, until finally the Roman Empire fell apart. The Roman army pulled out of Britton and went back to Rome in the year 410. The Celtic people were glad to get their homeland back again. But their joy was not to last.

Very soon, new invaders attacked the Celts. The invaders were called the Angles and the Saxons. They spoke Anglo-Saxon, which is a Germanic language. German is another very old language. The Anglo-Saxon invaders chased the unhappy Celts to Scotland and Ireland and Wales and settled in Britton. Their language was called Anglo-Saxon, but over the years its name changed to English. So, about 1,500 years ago, the English language was born. It was a German language, spoken by the Anglo-Saxons.

There was no rest for the Anglo-Saxons in Britton. For more than 100 long years the super-tall Vikings attacked the Anglo-Saxons, sailing right up to London in their sleek and swift ships. The Vikings (from Norway and Denmark) also spoke a form of German. Finally, the Vikings settled in England and married the Anglo-Saxons. So, by the year 1000 (over 1,000 years ago) everyone in England, the Vikings and the Anglo-Saxons, were speaking one kind of German or another! The English language was, at birth, almost totally German. Most of those early German words have died or become extinct. Today, only about 20 percent of those German words are left in our language: *live, love,* and *laugh* are all Germanic words from the days of the Anglo-Saxons and the Vikings. From the Germanic-speaking Vikings came words like *sky, skin,* and *skull.*

Then the Roman Catholic Church sent missionaries to England. The priests spoke Latin. Remember, the Roman Empire had ended, but the Roman language (Latin) continued. Latin was used by the church. Soon, Latin religious words began to mix with the German words in our language, words like *verse, priest,* and *commandment.* Words that were borrowed from the long-gone Greeks also joined our language through the church, words like *school, chorus,* and *psalm.*

Then, in 1066, England was invaded by people who spoke French. For more than 100 years, the invaders insisted that the English people speak French (not English). French is a Latin-based language. So, thousands of French and Latin words joined the English language.

About 60% of the words in the English language are from Latin or French. The word *parliament* comes from the French word *parlez,* which means "to talk." *Parlez-vous Francais?* The word *unique* is French. Do you see the prefix *uni-* at the beginning? *Uni-* is Latin for "one." So, if something is unique, it is the only one of its kind.

French was mainly the language used in the courts and government, in London. It was spoken by people who were rich and well educated. The more common people (the servants and the serfs) spoke Anglo-Saxon Germanic English. So today we use a lot of Anglo-Saxon words for common everyday things. Words like *shoe* and *house* come from the old Anglo-Saxon English. We got a lot of "fancy" words from the French—words like *chandelier* and *ballet.* From Latin, we got textbook words like *subterranean, investigation,* and *prediction.* And from Greek we got words like *telescope, biology, astronomer, electricity, museum, apostrophe,* and *paragraph.*

So, you see, English is like a mixing bowl full of words that came from all over the globe. English is a Germanic language based in old Anglo-Saxon, but it is strongly spiced with Latin, Greek, and French. Adding even more flavor to the mix, we borrow words constantly from many other languages. From native tribes in Haiti and North America came words like *tomato, potato, tobacco, woodchuck,* and *moose.* Words like *taco, rodeo, guitar,* and *bronco* come from Spanish. The words *or-*

From Ebbers, S.E. (2012, February 19). Invaders of the English language. *Vocabulogic Edublog.* Retrieved May 30, 2012, from http://vocablog-plc.blogspot.com/2012/02/invaders-of-english-language.html; adapted by permission.

(page 1 of 2)

ange, sugar, chess, and *algebra* are Arabic. English has adopted Chinese and Japanese words including *ketchup, tea, tsunami, judo, sushi, tofu,* and *karate.* People also add new words all the time; a few years ago no one had heard of words like *blog, unfriend, iPod, brunch, gigabyte,* and *readathon.* The English language is constantly growing and changing. It is a rich, spicy, living language!

From Ebbers, S.E. (2012, February 19). Invaders of the English language. *Vocabulogic Edublog.* Retrieved May 30, 2012, from http://vocablog-plc.blogspot.com/2012/02/invaders-of-english-language.html; adapted by permission.

(page 2 of 2)

In *Effective Instruction for Middle School Students with Reading Difficulties: The Reading Teacher's Sourcebook*
by Carolyn A. Denton, Sharon Vaughn, Jade Wexler, Deanna Bryan, and Deborah Reed (2012).
Published by Paul H. Brookes Publishing Co., Inc. 1-800-638-3775; www.brookespublishing.com

285

Word-Part Clue Evaluation Chart

Word	No prefix and root word	Prefix and root word	Prefix + root = meaning	Prefix + root ≠ meaning

From Diamond, L., & Gutlohn, L., *Vocabulary Handbook*, 89, 118, 120, Copyright © 2006 by CORE, published by Paul H. Brookes Publishing Co., Inc. Adapted by permission of the publisher.

In *Effective Instruction for Middle School Students with Reading Difficulties: The Reading Teacher's Sourcebook*
by Carolyn A. Denton, Sharon Vaughn, Jade Wexler, Deanna Bryan, and Deborah Reed (2012).
Published by Paul H. Brookes Publishing Co., Inc. 1-800-638-3775; www.brookespublishing.com

Context Clue Strategy

1. Reread the sentence that contains the unknown word. Be on the lookout for signal words or punctuation.

2. Reread the sentences before and after the sentence that contains the unknown word.

3. Based on the clues, try to figure out the meaning of the word.

4. Insert your meaning in the original sentence to see whether it makes sense.

(page 1 of 1)

In *Effective Instruction for Middle School Students with Reading Difficulties: The Reading Teacher's Sourcebook*
by Carolyn A. Denton, Sharon Vaughn, Jade Wexler, Deanna Bryan, and Deborah Reed (2012).
Published by Paul H. Brookes Publishing Co., Inc. 1-800-638-3775; www.brookespublishing.com

287

Types of Context Clues

Type of context clue	What to look for	Signal words	Sample sentence
Definition	A definition in the sentence	*Is, are, is called, means, or* Signal punctuation: Set off by commas	Brick made of sun-dried clay *is called* **adobe**. The Native Americans used **adobe**, *or* bricks made of sun-dried clay, to build their homes.
Synonym	A word with a similar meaning to the unknown word	*Also, as, like, same, similarly, too*	The Zuni built their homes with brick made of sun-dried clay. The Hopi *also* used **adobe** to build their homes.
Antonym	A word or phrase with the opposite meaning of the unknown word	*But, however, in contrast, on the other hand, though, unlike*	The Hopi lived in single-family houses, *but* the Iroquois lived in **longhouses**.
Example	Several examples in a list	*Such as, for example, for instance, like, including*	The Pueblo people grew many **crops** *such as* corn, beans, and squash.
General	General or inexact clues		After 1700, the Pueblos got sheep from the Spanish, and wool replaced cotton as the most important **textile**.

From Baumann, J.F., Font, G., Edwards, E.C., & Boland, E. (2005). Strategies for teaching middle-grade students to use word-part and context clues.
In Teaching and learning vocabulary : bringing research to practice by Hiebert, Elfrieda H.; Kamil, Michael L. Copyright 2012 Reproduced with permission of
TAYLOR & FRANCIS GROUP LLC – BOOKS in the format Textbook via Copyright Clearance Center.

In *Effective Instruction for Middle School Students with Reading Difficulties: The Reading Teacher's Sourcebook*
by Carolyn A. Denton, Sharon Vaughn, Jade Wexler, Deanna Bryan, and Deborah Reed (2012).
Published by Paul H. Brookes Publishing Co., Inc. 1-800-638-3775; www.brookespublishing.com

Guide for Context Clues Practice

Unfamiliar word	Signal word or punctuation	Type of context clue: Definition, synonym, antonym, example, or general	My definition

From Baumann, J.F., Font, G., Edwards, E.C., & Boland, E. (2005). Strategies for teaching middle-grade students to use word-part and context clues. In Teaching and learning vocabulary : bringing research to practice by Hiebert, Elfrieda H.; Kamil, Michael L. Copyright 2012 Reproduced with permission of TAYLOR & FRANCIS GROUP LLC – BOOKS in the format Textbook via Copyright Clearance Center; and Diamond, L., & Gutlohn, L., *Vocabulary Handbook*, 142, Copyright © 2006 by CORE, published by Paul H. Brookes Publishing Co., Inc. Adapted by permission of the publisher

(page 1 of 1)

In *Effective Instruction for Middle School Students with Reading Difficulties: The Reading Teacher's Sourcebook*
by Carolyn A. Denton, Sharon Vaughn, Jade Wexler, Deanna Bryan, and Deborah Reed (2012).
Published by Paul H. Brookes Publishing Co., Inc. 1-800-638-3775; www.brookespublishing.com

289

The Outside-In Strategy

If you read a word that you do not understand:

1. Look OUTSIDE the word for context clues. Reread the sentence and the surrounding sentences.

2. Look INSIDE the word for word-part clues. Can you break the word into parts? (If not, go to Step 3.)

    a. Is there a PREFIX? What does it mean?

    b. Is there a SUFFIX? What does it mean?

    c. Is there a ROOT or BASE WORD? What does it mean?

    d. Put the meanings of the word parts together. What is the meaning of the whole word?

3. GUESS what the word means.

4. INSERT your meaning into the original sentence to see whether it makes sense.

5. If needed, use the DICTIONARY to confirm your meaning.

From Baumann, J.F., Font, G., Edwards, E.C., & Boland, E. (2005). Strategies for teaching middle-grade students to use word-part and context clues. In Teaching and learning vocabulary : bringing research to practice by Hiebert, Elfrieda H.; Kamil, Michael L. Copyright 2012 Reproduced with permission of TAYLOR & FRANCIS GROUP LLC – BOOKS in the format Textbook via Copyright Clearance Center; and Diamond, L., & Gutlohn, L., *Vocabulary Handbook*, 216, Copyright © 2006 by CORE, published by Paul H. Brookes Publishing Co., Inc. Adapted by permission of the publisher.

(page 1 of 1)

In *Effective Instruction for Middle School Students with Reading Difficulties: The Reading Teacher's Sourcebook*
by Carolyn A. Denton, Sharon Vaughn, Jade Wexler, Deanna Bryan, and Deborah Reed (2012).
Published by Paul H. Brookes Publishing Co., Inc. 1-800-638-3775; www.brookespublishing.com

The Outside-In Strategy Worksheet

Word: _____

Context sentence: _____

_____

1. **Look OUTSIDE the word for context clues.**

    a. Reread the sentence, looking for signal words and punctuation.

Signal words and punctuation:

    b. Reread the sentences before and after the sentence with the word in it.

Context clues:

2. **Look INSIDE the word for word parts you know. Tell what each word part means.**

Prefix:

Suffix:

Base word or root:

Put the parts together. What does it mean?

3. What do you think the word means? _____

    _____

4. Try your meaning in the sentence in the text. Does it make sense? _____

5. Check the word with a dictionary if you need to. Remember that many words have more than one meaning, so look for the one that goes with the sentence in the book. Were you right? _____

(page 1 of 1)

In *Effective Instruction for Middle School Students with Reading Difficulties: The Reading Teacher's Sourcebook*
by Carolyn A. Denton, Sharon Vaughn, Jade Wexler, Deanna Bryan, and Deborah Reed (2012).
Published by Paul H. Brookes Publishing Co., Inc. 1-800-638-3775; www.brookespublishing.com

291

Fluency Chart

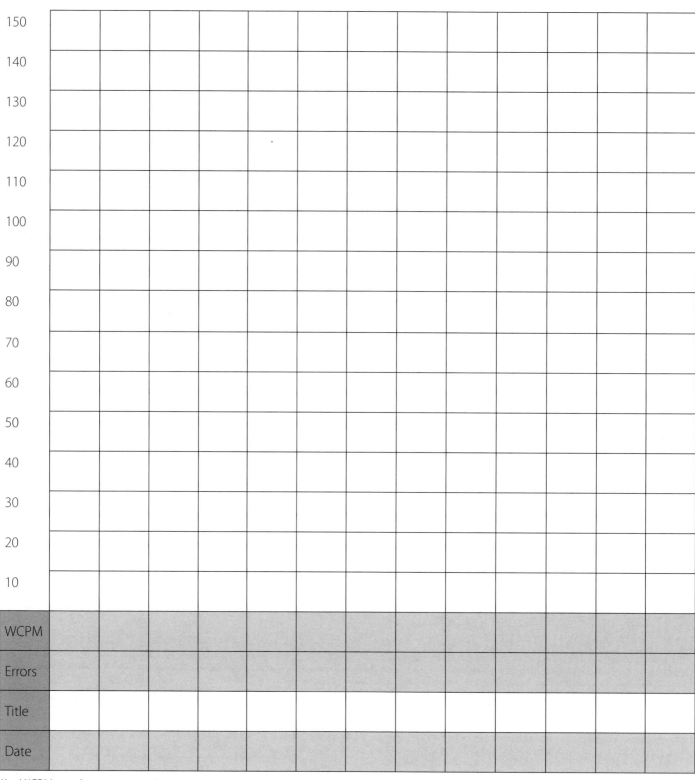

150											
140											
130											
120											
110											
100											
90											
80											
70											
60											
50											
40											
30											
20											
10											
WCPM											
Errors											
Title											
Date											

Key: WCPM, words correct per minute.

Vowel Sounds In Syllable Patterns

Closed syllables

Sound–spelling pattern	Key word
a	cat
e	let
i	sit
o	hot
u	cup
y	gym

Open syllables

Sound–spelling pattern	Key word
a	paper
e	me
i	hi
o	go, open
u	ruby
__y	my
___y	happy

Silent *e* syllables

Sound–spelling pattern	Key word
a__e	cake
e__e	these
i__e	like
o__e	note
u__e	cute, tube

Vowel-*r* syllables

Sound-Spelling Pattern	Key Word
ar	car
er	her
ir	bird
or	for
ur	church

Examples of words with consonant-*le* syllables

a<u>ble</u>, arti<u>cle</u>, ta<u>ckle</u>, ri<u>ddle</u>, gi<u>ggle</u>, spar<u>kle</u>, ap<u>ple</u>, ti<u>tle</u>, si<u>zzle</u>

Examples of words with *schwa*

<u>a</u>bout, tak<u>e</u>n, penc<u>i</u>l, <u>o</u>ther, less<u>o</u>n, beautif<u>u</u>l

Vowel team syllables

Sound–spelling pattern	Key word	Sound–spelling pattern	Key word
Patterns that spell long vowel sounds			
Long A		Long O	
ai	rain	oa	boat
ay	day	oe	toe
eigh	eight	ow	show
Long E		Long U	
ea	eat	ue	blue
ee	see	ew	flew
Long I		oo	cool
igh	night		
Patterns that spell other vowel sounds			
al, all	salt, tall	oi	oil
au	haul	oy	boy
aw	saw	ou	out
ea	head	ow	cow
oo	look		

Less common vowel teams

Sound–spelling pattern	Key word	Sound–spelling pattern	Key word
augh	daughter	ei	height
ea	great	ought	fought
ei	vein	ough	dough
ey	they	ough	rough
ey	key	ough	through
ie	chief	ou	soup
ei	either	ui	suit
uy	buy		

(page 1 of 1)

Effective Instruction for Middle School Students with Reading Difficulties: The Reading Teacher's Sourcebook
by Carolyn A. Denton, Sharon Vaughn, Jade Wexler, Deanna Bryan, and Deborah Reed. Copyright © 2012 University of Texas System/Texas Education Agency.
All rights reserved. Published by Paul H. Brookes Publishing Co., Inc. 1-800-638-3775; www.brookespublishing.com

Syllable Types Chart

Syllable type	Examples	
Closed	**pic-nic**	**ab-sent**
Open	**ve-to**	**a**-pron
Silent *e*	de-**bate**	**base**-ball
Vowel team	re-**frain**	car-**toon**
Vowel-*r*	en-**ter**	**or**-phan
Consonant-*le*	bot-**tle**	bea-**gle**
Other	gar-**bage**	fur-**ni-ture**

Guidelines for Reviewing a Reading Program

USING THE GUIDELINES

When reviewing a reading program thoroughly, it is not sufficient to examine only a sample of lessons. In order to determine whether a program is aligned with current reading research, it is essential to review all the teacher and student materials. This document was developed to help navigate a reviewer through the lengthy but important process of reviewing a reading program. It was designed to be utilized in conjunction with the resources listed below. When using this document, place a check mark in either the yes or no column after each question. If the answer is not clear or not evident, write "not evident" in the comments column and leave the yes/no columns blank. It is very important to use the comments column to detail specific examples, note questions, etc. When a question is marked "no" or "not evident" it is a concern that the program may not be fully aligned with current reading research. That is, if a reading program is aligned with current reading research, then "yes" will be marked on most or all of the questions with evidence to support this assertion written in the comments column. No program is perfect, and sometimes teachers will need to make adaptations to their instruction such as providing additional cumulative practice opportunities.

The following resources on the Florida Center for Reading Research Web site (http://www.fcrr.org) will assist educators who use this tool to guide their review of a reading program:
- Glossary of Reading Terms (boldface words in the Guidelines are found in the Glossary).
- Continuum of Phonological Awareness Skills.
- Continuum of Word Types.
- FCRR Reports (reviews of reading programs already posted).
- References and Resources for Review of Reading Programs.

OVERALL INSTRUCTIONAL DESIGN OF THE READING PROGRAM

Characteristic	Yes	No	Comments (e.g., specific examples, strengths, concerns, questions)
Is there a clear "road map" or "blueprint" for teachers to get an overall picture of the program (e.g., scope and sequence)?			
Are goals and objectives clearly stated?			
Is instruction consistently explicit (including direct explanations and models, clear examples, guided practice, and independent practice)?			
Is instruction consistently systematic (progressing from easier to more challenging skills, with confusing elements separated, teaching necessary preskills prior to introducing complex strategies)?			
Are there consistent, "teacher-friendly" instructional routines that include direct instruction, modeling, guided practice, student practice and application with feedback, and generalization?			
Are there aligned student materials?			
Are there ample guided practice opportunities, including multiple opportunities for explicit teaching and teacher feedback?			
Are teachers encouraged to give immediate corrective feedback and/or instructional scaffolding?			

In *Effective Instruction for Middle School Students with Reading Difficulties: The Reading Teacher's Sourcebook*
by Carolyn A. Denton, Sharon Vaughn, Jade Wexler, Deanna Bryan, and Deborah Reed (2012).
Published by Paul H. Brookes Publishing Co., Inc. 1-800-638-3775; www.brookespublishing.com

OVERALL INSTRUCTIONAL DESIGN OF THE READING PROGRAM *(continued)*

Characteristic	Yes	No	Comments (e.g., specific examples, strengths, concerns, questions)
Is scaffolding a prominent part of the lessons?			
Are there specific instructions for scaffolding?			
Are all of the activities (e.g., centers) reading-related (i.e., word building, fluency practice), and are they designed to provide independent practice in objectives that have already been taught and practiced with teacher support?			
Is differentiated instruction prominent?			
Is instruction individualized based on assessment?			
Is instruction provided to small groups of students with similar needs?			
Are there guidelines for flexible grouping based on assessment results, with movement from group to group based on student progress?			

TEXT READING

Characteristic	Yes	No	Comments (e.g., specific examples, strengths, concerns, questions)
Do the instructional routines of the program include daily text reading?			
Does the program include a variety of high-quality text for students to read?			
Is text available at a variety of reading levels so that each student can read on his or her independent and instructional levels?			
Does the level of difficulty of the text increase as students' skills are strengthened?			
Are sufficient quantities of both narrative and informational text included?			
Does the program include text in which students can successfully apply word identification skills and strategies?			
Does the program include text appropriate for fluency practice?			
Does the program include text to support vocabulary instruction?			
Does the program include text that is suitable for instruction and application of various comprehension strategies?			

From the Florida Center for Reading Research, http://www.fcrr.org

In *Effective Instruction for Middle School Students with Reading Difficulties: The Reading Teacher's Sourcebook*
by Carolyn A. Denton, Sharon Vaughn, Jade Wexler, Deanna Bryan, and Deborah Reed (2012).
Published by Paul H. Brookes Publishing Co., Inc. 1-800-638-3775; www.brookespublishing.com

INSTRUCTION IN DECODING, WORD IDENTIFICATION, AND SPELLING

Characteristic	Yes	No	Comments (e.g., specific examples, strengths, concerns, questions)
Is there a component of the program devoted to instruction in word identification, decoding, and spelling?			
Overall, does instruction progress from easier word reading skills and activities to more difficult ones?			
Is instruction and practice in word reading, decoding, and spelling provided for about 10 to 20 minutes daily?			
Does the program include explicit, systematic instruction in common sound-spelling patterns (e.g., vowel teams, letter combinations)?			
Does the program include placement tests and/or mastery tests that can be used to individualize instruction so that students are taught the specific sound-spelling patterns they do not know?			
Does the program provide opportunities to practice reading decodable words in isolation as well as in text?			
Does the program include explicit, systematic instruction to support the automatic recognition of high-frequency words, particularly those that are not decodable (e.g., was, of)?			
Does the program teach students to use structural analysis strategies to read multi-syllable words?			
Does the program include explicit instruction In the recognition of syllable types?			
Are there ample opportunities to read multisyllabic words daily?			
Does the program include instruction in using meaningful word parts, such as prefixes, suffixes, and basic roots, to pronounce unknown words and infer word meanings?			
Are word parts that occur with high frequency (such as *un, re,* and *in*) introduced over those that occur in only a few words?			
Are decoding and word identification skills and strategies applied while reading connected text that contains many examples of the sound-spelling patterns and word types that have been taught?			
Does the program include instruction and practice activities focused on spelling the same word types that students are taught to decode (e.g., word sorts, word-building activities, analogical reasoning activities)?			
Are students required to apply their word knowledge as they write sentences and more extended writing assignments?			

In *Effective Instruction for Middle School Students with Reading Difficulties: The Reading Teacher's Sourcebook*
by Carolyn A. Denton, Sharon Vaughn, Jade Wexler, Deanna Bryan, and Deborah Reed (2012).
Published by Paul H. Brookes Publishing Co., Inc. 1-800-638-3775; www.brookespublishing.com

FLUENCY INSTRUCTION

Characteristic	Yes	No	Comments (e.g., specific examples, strengths, concerns, questions)
Is fluency assessed regularly?			
Does the program include instruction and activities designed to promote reading fluency?			
Does fluency-based instruction focus on developing accuracy, rate, and prosody?			
Are ample practice materials provided at appropriate reading levels (independent and/or instructional)?			
Does fluency instruction include regular oral reading practice with feedback from a teacher or other more-able reader, including repeated reading of the same text and continuous wide reading for exposure to many different texts?			
Does fluency instruction include modeling and guided practice in fluent, phrased reading with expression, with feedback?			
Do fluency-building routines include goal setting and self-monitoring to promote reading accuracy and rate, including regular timed readings?			

VOCABULARY INSTRUCTION

Characteristic	Yes	No	Comments (e.g., specific examples, strengths, concerns, questions)
Is vocabulary instruction incorporated into the program?			
Are a limited number of words selected for robust, explicit vocabulary instruction?			
Are only important (words students must know to understand a concept or text), useful (words that may be encountered many times), and challenging (e.g., multiple meanings) words taught?			
Is instruction provided to promote the knowledge and use of academic vocabulary, words that students encounter often in academic texts, tests, and other school contexts?			
Does the instructional routine for vocabulary include: introducing the word, presenting a student-friendly explanation, illustrating the word with examples (and non-examples), and checking the students' understanding?			

298   In *Effective Instruction for Middle School Students with Reading Difficulties: The Reading Teacher's Sourcebook*
by Carolyn A. Denton, Sharon Vaughn, Jade Wexler, Deanna Bryan, and Deborah Reed (2012).
Published by Paul H. Brookes Publishing Co., Inc. 1-800-638-3775; www.brookespublishing.com

VOCABULARY INSTRUCTION *(continued)*

Characteristic	Yes	No	Comments (e.g., specific examples, strengths, concerns, questions)
Is vocabulary instruction provided in the context of read-aloud texts, student-read texts, and content area texts?			
Are vocabulary words reviewed cumulatively?			
Are multiple exposures to vocabulary words provided in different contexts?			
Are there activities for distinguishing and interpreting words with multiple meanings?			
Does the program include the study of word origins, derivations, synonyms, antonyms, and idioms to determine and clarify the meanings of words and phrases?			
Are word-learning strategies taught, and are ample opportunities provided to practice and apply these strategies?			
Is systematic and explicit instruction in morphemic analysis provided to support the understanding of word meanings through knowledge of roots, prefixes, and suffixes?			
Is there explicit instruction in the use and limitations of analyzing context clues to determine word meanings?			
Does the program include the use of grade-appropriate dictionaries as well as student-friendly explanations of word meanings?			
Is vocabulary taught both directly and indirectly?			
Is word awareness supported through strategies such as having students keep vocabulary logs and through practice activities that are engaging, provide multiple exposures to words, encourage deep processing, and connect word meanings to prior knowledge?			
Are opportunities provided to engage in oral vocabulary activities?			
Is high-level terminology used to bring richness of language to the classroom?			
Are there ample activities provided to practice writing vocabulary words in sentences and extended text?			
Is exposure to diverse vocabulary provided through listening and reading both narrative and informational text?			

In *Effective Instruction for Middle School Students with Reading Difficulties: The Reading Teacher's Sourcebook*
by Carolyn A. Denton, Sharon Vaughn, Jade Wexler, Deanna Bryan, and Deborah Reed (2012).
Published by Paul H. Brookes Publishing Co., Inc. 1-800-638-3775; www.brookespublishing.com

COMPREHENSION INSTRUCTION

Characteristic	Yes	No	Comments (e.g., specific examples, strengths, concerns, questions)
Is comprehension monitoring taught?			
Is explicit instruction in reading comprehension strategies provided?			
Are students taught how to determine which strategies to use in different situations (metacognition)?			
Is strategy instruction cumulative over the course of the year?			
Are sufficient opportunities to practice and apply strategies provided?			
Are there ample opportunities to read, discuss, and respond to narrative and informational text?			
Is prior knowledge activated before reading?			
Are there ample opportunities to engage in discussions relating to the meaning of text?			
Does the teacher model making inferences to explain and integrate ideas across a text? Are students taught to connect ideas across a single text and to make inferences by using information from the text along with their background knowledge?			
Is explicit instruction in recognizing different text structures included?			
Are graphic organizers used, including story maps and diagrams of various informational text structures?			
Are there frequent opportunities to discuss elements of narrative text and compare the use of these elements in different narratives?			
Are students taught to generate different kinds of questions and answer their own questions during reading to improve engagement with and processing of text?			
Are opportunities provided to interpret information from charts, graphs, tables, and diagrams and connect it to information in text?			
Is a strategy for finding main ideas explicitly taught (e.g., using pictures, then individual sentences, then paragraphs, etc.)?			
Are ample opportunities provided to employ main idea strategies using increasingly complex texts, including text in which the main ideas are not explicitly stated?			
Are summarization strategies taught? Do students routinely produce written or oral summaries of texts they have read?			
Is there an element of the program that requires students to follow specific oral directions in order to perform or complete activities to promote listening comprehension?			
Are there ample opportunities to listen to text read aloud and to discuss and respond to these texts?			

From the Florida Center for Reading Research, http://www.fcrr.org

(page 6 of 8)

300

In *Effective Instruction for Middle School Students with Reading Difficulties: The Reading Teacher's Sourcebook*
by Carolyn A. Denton, Sharon Vaughn, Jade Wexler, Deanna Bryan, and Deborah Reed (2012).
Published by Paul H. Brookes Publishing Co., Inc. 1-800-638-3775; www.brookespublishing.com

MOTIVATION AND ENGAGEMENT

Characteristic	Yes	No	Comments (e.g., specific examples, strengths, concerns, questions)
Does the program foster intrinsic motivation in students (e.g., student selection of books, various genres of book titles, multicultural/international book titles, opportunities to learn about topics of significant interest to individual students)?			
Is there a component of the program that fosters extrinsic motivation in students (e.g., external recognition, rewards, or incentives)?			
Are there ample opportunities for students to engage in group activities to promote active student involvement and motivation?			
Are there opportunities for students to set individual goals (usually along with the teacher) and receive feedback on progress toward their goals?			

ASSESSMENT

Characteristic	Yes	No	Comments (e.g., specific examples, strengths, concerns, questions)
Is high-quality assessment included in the program?			
Are the assessment instruments reliable and valid?			
Do the assessments measure progress or mastery of objectives in word identification, fluency, vocabulary, and comprehension?			
Does the program include diagnostic assessments to provide specific information about individual students' instructional needs (such as which sound-spelling patterns or vocabulary words they do not know)?			
Does assessment aid teachers in making individualized instruction decisions?			
Does the program provide teacher guidance in how to use assessment results effectively?			

In *Effective Instruction for Middle School Students with Reading Difficulties: The Reading Teacher's Sourcebook*
by Carolyn A. Denton, Sharon Vaughn, Jade Wexler, Deanna Bryan, and Deborah Reed (2012).
Published by Paul H. Brookes Publishing Co., Inc. 1-800-638-3775; www.brookespublishing.com

PROFESSIONAL DEVELOPMENT FOR THE READING INTERVENTIONIST

Characteristic	Yes	No	Comments (e.g., specific examples, strengths, concerns, questions)
Is professional development available from the publisher or another source to prepare teachers to implement the program with high fidelity?			
Are strategies included for providing in-class coaching or some form of ongoing support as teachers learn to implement the program?			
Are teachers taught how to administer and interpret assessments that accompany the program?			
Is professional development for the program customized to meet the varying needs of the participants (e.g., first-year teachers, coaches, principals)?			
Does the professional development help the teacher understand the rationale for the instructional approach and strategies utilized in the program (e.g., articles, references, and reliable Web sites) as well as how to implement them?			
Does the program provide materials (e.g., principal checklists, a video/CD with modeled lessons, printed teaching charts, graphs, transparencies) to supplement the professional development and facilitate high-fidelity implementation?			

In *Effective Instruction for Middle School Students with Reading Difficulties: The Reading Teacher's Sourcebook*
by Carolyn A. Denton, Sharon Vaughn, Jade Wexler, Deanna Bryan, and Deborah Reed (2012).
Published by Paul H. Brookes Publishing Co., Inc. 1-800-638-3775; www.brookespublishing.com

Index

Page numbers followed by *f* and *t* indicate figures and tables, respectively.

Permissions

Sample Lesson on Before-, During-, and After-Reading Comprehension: Previewing Text and Question Generation, beginning on page 61: This approach is based on the work of Raphael, T.E. (1986). Teaching question answer relationships, revisited. *Reading Teacher, 39*; and Raphael, T.E., & Pearson, P.D. (1985). Increasing students' awareness of sources of information for answering questions. *American Educational Research Journal, 22,* 217–235. The ideas and materials for previewing and question generation were adapted with permission from materials developed by the Teacher Quality Research Project through funding from the U.S. Department of Education's Institute of Education Sciences, grant contract number R305M050121A (*Enhancing the quality of expository text instruction and comprehension through content and case-situated professional development;* D. Simmons, S. Vaughn, & M. Edmonds, 2006).

Sample Lesson on Before-, During-, and After-Reading Comprehension: Generating Level 1 (Right-There) Questions, beginning on page 69: This approach is based on the work of Raphael, T.E. (1986). Teaching question answer relationships, revisited. *Reading Teacher, 39*; and Raphael, T.E., & Pearson, P.D. (1985). Increasing students' awareness of sources of information for answering questions. *American Educational Research Journal, 22,* 217–235. The ideas and materials for previewing and question generation were adapted with permission from materials developed by the Teacher Quality Research Project through funding from the U.S. Department of Education's Institute of Education Sciences, grant contract number R305M050121A (*Enhancing the quality of expository text instruction and comprehension through content and case-situated professional development;* D. Simmons, S. Vaughn, & M. Edmonds, 2006).

Sample Lesson on Before-, During-, and After-Reading Comprehension: Generating Level 2 (Putting-It-Together) Questions, beginning on page 76: This approach is based on the work of Raphael, T.E. (1986). Teaching question answer relationships, revisited. *Reading Teacher, 39*; and Raphael, T.E., & Pearson, P.D. (1985). Increasing students' awareness of sources of information for answering questions. *American Educational Research Journal, 22,* 217–235. The ideas and materials for previewing and question generation were adapted with permission from materials developed by the Teacher Quality Research Project through funding from the U.S. Department of Education's Institute of Education Sciences, grant contract number R305M050121A (*Enhancing the quality of expository text instruction and comprehension through content and case-situated professional development;* D. Simmons, S. Vaughn, & M. Edmonds, 2006).

Sample Lesson on Before-, During-, and After-Reading Comprehension: Generating Level 3 (Making-Connections) Questions, beginning on page 81: This approach is based on the work of Raphael, T.E. (1986). Teaching question answer relationships, revisited. *Reading Teacher, 39*; and Raphael, T.E., & Pearson, P.D. (1985). Increasing students' awareness of sources of information for answering questions. *American Educational Research Journal, 22,* 217–235. The ideas and materials for previewing and question generation were adapted with permission from materials developed by the Teacher Quality Research Project through funding from the U.S. Department of Education's Institute of Education Sciences, grant contract number R305M050121A (*Enhancing the quality of expository text instruction and comprehension through content and case-situated professional development;* D. Simmons, S. Vaughn, & M. Edmonds, 2006).

Sample Lesson on During Reading: Mental Imagery Log, beginning on page 86: Adapted with permission from The University of Texas Center for Reading and Language Arts. (2003b). *Special education reading project (SERP) secondary institute—Effective instruction for secondary struggling readers: Research-based practices.* Austin, TX: Author.

During Reading: Main Idea Strategy, beginning on page 91: Vocabulary routine adapted with permission from Archer, A.L., Gleason, M.M., & Vachon, V. (2005b). *REWARDS Plus: Reading strategies applied to social studies passages.* Longmont, CO: Sopris West. Main idea strategy adapted with permission from Klingner, J.K., Vaughn, S., Dimino, J., Schumm, J.S., & Bryant, D. (2001). *Collaborative strategic reading: Strategies for improving comprehension.* Longmont, CO: Sopris West.

Sample Lesson on After Reading: Summarizing Text, beginning on page 113: Adapted with permission from Archer, A.L., Gleason, M.M., & Vachon, V. (2005b). *REWARDS Plus: Reading strategies applied to social studies passages.* Longmont, CO: Sopris West.

Sample Lesson on After Reading: Wrap-Up/Main Idea Log, beginning on page 118: Adapted with permission from The University of Texas Center for Reading and Language Arts. (2003b). *Special education reading project (SERP) secondary institute—Effective instruction for secondary struggling readers: Research-based practices.* Austin, TX: Author.

Sample Lesson on Word Knowledge: Semantic Mapping, beginning on page 130: This is a commonly used technique. For more information and ideas see Johnson, D., Pittelman, S., & Heimlich, J. (1986). Semantic mapping. *The Reading Teacher, 29,* 778–783; and Stahl, S.A., & Vancil, S.J. (1986). Discussion is what makes semantic maps work in vocabulary instruction. *The Reading Teacher, 40*(1), 62–67.

Sample Lesson on Word Knowledge: Semantic Feature Analysis, beginning on page 138: This is a commonly used technique. For more information and ideas see Anders, P.L., & Bos, C.S. (1986). Semantic feature analysis: An interactive strategy for vocabulary development and text comprehension. *Journal of Reading, 29,* 610–161.

Sample Lesson on Word Knowledge: Generating Examples and Nonexamples, beginning on page 147: Adapted with permission from Frayer, D.A., Frederick, W.C., & Klausmeier, H.G. (1969). *A schema for testing the level of concept mastery* (Technical report No. 16). Madison, WI: University of Wisconsin Research and Development Center for Cognitive Learning.

Sample Lesson on Word Consciousness: Prepared Participation, beginning on page 154: This sample lesson plan is based on the work of Feldman, K., & Kinsella, K. (2005). *Narrowing the language gap: The case for explicit vocabulary instruction.* New York: Scholastic. A description of the strategy can be found at http://teacher.scholastic.com/products/authors/pdfs/Narrowing_the_Gap.pdf

Sample Lesson on Word Consciousness: Possible Sentences, beginning on page 158: This sample lesson plan is based on the work of Moore & Moore (1986) and Stahl & Kapinus (1991). A description of the strategy can be found in Stahl, S.A., & Kapinus, B.A. (1991). Possible sentences: Predicting word meanings to teach content area vocabulary. *The Reading Teacher, 45,* 36–43.

Sample Lesson on Word Learning: The Word-Part Strategy, beginning on page 164: For additional information see Kieffer, M.J., & Lesaux, N.K. (2010). Morphing into adolescents: Active word learning for English-language learners and their classmates in middle school. *Journal of Adolescent & Adult Literacy, 54*(1), 47–56, Kieffer, M.J., & Lesaux, N.K. (2007). Breaking down words to build meaning: Morphology, vocabulary, and reading comprehension in the urban classroom. *The Reading Teacher, 61*(2), 134–144, and Baumann, J.F., Font, G., Edwards, E.C., & Boland, E. (2005). Strategies for teaching middle-grade students to use word-part and context clues. In E.H. Hiebert & M.L. Kamil (Eds.), *Teaching and learning vocabulary: Bringing research to practice.* Mahwah, NJ: Lawrence Erlbaum Associates.

Sample Lesson on Word Learning: Using Context Clues, beginning on page 174: This is a commonly used technique. For more information and ideas see Baumann, J.F., Font, G., Edwards, E.C., & Boland, E. (2005). Strategies for teaching middle-grade students to use word-part and context clues. In E.H. Hiebert & M.L. Kamil (Eds.), *Teaching and learning vocabulary: Bringing research to practice.* Mahwah, NJ: Lawrence Erlbaum Associates.

Sample Lesson on Word Learning: The Outside-In Strategy, beginning on page 182: This is a commonly used technique. For more information and ideas see Ebbers, S., and Denton, C.A. (2008). A root awakening: Effective vocabulary instruction for older students with reading difficulties. *Learning Disabilities Research and Practice, 23*(2), 90–102, and Baumann, J.F., Font, G., Edwards, E.C., & Boland, E. (2005). Strategies for teaching middle-grade students to use word-part and context clues. In E.H. Hiebert & M.L. Kamil (Eds.), *Teaching and learning vocabulary: Bringing research to practice.* Mahwah, NJ: Lawrence Erlbaum Associates.

Sample Lesson on Partner Reading, beginning on page 195: This is a commonly used technique. For more information and ideas see Fuchs, L.S., Fuchs, D., & Kazdan, S. (1999). Effects of peer-assisted learning strategies on high school students with serious reading problems. *Remedial and Special Education, 20*(5), 309–18. And see Fuchs, D., Fuchs, L.S., Thompson, A., Svenson, E., Yen, L., Al Otaiba, S.,...Saenz, L. (2001). Peer-assisted learning strategies in reading: Extensions for kindergarten, first grade, and high school. *Remedial and Special Education, 22*(1), 15–21; and Greenwood, C.R., Delquadri, J.C., & Hall, R.V. (1989). Longitudinal effects of classwide peer tutoring. *Journal of Educational Psychology, 81,* 371–383.

Sample Lesson on Readers' Theater, beginning on page 197: This is a commonly used technique. For more information and ideas see Worthy, J., & Broaddus, K. (2002). Fluency beyond the primary grades: From group performance to silent independent reading. *Reading Teacher, 55,* 334–343.

Sample Lesson on Word Recognition: The Multisyllable Word Reading Strategy, beginning on page 210: This is a commonly used technique. For more information see Archer, A.L., Gleason, M.M., & Vachon, V. (2005a). *REWARDS: Multisyllabic word reading strategies.* Longmont, CO: Sopris West.